Law for Executives

LAW
FOR EXECUTIVES

edited by

RUSSELL F. MOORE
Member of the New York Bar

American Management Association, Inc.

Contents

Introduction

Lester E. Denonn

THERE IS AND SHOULD BE A MARKED DIFFERENCE BETWEEN THE INDIVIDUAL'S relationship to the medical profession and his reliance on the legal profession. The layman has checkups and dashes to a doctor when he feels unusual pain or disturbing symptoms, but he does not consider medicine as such unless its morbidities have some compelling interest for him. As to the law, on the other hand, the competent executive should have familiarity that goes beyond mere passing concern. The many ramifications of the business that looks to him for leadership are involved in legal problems and pitfalls at every turn. He should be conversant with these legal morasses so that he will know when to consult his firm's legal department or his general counsel, and he should school himself so that he can ask intelligent questions of his legal advisers.

It is just such an informative background that this book admirably serves to furnish. With it, the lay reader will not become a lawyer overnight, but he will develop a feel for the ever present legal aspects and will have a better basis for appreciating the legal advice he should seek.

Even if the executive is a trained lawyer, he can derive great value from this book. If he has been away from the active practice of the law, he will find his perusal of this volume worthwhile in bringing him abreast of current problems.

LESTER E. DENONN is with the New York law firm of Simpson, Thacher & Barlett.

7

Whether layman or nonpracticing lawyer, the reader will appreciate that the lucidity of the exposition of the problems covered in this book is of great advantage. It is rare that one can sit down to read a law book for laymen that does not get bogged down in technicalities. This work does not. It invites careful reading and assures reward for the effort.

The wise executive should be aware that, as an officer and director, he is wide open to possible personal liability for his actions ostensibly on behalf of the corporation. He owes well-defined responsibility to the corporation and to its stockholders. There are areas where the line is extremely narrow on the question of conflict of interest, and he may face the charge of personal aggrandizement. What can he do to minimize this possible liability, and to what extent can he be indemnified by the corporation against personal loss? These are some of the questions posed in the chapter on the liability of officers and directors.

The merger-minded executive with obvious good intent to attain diversification for his company must tread lightly and cautiously lest he run afoul of the statutes governing antitrust. He must likewise be aware of trade regulations, competitive restrictions, and price-fixing problems. What is a "tie-in," and how far can one go? The chapter on antitrust and trade regulations considers some of the fundamentals involved in these vital areas of concern.

The Uniform Commercial Code endeavored to fix a basis for product liability that would establish some measure of uniformity, but the cases have gone beyond the statute and have brought the manufacturer closer and closer to the problems of possible liability. The subjects of privity, warranties, negligence, strict liability, and avenues of defense are important to the executive, as is well demonstrated in the chapter on product liability.

The pages devoted to the law of advertising introduce the executive to a field that he might offhandedly toss aside as of little concern to him. It has its problems, and various bodies of the law must be brought to his attention so that he can be guided safely over the shoals and recognize the import of some of the leading cases.

Apropos of advertising is the question of the proper packaging and labeling of products, a subject which has received growing consideration by statute and regulation. The daily production and marketing decisions of the executive are constantly involved in this subject, so he should welcome the opportunity to become familiar with this area of the law through the medium of the chapter devoted to it.

Once in a while, amid all these varying and perplexing problems, the executive has time to sit back and ask himself: "How about me?" This is a proper question and raises the subject of legal problems of executive compensation. Incentive he has and incentive he needs, but the tax collector is looking over his shoulder to see what he is getting and how he is getting it. Here are problems for both the corporation and the individual executive.

There is a personnel manager down the hall from the executive. Has he any legal problems today, or can he just sit back and twiddle his thumbs while applicants take intelligence tests? Far from it. If he has not heard about "equal opportunity" by this time, he should be thoroughly schooled by the executive who has profited by reading the chapter on the subject. And don't forget that the little old problem of sex discrimination appears also. We have comparatively new statutes in the employment area that must be grappled with to insure compliance.

The executive perforce knows that he labors all the time and needs no reminder of it, but he can nonetheless profit by reading about labor law and its perplexities as well as the problems involved in administrative procedures and at the bargaining table.

Don't miss the story of John Lombe and the dramatic events in his short life. It is an episode in English economic history and a fitting introduction to the plaguing subject of the protection of industrial property and trade secrets. Here is a topic of vital concern to the law and business. And, for further protection of business interests, there is need to be guided in the field of patents, trademarks, and copyrights, nationally and internationally.

Tax havens serve functions other than providing rather good vacations. The alert businessman today is ever mindful of international trade possibilities; for him, the taxation of income from international business transactions is of increasing significance.

Once in a while, when the executive is tired of the foregoing areas of business problems and their legal aspects, he can sit back and relax and think of himself for a change; but his repose is not long-lasting. He soon turns to the inevitable and wonders about estate planning, as discussed for him in the chapter devoted to its many facets.

The astute executive who may have ventured to read this far and to have glanced at the table of contents is bound to exclaim, "But I can't find any chapter devoted to tax law as such." That topic, gentle executive, has been reserved for this introduction and can be treated in a single sentence. When you arrive each day at your regal office, gaze upon the Braques, Klees, and Picassos that adorn the walls, continue breathing, or engage in any other activity, be sure to consult your tax counsel to be advised fully as to the tax consequences.

There is something in this book for every executive who seeks a better understanding of the legal problems involved in the field of his daily activities as well as a comprehensive and informative bird's-eye view of the legal complexities of modern business activities in their manifold ramifications.

Liability of Officers and Directors

Herbert Goldenberg and
George M. Szabad

T HERE HAS BEEN A GROWING CONCERN WITH THE SUBJECT OF THE PERSONAL liability of corporate directors and officers. This concern has been expressed in news items in the general and financial press, discussions in management group seminars, questions posed by corporate officers and directors to their attorneys, and an increasing number of articles on the subject.

This chapter will not discuss these problems in detail. Rather, it will attempt to set forth in broad outline the basic standards of responsibility required of management, the techniques generally available and utilized to enforce these standards, the types of conduct which are likely to lead to liability, and the availability of means to minimize the risk of liability.

HERBERT GOLDENBERG is a member of the firm of Blum, Haimoff, Gersen & Szabad in New York City. GEORGE M. SZABAD is vice president, counsel, secretary, and a director of Burndy Corporation, and he is also a member of the firm of Blum, Haimoff, Gersen & Szabad. The authors, gratefully acknowledge the participation of Mr. Edward Greenbaum, a member of Blum, Haimoff, Gersen & Szabad, in the preparation of the chapter.

11

Standards of Management Responsibility

By "standards" of responsibility we mean the kind of conduct required of corporate managers in the exercise of their authority, as distinct from the "scope" of their responsibility (that is, the nature and extent of their authority).

The scope of management's responsibility may differ appreciably from state to state and from corporation to corporation. Most corporate statutes entrust the general management of a corporation in the first instance to its directors, but there is less uniformity among state laws concerning the extent to which the directors' powers may be restricted or delegated by means of charter provisions, bylaws, stockholders' agreements, or corporate resolutions. Where corporations are given discretion regarding allocation of authority, the scope of management responsibility will depend upon the manner in which the particular corporation has been organized.

In the matter of standards of conduct for corporate managers, however, a greater degree of generalization is possible. The officer or director will not ordinarily be held to a strict standard of accountability to the corporation's creditors or stockholders as would be an insurer who is liable regardless of his personal actions. Nor, on the other hand, may he regard his position as a mere honorarium with no affirmative obligation to exercise his authority. The standards of responsibility for corporate managers lie between these two extremes and, subject to certain exceptions and qualifications, may be said to consist of two elements: (1) good faith and (2) due care.

Good Faith

We are now discussing good faith as a duty owed to the corporation and its stockholders. The duty of the officers and directors to third persons under general principles of law and special statutes will be considered elsewhere in this chapter.

Basic to the concept of good faith as so limited is the quasi-fiduciary nature of the relationship of the director or officer to the corporation he serves. This relationship imposes upon him the strictest responsibility to regard the welfare of the corporation as paramount and to subordinate all other interests to it. In this context, "good faith" can be equated with loyalty. Personal honesty, which is the most obvious component of good faith, is only a specific example of loyalty to the corporation rather than to the manager's personal interests.

Good faith and individual loyalty are obviously subjective in nature. In other words, they are expressions to describe a state of mind. By its nature, an individual's state of mind is not susceptible to any direct proof other than the individual's testimony. It is, however, subject to indirect proof by "circumstantial evidence"—that is, evidence of circumstances from which the existence of a particular state of mind may legitimately be inferred. The amount and kind of circumstantial evidence that will suffice to indicate violation of the standard of undivided loyalty constitute a more meaningful area of inquiry than the subjective standard itself.

Proof of the mere existence of adversity of interest is insufficient to indicate a breach of duty. The manager is permitted to serve his personal interests in receiving compensation for his services; and, even if he does not vote upon the amount he himself is to receive, he may well be in a position to fix the compensation of those who will in turn determine his salary and emoluments. Moreover, the corporation may derive considerable advantage from the services of persons, particularly outside directors, who have a built-in potential for adverse interest because of a connection with an enterprise that does business with the corporation or renders professional, investment, or financial services to it.

It is clear, therefore, that the mere existence of conflict of interest will not necessarily vitiate a transaction between the corporation and an officer or director. Most jurisdictions recognize that such a transaction will be upheld if the corporation had independent and disinterested representation and if the transaction is fair to the corporation.

The concept of independent representation implies that the corporation has acted in the transactions through those of its directors who were not interested in its benefits and who were independent in the sense that they were not under the control or undue influence of any interested directors. Generally, there must be a quorum, none of whose members has an interest in the transaction. However, charter provisions, bylaws, and the corporation laws of several states extend the concept of independent representation to uphold transactions with respect to which interested directors are counted in determining the presence of a quorum, even if their votes are recorded, as long as such votes are not required to authorize the transaction. If independent representation may not be attained, approval by stockholder action will generally be regarded as its equivalent.

A transaction will be considered a fair one if there has been full disclosure of all relevant information to the corporation's disinterested representatives concerning the subject of the transaction and the nature and extent of any officer's or director's adverse interest. In addition, fairness requires that the corporation derive a reasonable benefit or consideration from the transaction. An officer or director will not be permitted to secure an unconscionable advantage at the corporation's expense, even if there has been independent representation and full disclosure.

DUE CARE

A number of states require nothing more of an officer or director than "good faith." Most, however, impose an additional objective standard: the exercise of some degree of care. This obligation to exercise care may, for the purpose of analysis, be further broken down into "diligence" and "prudence."

Diligence. To the extent that the law of a jurisdiction holds the director or officer to a standard of care, the duty to be diligent will be more rigorously applied than the duty to be prudent. Diligence includes reasonable attendance at meetings, efforts to keep informed about corporate affairs, examination of reports submitted for consideration, familiarity with charter and bylaws, and, in general, a degree of participation in corporate management that will demonstrate the acknowledgment of one's stewardship.

Prudence. The duty to be prudent exposes the officer or director to risk of liability for errors of judgment which result in loss to the corporation, even where there has been no lack of diligence. Prudence is generally defined as that degree of care which an ordinarily prudent man would exercise in the conduct of his own affairs. This standard, which is usually imposed on persons, such as trustees, acting in a fiduciary capacity, would appear to impose liability for ordinary negligence. However, corporate officers and directors are quasi-fiduciaries, rather than full-fledged fiduciaries, and so are not held to as rigorous a standard of care as trustees. Thus, although statutes and court decisions continue to speak of prudence, officers or directors are not likely to be held liable for errors or mistakes of judgment which an ordinarily prudent man would not have made in the conduct of his own business. To put it differently, they will not be held liable for losses resulting from ordinary negligence. The impact of the requirements of prudence has been mitigated by the development of the "business judgment" rule.

Business judgment rule. The business judgment rule is a doctrine enunciated in judicial decisions which exonerates directors and officers from liability for the consequences of exercising their business judgment unwisely although honestly and with loyalty to the corporation (that is, in good faith). As to the concept of due care, the business judgment rule has been declared, in some court opinions, to presuppose that judgment has been exercised—in other words, that the business decision, even if erroneous or imprudent, was not a reckless or grossly negligent one. It appears, therefore, that the corporate officer or director is meeting the standards of his responsibility to his corporation and its stockholders if he acts in good faith and with reasonable diligence, even if his judgment is poor.

STANDARDS OF RESPONSIBILITY TO THIRD PERSONS

A corporate officer or director is not insulated from his responsibility as an individual to avoid wronging third persons. If, by his own acts or omissions, he has personally participated in the commission of a wrongful act or tort—a noncontractual breach of legal duty such as improperly ordering an arrest on corporate premises—he will not be insulated from liability merely because he was acting on behalf of the corporation, and the corporation is also liable. In these situations, however, his responsibility is that of an individual, and he must personally be a participant in the wrongful conduct.

The corporate officer or director does not owe undivided loyalty to such third persons unless he happens to have fiduciary relationship toward them. Nor would he ordinarily need to concern himself about the adequacy of the benefits received by third persons out of a transaction with the corporation. His quasi-fiduciary responsibility to the corporation and its stockholders does not extend to third persons who deal with the corporation or with him as an officer or director of the corporation. There are, however, particular statutory provisions which may impose special responsibilities or liabilities on corporate officers or directors as a matter of public policy. Some of these provisions will be mentioned later.

Methods of Enforcing Liability

As has been indicated, the corporate officer or director bears a quasi-fiduciary responsibility to the corporation and its stockholders and a responsibility for his individual acts or omissions to third persons, plus special obligations or liabilities prescribed by statute. A discussion of responsibility, which describes the requisite standard of behavior, is incomplete without a discussion of accountability, the means by which the duty to maintain such standards may be enforced. Of course, there are sanctions other than legal liability for the violation of such duty. Discharge from office and forfeiture of economic benefits may be more significant than liability. However, accountability as used here means enforcement of legal liability.

ACCOUNTABILITY TO CORPORATION AND STOCKHOLDERS

It has been stated that the quasi-fiduciary duty of good faith and due care on the part of a corporate officer or director is owed to the corporation and its stockholders. However, enforcement at law must be brought by or in the name of the corporation. The stockholders ordinarily have no right, either individually or collectively, to sue in their own behalf for breach of a fiduciary duty to the corporation. It may happen, however, that the corporation would decline to bring an action, either because the prospective defendants control the board or because those in control of the corporation consider the action inadvisable or lacking in merit. In such event, statutory provisions authorize the bringing of such action *on behalf* of the corporation, a proceeding known as a "derivative" action. Such actions are most commonly brought by minority stockholders after the corporation has refused to act for itself, and they are known as stockholders' derivative suits. In certain instances, however, derivative actions on behalf of the corporation may be brought by creditors or even by the state attorney general or other public official.

While accountability for breach of the fiduciary duty is to the corporation alone, the same act may constitute a separate and distinct wrong to one or more stockholders, independent of the wrong to the corporation. For redress of such personal wrong, the stockholder may bring an individual action in his own behalf or a representative action for himself and all other stockholders similarly situated. Examples of stockholders' individual or representative actions would include a suit against directors based upon the alleged exclusion of the plaintiff stockholders from proper participation in the affairs of the corporation, or violation of pre-emptive rights of stockholders to purchase corporate securities, or wrongful refusal to transfer ownership of shares on the books of the corporation.

ACCOUNTABILITY TO NONSTOCKHOLDERS

As indicated earlier, the corporate officer or director who commits a personal tort—such as fraud or actionable negligence—while acting on behalf of the corporation will be jointly liable with the corporation to pay damages to the person injured. This liability ordinarily is limited to torts, since, in contractual matters, corporate officers and directors are known to be acting as agents who assume no personal obligations. Enforcement in such cases is by direct action against both the corporation and the officer or director or against either of them.

Special statutes which provide for either civil or criminal liability for certain acts or omissions of corporate officers or directors and the liability of officers and directors to creditors will be considered later.

Conduct Which May Lead to Liability

LIABILITY TO CORPORATION AND STOCKHOLDERS

There has been a wide variety of factual transactions which have given rise to suits asserting liability of officers and directors. Such liability, as has been indicated, is predicated on absence of good faith or failure to exercise due care. It may be of some value to mention briefly certain areas in which these standards have been applied.

Misappropriation and fraud. The most obvious ground on which liability may be asserted under the heading of breach of good faith is, of course, actual misappropriation of corporate property through the commission of larceny, fraud, bribery, and the like—instances of dishonesty. As has been pointed out, however, good faith means more than personal honesty. Without any corrupt intent, a corporate officer or director may, nevertheless, be held to have failed to meet his obligation of loyalty to the corporation.

Self-dealing. After actual misappropriation cases, the most obvious area of risk of liability is the self-dealing situation. Here the officer or director is receiving a direct or indirect benefit, personally, in a transaction with the corporation. Such cases include actions by or on behalf of the corporation to recover compensation deemed excessive in relation to the services rendered, to demand an accounting for profits from doing business with a concern in which the officer or director has a personal interest, or to claim the profits realized on investments made by the officer or director individually with funds borrowed from the corporation. In such matters, proof of good faith, as stated previously, requires evidence that the corporation acted through disinterested representatives, that there was full and fair disclosure of all available information on the subject of the transaction, and that the corporation derived fair value from its dealings with the officer or director.

Trading on status or information. Thus far consideration has been given to the impact of the good faith requirement in transactions involving both the corporation and the officer or director. Most sophisticated corporate executives are aware of the possibility of challenge in such cases, but fewer recognize the danger in dealings with third persons—not the corporation—which may be construed as trading upon the executive's status or his information as an insider.

An example of trading on status would be the management group's sale of a controlling block of stock at a price which exceeds fair market value. The excess is often claimed by or on behalf of the corporation as a secret premium or payment for the resignations of these directors who are selling.

Section 16 of the Securities Exchange Act of 1934 is specifically designed to prevent unfair use of corporate information by insiders in connection with the purchase and sale of securities of corporations which are traded on national securities exchanges or of over-the-counter companies with total assets of more than a million dollars and with 500 or more stockholders. This law requires all directors and officers of such corporations and persons holding more than 10 percent of any class of their equity securities (the insiders) to report all transactions in such securities and renders the insiders liable to the corporation for any "short swing" profits realized in such securities dealings—that is, any purchase or sale and purchase of stock or other equity security of the corporation occurring within six months, where the sale price is higher than the purchase price. In such cases, no proof is required that the insider actually used inside information. In fact, the insider is held liable even if he proves that he did not utilize or even possess confidential corporate information.

Unlike Section 16, Rule 10b-5 (issued by the Securities and Exchange Commission under Section 10 of the Securities Exchange Act and applied in the much publicized *Texas Gulf Sulphur Company* case) is directed to the actual misuse of inside information. Under this rule, a person possessing confidential corporate information, whether or not he is an officer or director, who profits from such information in connection with the purchase or sale of the company's securities may be held liable for the profitable advantage he gains. However, his liability would not be to the corporation or its stockholders but to the buyer or seller of his company's securities.

In the *Texas Gulf Sulphur Company* case, the insiders, including officers and directors, were found by the court to have utilized confidential information about an important mining discovery so as to purchase stock (and calls on the stock) of the company before the information was made public and the price of the stock rose. The Court of Appeals also held that the officers violated the law when they accepted stock options without disclosure of the crucial information to the Stock Option Committee or the Board of Directors, which granted the options. An officer or director is well advised, therefore, not to trade in his company's stock or to accept options whenever there is any undisclosed information which, when made public, might materially affect the price of the stock.

In a recent New York case, it was held that directors could be held liable to account to the corporation itself for their profits from sales of their own stock in the corporation if these profits were caused by the directors' failure to give their stockholders and the investing public inside information as to the declining earnings of the corporation. The directors are liable even though such sales had no adverse effect on the corporation or its business. In reaching this conclusion, the court acknowledged that the directors might be exposed to double liability if the purchasers of their stock sued them for failure to disclose material information. [*Diamond* v. *Oreamuno, et al.*, 29 A.D. (2d) 285, 287 N.Y.S. 2d 300 (1st Dept. 1968)]

Corporate opportunities. As the preceding discussion indicates, the corporate executive may not take advantage of his position in seeking personal gain. The obverse of that proposition is equally true: The officer or director may not *disregard* his position in seeking personal gain. He may not appropriate for himself a "corporate opportunity"—that is, a business opportunity in which the corporation had a pre-existing interest or which is manifestly in the corporation's interest in view of its business and history. Naturally, the determination of whether an opportunity is a corporate opportunity will depend upon the particular facts of each case, including the corporation's financial ability to undertake the enterprise, its prior policy with respect to similar undertakings, and the willingness of the other parties involved to deal with the corporation. The basic consideration in the corporate opportunity situation is the good faith of the corporate director or officer—has he, in appropriating the opportunity for himself, placed his personal interest ahead of his loyalty to the corporation? As in other good-faith situations, full disclosure to and approval by disinterested independent representatives will avoid later claims of liability in an action by, or in the name of, the corporation.

Another aspect of the corporate opportunity doctrine is the limitation on the right of directors to engage in business competing with that of the corporation. While there is no blanket prohibition against competition by a director where there has been full disclosure, competition may not be carried out to such extent as to involve disloyalty to the corporation's interests. Officers usually have no right to compete at all, since their full-time services are normally required by the corporation.

Management use of corporate funds in proxy contests. The general trend of cases upholds the right of management to use corporate funds in proxy contests, particularly where the issue involves a good-faith dispute over questions of corporate policy rather than mere selection of persons who will run the company. Thus, to the extent that any doctrine may be distilled from the cases, the paramount consideration is whether the expenditures were made, bona fide, in the interests of the corporation or in the personal interests of the management.

Lack of due care. As indicated previously, liability to the corporation for errors in business judgment would most likely be limited to instances of gross negligence on the part of the executive. However, liability need not necessarily be predicated on waste or dissipation of corporate assets resulting from business decisions. Loss to the corporation may result from activities beyond the powers granted or implied in the corporate charter (so-called *ultra vires* acts) or from doing business in a state in which the corporation was not qualified to act. In these situations, the executives may be held liable because of their lack of diligence regarding the existence of corporate power and authority, even though the decision to embark upon the enterprises would not otherwise have rendered them liable. Directors may also be held liable for want of diligence if they permit excessive accumulations of earned surplus and the corporation is surcharged with tax penalties on the constructive dividends.

Conceivably, directors may be considered grossly negligent in selecting obviously improper persons as officers or employees. Similarly, directors who permit a dominant controlling director to mismanage the affairs of the corporation may well be deemed culpable.

LIABILITY TO CREDITORS

Acts leading to impairment of the capital of the corporation may expose directors to personal liability to the creditors of the corporation or to the shareholders, whose position, in such cases, would be comparable to that of the creditors.

Typically, the director may be charged with liability if he votes for improper declaration of dividends when the surplus usually required for that purpose is not available, or if he votes for the corporation's purchase or redemption of its own stock in a manner contrary to law (such purchases may be made out of stated capital only for limited purposes; otherwise, purchases must be made from surplus). If he votes for the distribution of assets to stockholders on liquidation without making adequate provision for payment of debts of the corporation or in favor of loans to directors without stockholder approval, he is also liable.

SPECIAL STATUTORY OBLIGATIONS

A number of statutory provisions impose special civil or criminal responsibility on corporate management. An exhaustive listing is impossible, but a few examples will serve to indicate the need for consulting corporate counsel as to the existence of such provisions in the jurisdiction involved.

A major area of concern is the liability created in tax statutes, such as Section 6672 of the Internal Revenue Code of 1954, which renders corporate officers liable for a penalty equal to 100 percent of a tax which the corporation is obligated to collect and pay over, such as withholding taxes, where the failure to collect or pay over the tax was knowingly and intentionally participated in by the officers. State laws have comparable provisions.

In addition, there may be special statutory fines or similar penalties imposed upon corporations for violating particular requirements of law, which may be charged against corporate executives as well. Thus, for instance, the president, secretary, and treasurer of a corporation are personally liable for payment of the special assessment exacted from corporations for failure to secure Workmen's Compensation Insurance. A comparable, although not identical, provision is contained in the New York law governing disability benefits.

Section 11 of the Securities Act of 1933 imposes liability on directors and certain officers who are required to sign a registration statement. Falsification or material omission in a registration statement issued in connection with a public offering of the corporation's securities renders these persons liable. A similar but less severe liability is imposed for false or misleading statements in periodic reports required to be filed with the Securities and Exchange Commission under the Securities Exchange Act of 1934.

The Securities Act of 1933 also limits the freedom of a director or officer to sell his own stock in his corporation. If he is deemed to be in a "control" relationship with his corporation and his transaction amounts to a public distribution of his stock, he may be held liable for civil and criminal penalties by failing to comply with the registration requirements of the Act.

Section 16 of the Securities Exchange Act of 1934 and state laws impose penal sanctions for short sales of their own company's securities by officers or directors.

The action of a director in voting in favor of declaring dividends out of capital in violation of law may constitute a misdemeanor on his part, as well as a basis of liability to corporate directors. Another criminal act in certain jurisdictions would be the issuance of capital stock without receipt of full consideration. The action by directors in favor of purchase or redemption by the corporation of its own shares out of capital in violation of law may also be a crime. All of these prohibited actions tend to impair the capital of the corporation in fraud of creditors. In addition, issuing capital stock in excess of the authorized capital is a criminal act by the officers and directors participating in it.

Corporate officers and directors may also be held both criminally and civilly liable for violation of the antitrust laws. Section 14 of the Clayton Act specificacally provides for the criminal liability of officers and directors, but prosecutions under the Sherman Act have also been upheld. On rare occasions, jail sentences have been imposed for antitrust violations imposed on corporate officers. In addition, the courts have sustained actions to impose civil liability upon corporate officers and directors for violation of the antitrust statutes even though there is no specific provision imposing civil liability on corporate officers or directors to compare with the express language concerning criminal responsibility of such persons.

The foregoing enumeration touches upon the major areas in which the corporate officer or director may be exposed to personal responsibility in the collection and payment of taxes, in the providing of Workmen's Compensation and other protection for employees, in the preservation of capital for the protection of creditors, in dealings with the securities of the corporation, and in matters which are governed by the antitrust statutes. Each of these areas should be carefully explored, and corporate officers and directors must devote particular attention to them or risk personal responsibility, either criminal or civil, or both.

Minimizing Risk of Liability

There are three broad areas in which the corporate official may be protected in whole or in part from legal liability. The first of these, of course, concerns his actual conduct in the performance of his duties as corporate executive; the second involves the possibility of his receiving indemnification from the corporation for the loss and expense of litigation; and the third involves procurement of insurance against liability.

CONDUCT MINIMIZING RISK OF LIABILITY

The corporate executive may minimize the risk of liability by means of actions which establish a record, or furnish evidence, that he has, in fact, satisfied the standards imposed upon him by law. To demonstrate good faith the corporate official should, for example, endeavor to show affirmatively that the corporation had the benefit of independent representation, that he made full disclosure of information relating to the matter, and that the transaction was fair to the corporation. Such record may be made by insisting upon directors' minutes or other appropriate memoranda which reflect all those elements. Similarly, satisfaction of the obligation to be diligent may be demonstrated by a record of regular meetings and regular attendance at such meetings.

In order to satisfy the requirement of independent representation of the corporation, officers should require approval by the directors in transactions which are outside the ordinary course of the officers' duties. Similarly, directors who are interested in any such transaction should make known their interest and abstain from voting. The votes and the abstentions should be reflected specifically in the minutes. If independent representation in the board of directors is not available and if full disclosure has been made to the stockholders, ratification by a majority of the stockholders will usually satisfy the requirement of fairness, notwithstanding a dissent by a minority of the stockholders.

Diligence may be demonstrated by insistence upon the advice or opinions of specialists, such as counsel for the corporation or accountants, where necessary. By the use of such professional advice, the officer or director may be relieved of the responsibility of determining at his own peril the permissible scope of the corporation's powers, or its qualification to conduct business of any particular nature or in any particular jurisdiction, or any other matters which might result in losses to the corporation and which are basic to his obligation to exercise due care.

With respect to liability to third persons, the obligation of the corporate official may, in some cases, consist of no more than the same exercise of good faith and due care. In other cases, however, he may be exposed to a technical statutory liability despite the honesty of his intentions and his innocence of any knowledge of wrongdoing. To minimize risk of liability in such cases by means of his own actions, the corporate executive can do no more than to be particularly alert in matters pertaining to taxes, payroll, competition (that is, antitrust matters), preservation of capital for the benefit of creditors, and securities transactions in which provisions for such special liability are most likely to be found, and to avail himself of professional legal or accounting advice.

INDEMNIFICATION OF DIRECTORS AND OFFICERS

The charter or bylaws of corporations commonly contain provisions for indemnifying officers and directors for the expense incurred (including counsel fees) in suits brought against them for their actions in those capacities. The extent to which the corporation may validly agree to make such indemnification may be limited by statute, and, to some extent, there is a lack of uniformity among states regarding such statutory restrictions. In general, in a derivative action or a third-party action, civil or criminal, the corporation may properly indemnify the officer or director who has been vindicated by judgment. In all likelihood, such indemnity would also be proper where the action was withdrawn or discontinued without any recovery or voluntary settlement, although no judgment was actually rendered in favor of the corporate executive. In all probability, such indemnification could also be made where judgment in favor of the corporate official exonerates him from liability because of some ground other than the merits, such as the expiration of a period of limitations on the commencement of suit.

However, if a proceeding is settled by a compromise of liability or if a judgment is actually rendered against the officer or director, the right of the corporation to indemnify him will depend upon whether the action was brought by or on behalf of the corporation or whether it was brought by a third party (including a criminal action).

In a third-party action, civil or criminal, a corporation can generally indemnify the director if he has acted in good faith for a purpose which he reasonably believed to be in the corporation's best interests and, as far as criminal prosecutions are concerned, where he had no reasonable cause to believe that his conduct was unlawful. If these conditions are met, the corporation very likely will be permitted to indemnify him both for his legal expenses and for any sum he may be required to pay on account of a judgment, a fine, or a settlement. The Securities and Exchange Commission, however, has taken the view that indemnification provisions may contravene public policy to the extent that they permit indemnification against liability under the Securities Act of 1933. The commission has insisted that corporations offering securities for sale under the Act undertake to resist the payment of any claim for such indemnification unless the question is decided by a court of appropriate jurisdiction.

If the action was brought by or on behalf of the corporation and it is settled, the corporation will not, of course, be permitted to reimburse him for any sums he may be compelled to pay to the corporation by way of compromise, and it may reimburse him for his expenses only if such settlement has been approved by the court. If there is an adjudication against the officer and director, rather than a settlement in an action brought by or for the corporation itself, it is practically certain that the corporation will not be permitted to indemnify the officer or director either for the amount he is required to pay or for his expenses, since such judgment will constitute a judicial determination that he has violated his duty to the corporation.

INSURANCE AGAINST LIABILITY OF OFFICERS AND DIRECTORS

There has been increasing popular interest in directors' and officers' liability insurance. The coverage is divided into two parts. First, there is a coverage of the corporation's loss resulting from indemnification of its directors and officers for losses. Second, there is coverage of the personal liability of directors and officers when they are not indemnified by the corporation. Although the two types are covered by separate policies, they are usually sold as a package, with the corporation acting as agent for the directors and officers. Generally, policies provide for a deductible amount of $20,000 for each loss, and the insurance company will pay only 95 percent of the losses in excess of the deductible amount. The remaining 5 percent of loss in excess of the deductible amount must be borne by the insured parties.

Although some corporations and their counsel have taken the view that the corporation may pay the entire cost of such insurance, the more widely held position is that the insured directors and officers should pay a portion of the premium expense. Since the director or officer is insured only in situations in which he is not entitled to indemnification, it is argued that the corporation should not be allowed to indirectly indemnify its directors and officers for such liability by paying insurance premiums attributable to such coverage. Since the insurance companies do not allocate their premiums between the two types of coverage, the corporations and their directors and officers have been required to fix their own allocations. Because insurers have had very little loss experience in this comparatively new type of coverage, meaningful actuarial data are not available to assist in determining such allocation. Under a formula which has been generally accepted by many corporations and their officers and directors and has been recommended by insurance companies, 90 percent of the premium is allocated to the cost of the corporation's reimbursement coverage; 10 percent, to the protection afforded to directors and officers as a group for non-reimbursable expenses.

There are a number of exclusions from the coverage of the various policies being written. Some of the more important exclusions from the liability of the insurer include claims of libel and slander, claims based on or attributable to the directors' or officers' gaining in fact a personal advantage, claims for an accounting of profits from the purchase and sale of securities of the corporation under Section 16 of the Securities Exchange Act of 1934, and claims brought about by active and deliberate dishonesty of the insured as judicially determined.

In summary, although an officer or director cannot be protected by insurance for fraudulent or willful acts, he can be insured for negligence or mismanagement where he has not gained any personal profit or advantage. In cases where the officer or director is entitled to corporate indemnification as discussed here, the corporation in turn is insured for the amount required to be paid to the officer or director.

Antitrust
and Trade Regulation

Michael Malina

T HE SCOPE OF FEDERAL ANTITRUST REGULATION IS ALL-PERVASIVE, WITH
virtually every business of significance falling within its reach. With
the notorious exception of the Robinson-Patman Act, the relevant statutory
provisions are deceptively simple. Each can be set forth on one page, and
all are expressed in straightforward language apparently comprehensible
even to the uninitiated. Three-quarters of a century of judicial construction and active governmental and private enforcement have put substantial flesh on the bare-boned statutory texts.

Yet the risk of violation, even if unintentional, is so great that some
familiarity with the antitrust mysteries is a *sine qua non* for the conscientious executive. Accordingly, a brief survey such as this can be useful,
if only in alerting management to the fact that a problem of antitrust
dimension is present which an attorney should review. It should be noted
at the outset, however, that this review takes a conservative approach,
since antitrust litigation, even if successful, is expensive and should there-

MICHAEL MALINA is an attorney associated with Kaye, Scholer, Fierman, Hays &
Handler in New York City.

fore be avoided when possible. In the last analysis, antitrust turns on the peculiar facts of the given case, and the advice of counsel should invariably be sought.

The General Statutory Scheme

The basic antitrust statutes are few in number: The Sherman Act of 1890; the Clayton Act, first enacted in 1914 and significantly amended in 1936 by the Robinson-Patman Act and in 1950 by the Celler-Kefauver Antimerger Act; and the Federal Trade Commission Act of 1914.

The Sherman Act, which prohibits contracts, combinations, and conspiracies in restraint of trade, and monopolization, is a criminal statute. Violation can result in fines of up to $50,000 and, for individual transgressors, imprisonment of up to one year. In addition, court orders restraining future violations are also available. These provisions are enforced primarily by the Antitrust Division of the Justice Department.

The Clayton Act, which deals with specific types of restraints including exclusive dealing arrangements, tie-in sales, price discrimination, mergers and acquisitions, and interlocking directorates, carries only civil penalties and is enforced jointly by both the Antitrust Division and the Federal Trade Commission, but with the FTC in practice assuming almost total responsibility for the Robinson-Patman Act's strictures against anticompetitive price discrimination.

The Federal Trade Commission Act, administered solely by that agency, is a catch-all enactment which has been construed to include all the prohibitions of the other antitrust laws and, in addition, may be utilized to fill what may appear to be loopholes in the more explicit regulatory statutes.

Both the Antitrust Division and the Federal Trade Commission have broad investigatory powers to discover antitrust violations. Yet, despite the breadth of this authority, they are subject to constitutional and statutory limitations. It is therefore essential, when contacted by an enforcement agency, to consult counsel at once.

Over and above this awesome panoply of governmental enforcement, the Clayton Act arms any person who can establish that he has been injured by virtue of any antitrust violation with the substantial weapons of a private suit in the federal courts for treble the damages sustained plus reasonable attorneys' fees and a court order restraining future violations.

In recent years, particularly in the wake of the industrywide charges of price fixing leveled at the manufacturers of heavy electrical equipment, this treble-damage remedy has assumed a featured role on the antitrust stage. In many instances, the specter of substantial liability for treble damages, not to mention the cost of defending myriad such suits, is a far more effective deterrent to antitrust infraction than the threat of what may be only a minimal fine and an infrequently imposed jail sentence. Significantly, the Supreme Court has consistently been most hospitable to the "private attorney general," and recent developments indicate that the treble-damage arena will more and more be the forum in which important antitrust questions are litigated and resolved.

Rule of Reason and Per Se Offenses

Section 1 of the Sherman Act prohibits "every contract, combination . . . or conspiracy in restraint of trade. . . ." Such a sweeping interdiction, if literally applied, would invalidate practically every commercial arrangement. Accordingly, as early as 1911 the Supreme Court ruled that, despite the all-embracing statutory language, the Sherman Act reached only those trade restraints which are unreasonable. This so-called rule of reason has since been, at least in theory, the hallmark of judicial construction of the antitrust laws. Under its aegis, the anticompetitive consequences of a challenged practice are weighed against the business justifications upon which it is predicated, and a judgment with respect to its reasonableness is made.

However, such an approach has obvious shortcomings. For one thing, reasonableness is an ephemeral concept, and whether a particular course of conduct will ultimately be found to be reasonable is not easy to predict when new business arrangements are contemplated. Moreover, the task of enforcing a regulatory scheme based on such a theory can be staggering. The trial of particular cases often entails a microscopic examination of the entire market involved. In light of these difficulties and the blatantly anticompetitive nature of certain types of conduct, the courts have developed a doctrine of "per se" illegality which conclusively presumes such practices to be unreasonable. In other words, when a per se offense (such as price fixing among competitors) is charged, all the government must establish is that the defendant has, in fact, engaged in the proscribed practice; illegality follows as a matter of law, no matter how slight the anticompetitive effect, how small the market share of the defendants, or how proper their motives. In the past decade the scope of the per se doctrine has been constantly expanded, making the enforcement task less onerous, the legal treatment to be afforded contemplated conduct more certain, and the flexibility of the antitrust laws more limited.

Horizontal Restraints Among Competitors

Horizontal restraints of trade—that is, concerted actions among entities in actual or potential competition with one another—have traditionally been considered the most serious of antitrust infractions and constitute that category of violations most susceptible to criminal penalties. The reason for such harsh treatment is plain: The antitrust laws postulate a competitive economy in which rival firms compete with respect to prices, products, and services. Any arrangement which runs counter to this axiomatic conduct among competitive entities is accordingly suspect.

PRICE FIXING

Antitrust's capital crime is horizontal price fixing. Agreements among competitors with respect to prices for products or services are illegal per se. The prohibition is all-embracing, whoever may be involved and whatever the circumstances. Not only sellers but buyers as well are within the statute's scope. Both large and small companies in all industries, whether booming or depressed, are covered. Even price agreements intended to provide their participants with the countervailing power to meet larger, more powerful competitors are not permitted. Moreover, the reasonableness of the agreed-upon prices is beside the point. Agreements setting maximum prices in inflationary times and those setting minimum prices during depressions are equally prohibited. In short, price fixing, in any shape or form, is deemed anticompetitive and thus unlawful.

What is price fixing? What, then, is price fixing? To start with the obvious, competitors may not agree on the actual prices they will charge or pay for a product or service. But this self-evident example is only the beginning. As the Supreme Court has made explicit, agreements that *affect* prices are as unlawful as those that actually *set* them. Competitors may not agree on a price range within which they will compete, on a common list or book price from which discounts are free to vary, or even on the discounts themselves. Terms and conditions of sale which indirectly affect price cannot lawfully be the subject of agreement. Nor can competitors act in concert to limit supply in order to drive prices up. Even agreements on common standards may, if entered into for the purpose of affecting price, be violative of the law. The lesson is clear. No agreement with a competitor which can be construed as affecting price is completely free from antitrust risk. And the risk is great: criminal proceedings resulting in fines and possibly imprisonment, followed by claims for treble the damages provable by aggrieved customers.

The element of agreement. Given the broad sweep of the Sherman Act's prohibition of price fixing, the statutory requirement of "contract, combination or conspiracy" becomes crucial. In short, these words mean that there must be an agreement for the statute to apply. But the concept of agreement in the antitrust lexicon is a far cry from the notion as found, for example, in the law of contracts. And, practically speaking, it is as important to avoid conduct which might be construed to evidence agreement as to avoid agreement itself.

To run afoul of Section 1 of the Sherman Act, an agreement need not be in writing and be signed by each of the parties. In fact, it need not be formally entered into at all. It would indeed be rare in this day and age for competitors to draft such an agreement. Rather, the element of agreement is an ultimate fact to be proved, sometimes by direct evidence that the parties agreed, but most often circumstantially—by inferences logically drawn from all the relevant circumstances.

Thus, whenever competitors follow a similar course of conduct which would not ordinarily be taken in the absence of prior agreement, the possibility is present that an inference of conspiracy will be drawn. To the extent that any substantial contacts among the competing firms have taken place, there is a risk that an agreement will later be found. In fact, the Supreme Court has stated that a discussion of prices and the need for an increase among competitors followed within a few days by a uniform price rise is little less than proof positive of agreement. Accordingly, such contacts should be kept to a bare minimum if not avoided altogether.

One leading manufacturer, having been severely burned by the antitrust laws, instructed its sales personnel to have no contacts—even personal ones—with competitors if a competitor is seen on the street, cross to the other side. While this mandate may be somewhat extreme, certainly no price information of any kind should be exchanged with competition. Competitive price lists should be secured only from customers and should be clearly marked as to their source. If it is necessary to get in touch with a competitor, the purpose and substance of the contact should be recorded. The basic rule is to err on the side of fewer contacts.

Even if overt contacts with competitors are avoided, the risk that an agreement may be found is not totally eliminated. If competitors take uniform action which might not otherwise be expected in the circumstances, the inference of agreement can be drawn. Much has been written of the doctrine of "conscious parallelism," inferring conspiracy from parallel action among competitors. The Supreme Court has decided that, although such a state of facts is relevant to the question of agreement, it is not the substantive equivalent of conspiracy; in other words, parallel action alone will not conclusively prove a violation.

The problem arises most often in the context of the widespread industry practice of price leadership—one market leader announces a price change, and all other companies follow with identical moves shortly thereafter. If the leader's move is downward, there can be no legitimate inference of agreement if everyone follows, since it is to be expected that competition will be met. On the other hand, following the leader upward can present problems. If there is no evidence of discussions or other contacts among the various concerns, the inference of agreement is proper only if the circumstances in the market dictate a result other than the one that has been uniformly reached. For example, if a standardized product with roughly uniform production costs is involved, one would expect uniform pricing and the standard price leadership pattern would not raise any eyebrows. On the other hand, if the price leader announced a substantial increase in the face of sharply falling demand and a condition of chronic overcapacity, and then every other firm announced an identical increase, one might be hard put to convince a court or jury that each company's decision was made individually.

In the last analysis, if a price-fixing agreement is charged the defendant should be prepared to show facts supporting the exercise of an individual business judgment in making its pricing decision. And, whenever it is decided to follow a competitor's price move upward, discretion suggests that timing differ and, if practicable, certain details of the change not be carbon copies.

ALLOCATION OF MARKETS OR CUSTOMERS

Agreements among competitors dividing markets by territory or by customers are patently anticompetitive and hence illegal per se. If anything, such arrangements are even more restrictive than the most formal price-fixing agreement, since they leave no room whatsoever for competition of any kind.

Thus competing firms may not divide among themselves the geographical areas in which they sell, nor may they distribute customers or allocate business by percentages of the available market. All such understandings, whether direct or indirect, are unlawful.

Again, since agreement is a matter of inference and proof, one must be careful to avoid suspicious conduct. It is dangerous to refer customers to a competitor, since an agreement not to sell to them might be inferred. It is risky to use competitors as exclusive distributors, lest the conclusion be reached that an agreement not to compete underlay the arrangement. As with all questions of horizontal conspiracy, the prudent course is to avoid even the suspicion of a prohibited agreement.

Concerted Refusal to Deal

The horizontal boycott is a classic per se offense. The law prohibits agreement by two or more persons not to sell to or not to buy from an individual, a firm, or a group. Such an agreement amounts to a private licensing scheme and is thus contrary to the free-market principles underlying antitrust policy. Being per se illegal, such boycott agreements cannot be justified, whatever their raison d'être. Thus sellers may not agree to deal with a known price cutter. Similarly, buyers may not join in boycotting sellers whose prices are too high or whose goods are defective. Such decisions must be made individually. As with all horizontal restraints the element of agreement, once found to be present, is the kiss of death.

Trade Associations

Trade associations, by their very nature, bristle with antitrust problems. Practically by definition the requisite agreement is present, and the inquiry focuses on the nature of the members' concerted activity. In view of this constant antitrust concern, every trade association activity, even if it may appear wholly innocuous, should be closely supervised by an attorney. Agendas should be prepared in advance and reviewed with counsel—who should, if possible, be present at every meeting. Informal meetings outside the presence of counsel should be avoided. In addition, membership in a trade association should be open to all qualified firms, since arbitrary exclusion might be construed to be a group boycott, especially where membership confers a significant competitive advantage over nonmembers.

Per se offenses such as price fixing, market divisions, and refusals to deal are obviously improper for an association. Of course, trade associations may properly act, under supervision, in many areas. Among these, statistical reporting of various types—past costs, production, sales, and the like—is the most usual. But the identification of the individual firm's data should be buried in the association's reports, and forecasts of any kind should be avoided. Past prices can probably be reported; but, in light of the use of past price discussions to help prove price-fixing conspiracies, such statistics are dangerous and ought to be closely supervised. So also, standardization may be a proper association activity as long as standards which serve to affect prices or lessen competition are avoided and all members are free to disregard them.

It would be impossible in this brief review to catalogue the do's and dont's of trade association activities. The best advice is to consult counsel every step of the way.

Vertical Restraints

Antitrust analysis distinguishes between economic relationships among entities on the same level of distribution which compete with one another (horizontal relationships) and relationships among suppliers and customers on different distributional levels (vertical relationships). Vertical arrangements, not being among direct competitors, were for many years treated less severely than horizontal restraints although, to be sure, certain vertical restraints have been uniformly condemned. In recent years, the judicial attitude toward verticals has hardened considerably, and per se illegality seems more and more to be the rule rather than the exception.

Vertical Price Fixing

As is the case with horizontal price-fixing agreements among competitors, vertical price-fixing agreements, whereby a seller and a buyer agree with respect to the price at which the buyer will resell, have long been illegal per se. As is true with horizontal agreements, it does not matter how reasonable the agreed-upon price may be or how many good and sound reasons there are for the agreement. Moreover, indirect price fixing (such as limitations on price advertising) are as unlawful as direct agreements. Nor does it matter whether the fixed price is a maximum rather than a minimum, as the Supreme Court has recently reaffirmed. In the absence of a valid fair-trade program, if an agreement is found, illegality follows inexorably.

Accordingly, the crucial question again is whether an agreement exists. It has been made clear by the courts that a seller may properly suggest a resale price to his vendee; the fact that the suggested price is followed is not enough to show the presence of conspiracy. It is thus advisable, in mentioning resale prices, to use the word "suggested" in order to make the seller's intention clear.

Consignment sales. For many years it was accepted antitrust doctrine that, in consignments to a true agent (as opposed to a merely formal arrangement), a seller was free to set the price at which "his" products were sold, even though the agent was otherwise an independent businessman. In recent years, the Supreme Court has raised serious questions with respect to the continuing validity of this rule. Although no clear principle has yet evolved, vertical price fixing under a consignment device appears to be dangerous whenever the seller is in a position, by using economic leverage, to "coerce" the consignees into compliance. The prudent course is apparently to utilize consignment selling only if there is a good nonprice reason for doing so and, whenever such a method is followed, to treat the consignee as a true agent—the seller should pay taxes and insurance, maintain inventory control, and give approval on significant decisions.

Fair trade. The Congress has provided that, if state law permits, certain resale price maintenance contracts are exempt from the strictures of the federal antitrust laws. The key here is state law; only if the state provides for so-called fair trade is the exemption operative. In states with no such legislation, vertical price-fixing agreements continue to be illegal per se.

The variety of fair-trade programs available turns on state law. There are basically two types: "signer" states, in which only those resellers who actually agree to observe the seller's resale prices are bound to do so; and "non-signer" states, in which all resellers who have received notice of at least one fair-trade contract are bound by its terms. In general, if a seller desires to enforce a fair-trade program, he must do so without discrimination; intentionally permitting certain resellers to disregard established prices may jeopardize the entire scheme.

The federal legislation which provides the fair-trade exemption explicitly denies it to contracts between retailers, wholesalers, or persons in competition with each other. It is thus dangerous for sellers to fair-trade if they distribute through company-owned branches as well as independent retailers, particularly when the two types of outlets compete for the same customers.

ORDERLY MARKETING ARRANGEMENTS

In organizing the distribution of their products, sellers often resort to a variety of restrictions aimed at the orderly marketing of their goods. These restraints often limit intrabrand competition in the seller's goods among the various dealers in order to enhance the goods' position in the inter-brand competitive struggle with the goods of other sellers. Traditionally, orderly marketing arrangements are governed by rule of reason and con-demned only when unreasonable in the totality of the economic circum-stances of the market. Recent decisions have severely limited their utility, however, in that per se rules have been fashioned to condemn the most pervasive varieties of orderly marketing techniques.

Exclusive selling agreements. Sellers may grant an exclusive franchise to a particular dealer in a specified territory by agreeing to sell only to that dealer within its area of responsibility. Such restraints, which are limitations upon the seller's freedom, are governed by the rule of reason and are, in most circumstances, valid. Even if the seller is induced to grant such an "exclusive" by the dealer, the courts have not found an illegal concert of action. But if the seller enjoys a monopoly position in the product, so that alternative sources of supply are not available to the con-sumer, the restraint has been deemed unreasonable and hence prohibited.

Territorial and customer restrictions. Orderly marketing plans have often utilized arrangements whereby dealers agree to resell the product only within specified territories and to solicit business only from specified classes of customers. Thus these restrictions are upon the buyer. Prior to 1967 it was generally thought that such restraints were subject to the rule of reason with validity depending on economic justification, so long as the agreements were purely vertical and did not involve horizontal conspiracy among the dealers. To be sure, the Department of Justice took a dim view, asserting that most such schemes should be prohibited. In its *Schwinn* decision in 1967 the Supreme Court terminated the controversy by ruling that, once title to a product has been transferred, no limitation on its future sale is permissible—in other words, that territorial and customer restrictions ancillary to the sale of goods are illegal per se.

This ruling does not necessarily toll the death knell of orderly marketing. There are still means by which a seller can organize distribution. But such organization can no longer be made rigid and enforced strictly. It is now proper, for example, to assign to a dealer a territory of primary responsibility in which he must exercise his best efforts to promote sales. A quota system can be used to implement such a device, on condition that quotas are not so high as to raise an effective barrier to sales outside the territory. With certain products for which service or installation is important, dealers can be required either to install and service all machines they sell or, if they prefer, to pay a fee to a local dealer for assuming that obligation. Again, the amount of the fee must be reasonably related to the cost of the service lest it be deemed an indirect territorial restriction.

With respect to customer restrictions, it is no longer lawful for a seller to retain certain accounts (such as governmental entities) for itself and forbid dealers to solicit their business. However, if business reasons dictate such a result, it may be achievable by selling to such customers at a price so low as to be prohibitive to the dealer. Such pricing probably would not run afoul of the Robinson-Patman Act.

Since the *Schwinn* decision's rationale is premised on the invalidity of restrictions after title passes, and since the court specifically upheld Schwinn's territorial and customer restraints in agency and consignment sales, it has been suggested that the force of the ruling can be avoided by widespread consignment selling. Aside from the fact that consignment selling is not commercially feasible for many businesses, it is important to note that the court did not give a green light to such restrictions, but merely upheld their reasonableness on the basis of competitive factors present in that particular case. In light of the problems raised by consignments in other antitrust contexts—particularly when utilized by large firms —it cannot be said that such a method of distribution is immune from antitrust risk.

Exclusive dealing agreements. Exclusive dealing agreements, pursuant to which the buyer undertakes to purchase all his requirements for the product from the seller, are governed by Section 3 of the Clayton Act; this prohibits such contracts if they are likely to substantially lessen competition. The principal vice of exclusives is that, if they tie up a significant portion of the market, the seller's competitors will be foreclosed from market access and competitively disadvantaged.

The development of the law in this area has been muddled, to say the least. In an important decision in 1949 the Supreme Court ruled that, if a substantial share of total sales in the market (measured by percentages) is foreclosed, illegality follows; a finding of 6.7 percent foreclosure was deemed sufficient. Twelve years later, however, reliance on numbers alone was eschewed, and a test requiring a case-by-case evaluation of the exclusive's probable effect on competition was announced. Then in 1966 the court decided that, in cases brought by the Federal Trade Commission charging unfair methods of competition under Section 5 of the FTC Act, a violation of the Clayton Act need not be proved at all, and any exclusive dealing arrangement which forecloses the seller's competitors from a substantial number of outlets may be prohibited.

Since it matters very little to a company whether its conduct is declared unlawful by a court in a Justice Department proceeding or by the FTC, the prudent course is to avoid any widespread use of exclusive dealing arrangements or any single agreement or group of agreements which would tie up a large number of outlets. Antitrust risk would be minimized by requiring dealers to purchase absolute minimum quantities or by utilizing similar undertakings to assure adequate inventories.

Tying arrangements. Sellers with more than one product may seek to tie the sale of one (which the customer presumably desires) with that of the other (which he presumably does not want). Such tie-ins are governed not only by the general language of the Sherman Act, but by the more particular provisions of Section 3 of the Clayton Act, which prohibits such arrangements if the likely result is substantially to lessen competition.

The central problem with respect to tie-ins is one of definition. Certainly, a shoe producer may require that a left shoe be purchased with a right. The question boils down to whether purchasers ordinarily buy the products together, in which case there is no infraction; or whether two distinct products are being sold together, thus forcing the customer to buy both.

Tie-ins are plainly anticompetitive in that the leverage generated by economic power in one market is used to accomplish sales in another. Accordingly, they are given harsh antitrust treatment. Once it is established that a tie-in is present; that the seller, by virtue of uniqueness or customer appeal, has sufficient economic power in the desired product to accomplish the tie-in; and that a "not insubstantial" amount of sales is involved (amounts as small as $60,800 have been found to meet this standard), they are generally deemed unlawful. Moreover, the concept has recently been expanded to reach coercive arrangements where the defendant does not sell both products but has an interest in their sale. For example, when a gasoline company coerced its dealers to sell the products of a particular manufacturer of tires, batteries, and accessories for which the oil company received commissions, the Supreme Court invalidated the arrangement as an unfair method of competition under the Federal Trade Commission Act.

Despite this usual rule of invalidity it is incorrect to state, as courts often have, that tie-ins are unlawful per se. In rare instances, tie-ins justified by exceptional competitive circumstances have been upheld—for example, in new industries and as part of a franchise operation involving the licensing of the seller's trademark to franchisees. Nevertheless, most tie-ins are frowned upon and the device should generally be avoided.

Restraints ancillary to trademark licenses. Franchising operations usually involve a license granted to the franchisee to use the franchisor's trademark on a product or service. To insure that quality is maintained and to avoid impairment of the franchisor's goodwill, the franchisee is frequently required to purchase ingredients only from the franchisor or approved suppliers. The franchisor's vital interest in maintaining the goodwill of its trademark by such arrangements has been recognized by both the courts and the FTC, which have upheld those utilized by Carvel with respect to its franchised ice cream dealers.

RECIPROCITY

One of the burning issues in antitrust today is the treatment to be afforded reciprocal buying arrangements. Although there have been few decisions on the question, the Department of Justice and the FTC have vigorously opposed systematic or coerced reciprocal dealing.

Analytically, there are several types of reciprocity. At one extreme is so-called coercive reciprocity: A company with substantial buying power in one market uses the leverage generated by that power to force unwilling suppliers to purchase otherwise unwanted products as the price for continued dealing. The analogy to tie-in sales is plain, and such coercive reciprocity has long been held unlawful. At the other extreme, companies may deal with each other reciprocally by happenstance, with no understanding at all, express or implied. Such mere mutual patronage should, as a theoretical matter, raise no antitrust problems. Between these two poles lies a broad area of what may be called noncoerced conditioned reciprocity— the two companies voluntarily condition their purchases from each other on reciprocal treatment. It is the antitrust treatment of this situation which is currently being debated. Since the enforcement agencies have taken a strong stand in opposition to the practice, it is not advisable to utilize trade relations departments which seek to formalize reciprocal buying arrangements.

REFUSALS TO DEAL

Vertical boycott agreements, like their horizontal counterparts, are illegal per se. Thus a seller may not agree with certain of his purchasers that he will not sell to another (for example, a price cutter). If such an agreement can be shown, the refusal to deal is plainly prohibited.

On the other hand, a seller has traditionally been afforded the right, acting independently, to select those with whom he will do business. This right, however, has been severely limited by a series of judicial decisions so that, as a practical matter, it may not be very meaningful. For example, the cases say that a seller may announce his unwillingness to deal with anyone who does not comply with certain suggestions (such as resale prices) and may cut off those who do not act accordingly. But if such a seller is assisted *in any way* by others identifying the violators of his policy, independent action is not present and an unlawful combination may be found. Therefore, it is essential, when deciding to cut off a customer, to avoid any inference of concerted action with others. If complaints are received from dealers about another dealer, it is dangerous to answer them, to advise the alleged offender of the complaint, or to inform the complaining parties of the eventual outcome.

Even if no possible combination or agreement can be shown, some recent decisions have condemned purely unilateral refusals to deal if for an anticompetitive purpose. Violations have been found when sellers refuse to sell to dealers who will not observe suggested prices or deal exclusively. Since this is a frontier question, it would be prudent not to cut off any dealer for reasons related to questions of antitrust concern. The far safer course is to try to avoid dealing with such persons in the first place. In light of the rapid pace of the law's development on refusals to deal, the advice of counsel should be sought before any dealer is cut off for any reason.

Structural Offenses—Monopoly and Merger

The problems that have been dealt with thus far concern what may be deemed behavioral offenses—certain types of anticompetitive conduct which the antitrust laws forbid. Antitrust is also concerned with market structure, and it prohibits structural phenomena likely to substantially lessen competition or to create a monopoly. Whether or not the assumption is sound as a matter of law or economics (and lawyers as well as economists have widely divergent views on the question), antitrust is premised on the belief that a competitive economy can best be achieved by maintaining markets with a large number of small sellers. Hence, to a significant extent, the structural aspect of the law focuses on avoiding or remedying the concentration of market power in a few firms with large market shares.

MARKET DEFINITION

Analysis of market structure requires, in the first instance, a definition of the market to be examined. As a theoretical matter the question is, What is the arena of effective competition?

Product market. The fundamental issue in delineating a product market is to determine what products or groups of products are sufficiently related to confront each other in the marketplace. Thus cellophane was found to be in the same market as other packaging materials, and glass containers were held to compete with cans. The criteria which the decisions say are relevant include industry or public recognition interchangeability of function or use; peculiarities of use; uniqueness of production facilities; distinct classes of customers and price and intersensitivity to price change. But, in the current antitrust climate, the application of these criteria has not been all that an objective observer might wish. By sanctioning the use of submarkets within markets, the courts have provided a flexibility in market definition which is often totally divorced from meaningful market facts. Criteria found dispositive in one case have been virtually ignored in the next, with markets being defined in an ad hoc manner, generally leading to illegality. The moral, unfortunately, is that the defense of a merger or monopolization case on product market grounds is often an exercise in futility.

Geographic market. The judicial construction of geographic markets is of a piece with that concerning products. Although theoretically an analysis should be made to determine in what areas competition actually takes place, the Supreme Court has ruled that economically meaningful geographic markets need not be proved. Any section of the country in which the impact of the challenged structural change is felt will suffice. Accordingly, it is typically overly optimistic to rely on the impropriety of the alleged geographic market in defending a merger or monopolization case.

MONOPOLIZATION

Section 2 of the Sherman Act makes it unlawful to monopolize, attempt to monopolize, or conspire to monopolize a line of commerce. It is significant that the statute does not speak in terms of the existence of a monopoly; rather, its focus is on the act of monopolization, which requires something more. The offense, which is not purely structural, has two elements: (1) possession of monopoly power in the relevant market and (2) willful acquisition or maintenance of that power.

Monopoly power. The Supreme Court has defined monopoly power as the power to control prices or exclude competition. As a practical matter, such power is measured by the alleged monopolist's share of the relevant market. Absolute monopoly in the economic sense—100 percent of the market—is a rare phenomenon, raising the question of how large a share a firm must possess to come within the statutory concept. Although there is no hard and fast rule, any market share of 50 percent or higher is sufficient to be of concern. And it must be remembered that markets and submarkets can be constructed in such a way as to create unduly high percentage shares that bear little relationship to economic reality.

Willful acquisition or maintenance. Once monopoly power is found the question remains: Was it willfully acquired or maintained? This is ephemeral and difficult to determine. What is clear is that the statute does not require that monopoly power be abused or intentionally exercised to drive out competition, although such conduct, if present, is sufficient to make out a violation. Nor does the element of willfulness entail an evil intent to eliminate competitors. Conscious acts designed to further or maintain a dominant market position will suffice—for example, acquisitions of competitors, exclusive dealing arrangements, or unreasonably low pricing tactics. On the other hand, monopoly power achieved through growth or development as a consequence of a superior product, business acumen, or historic accident is permissible. But concrete examples of such circumstances are few and far between.

MERGERS

Probably the most controversial aspect of antitrust today is the treatment afforded corporate mergers and acquisitions under Section 7 of the Clayton Act. The statutory language prohibits acquisitions, whether of stock or assets, where the likely result is a substantial lessening of competition or a

an abstractionist picture. The important thing is to put each piece in its proper place; concern for the ultimate picture will only lead to wrong results. With this warning in mind, the basic elements of the statutory scheme can be reviewed.

THE FUNDAMENTAL ELEMENTS OF VIOLATION

The Robinson-Patman Act prohibits discriminations in price among purchasers of commodities of like grade and quality which are likely to result in substantial injury to competition. Each of the elements is separate and must be found before the statute is violated.

Discrimination. For purposes of the Robinson-Patman Act, price discrimination means a difference in the price actually charged a purchaser, no more and no less. The term imports no element of bad intent. If there are at least two sales at different prices, this element of the statute is met.

As a general rule, price means actual price paid by the purchaser. If the seller wishes to utilize a delivered price system which absorbs varying amounts of freight costs in sales to different customers, there is no discrimination so long as every buyer pays the same delivered price. Conversely, it is permissible to sell f.o.b. seller's plant at the same price to all regardless of freight. Only the invoiced price paid by the purchaser matters.

The price difference must be between different purchasers. This means that a refusal to sell except at a higher price which does not culminate in a sale or a mere offer to sell on discriminatory terms cannot be deemed a price discrimination. As a general rule, only prices to purchasers directly from the seller are relevant. But if the seller exercises a degree of control over the resale terms, even though sales are made through an intermediary such as a wholesaler, the wholesaler's customers may be deemed "indirect purchasers" from the seller.

Like grade and quality. Price differences are not within the Act unless the goods sold to the different purchasers are of "like grade and quality." This requirement relates solely to the physical characteristics of the goods. Are they sufficiently alike for the law to require that their pricing be identical? Stated conversely, is there a significant commercial difference in the physical characteristics of the goods to justify a price differential? The fact that identical goods may be sold under differing brands and may have varying degrees of customer acceptance is beside the point at this stage of the inquiry. If the goods are fundamentally alike in physical and chemical composition, they are of like grade and quality.

Injury to competition. Discriminations in sales of goods of like grade and quality are unlawful only if they are likely to result in substantial injury to competition. Essentially, such injury can be of two types: (1) to buyers' competition (injury in the secondary line); and (2) to sellers' competition (injury in the primary line).

When secondary-line injury is charged, the inquiry focuses on the competitive harm suffered by the disfavored purchaser who pays the higher price in relation to his favored competitor. Thus, for secondary-line injury to be present, the discrimination must be between competing purchasers. If both purchasers are ultimate consumers and do not compete, no violation can be found. Not only must the purchasers compete geographically; they must, as a general rule, be on the same functional level. A wholesaler who buys at a lower price does not compete with a retail customer of the same seller, even though a price discrimination is present. On the other hand, if a direct-buying retailer is charged less than a wholesaler whose retail customers compete with the favored retailer, injury is likely to be found.

Given a discrimination between competing buyers, the case law is quite harsh. Injury is virtually presumed if the amount of the discrimination is substantial or, even when small and continuous, if the industry is characterized by small profit margins or fierce resale price competition. If, on the other hand, the lower price is reasonably available to all purchasers—for example, if the smallest can buy enough to gain the highest quantity discount—the discrimination would result from the disfavored buyer's own choice, and injury to competition would be hard to establish.

Primary-line injury focuses on damage to competition between the seller and his competitors who may lose business because of the low discriminatory price. Here the discrimination need not be between competing purchasers; in fact, the usual primary-line case involves area discrimination where the seller lowers his price in one area in order to attract more business. Here, Robinson-Patman flirts with a direct conflict with the basic antitrust premise of open price competition, and accordingly primary-line injury requires a stronger showing of likely impairment of competition than in a secondary-line case. Mere diversion of some business from one competitor to another is insufficient. But, if the lower prices are predatory—at or below cost or aimed at destroying a competitor—or if the market's price level is driven so low as to endanger the competitive health of other sellers, primary-line injury may be established.

THE STATUTORY DEFENSES

In the event that each of the elements of a Robinson-Patman violation is proved, there are two defenses which, if established, permit the defendant to prevail despite the injury to competition which may result: cost justification and meeting competition.

Cost justification. The statute expressly permits discriminations which "make only due allowance for differences in the cost of manufacture, sale or delivery resulting from the differing methods or quantities" sold or delivered to the purchasers. Cost justification is extraordinarily complex. Suffice it to say that successful defense involves intricate accounting techniques hobbled by stringent rules.

Meeting competition. If the lower price was made in good faith to meet the equally low price of a competitor, the seller has an absolute defense to a Robinson-Patman charge even if every other element of a violation is proved.

The key to the defense is the seller's good faith. He must obtain sufficient facts to justify a reasonable belief that his lower price is equal to—not lower than—that of his competitor. In other words, it is permissible to meet, but not to beat, the competitor's price. It is thus advisable to make a record of every available fact demonstrating the identity of the competitor and its price. These facts should be sought from the customer, rather than the competitor, if a price-fixing charge is to be avoided. The competitor whose price is met must compete directly with the seller; it is not permissible to give a dealer a lower price to allow him to meet his own competition. And, if the seller has reason to believe that the competitor is also discriminating and that his price is unlawful, the defense will not be available.

PROMOTIONAL ALLOWANCES

The statute also prohibits the granting of promotional materials and allowances (such as for cooperative advertisements) to competing customers except upon proportionally equal terms. In this area the law is quite strict, decreeing per se illegality once nonproportional payments are found. Injury to competition need not be shown, although the good-faith meeting of competition is a defense.

If it is decided to grant such allowances at all, they should be affirmatively offered to all competing customers, not just to those who ask for them. Prudence dictates that the offer be pursuant to a written plan which, as a routine matter, is provided to every customer. Moreover, the payments must be "functionally available" to all. This means it is not permissible to offer payments for television advertising to all customers if only a few large ones can afford it. A substitute must be provided for the smaller purchaser, such as newspaper space in local papers, leaflets, or the like. Even the smallest purchaser must be included, or the plan may be deemed illegal. The statute's requirement of proportional availability must also be met. The safe way to do so is to key payments to periodic sales volume either in dollars or in units. Thus, for example, the seller may offer to pay for half the cost of cooperative advertisements up to a ceiling of 3 percent of annual volume. So long as every customer is in the same boat, almost any variation will be permitted.

These guidelines apply equally to the furnishing of promotional facilities such as racks or demonstrators. Again, if such facilities are to be furnished at all, they must be made available to every purchaser on proportionally equal terms.

BUYER LIABILITY

The stated goal of the Robinson-Patman Act is to curb the power of large buyers. It is thus not surprising that the statute makes it unlawful for a buyer to induce a violation. The tests of illegality are essentially the same. If the seller's discrimination is unlawful and the buyer knowingly induced the illegal price, the buyer may be found in violation of the law.

✦ ✦ ✦

This brief review has necessarily touched upon only the fundamental outlines of antitrust doctrine. The purpose has been to alert the businessman to antitrust risks lurking in commercial conduct. Perhaps the best advice is to seek to avoid the exposure and costs of litigation by the application of prophylaxis. Given awareness of the problem and a modicum of ingenuity, often a feasible alternative can be found to minimize antitrust risk.

Product Liability

Richard M. Markus

T HE AMERICAN TECHNOLOGICAL CORNUCOPIA HAS BEEN ABLE TO PRODUCE
    fantastic new merchandise at incredible speed with increasing effi-
ciency. At the same time, the American consumer has demanded greater
excellence in quality control and product reliability, with an increasing
awareness of the availability and need for safety in every form of activity.
Therefore, it is hardly surprising that the Congress, the state legislatures,
and the courts have reflected these public attitudes by requiring more
stringent safety standards for products and their advertising. There seems
to be a direct correlation between technical progress and the development
of the law of product liability.

Significance to Management

At its present stage of development, potential product liability should
be an important consideration for management in making decisions about
production and sales. The rapid expansion of this field and the increasing
number of product claims make the need for such consideration particularly

RICHARD M. MARKUS is a partner in the Cleveland law firm of Sindell, Sindell,
Bourne, Markus, Stern & Spero. The research assistance of Thomas S. O'Neill is acknowledged
with appreciation.

impressive. It is obvious at the outset, for example, that such potential responsibility makes effective quality control an economic necessity. But the impact of this field of law is being felt increasingly in virtually every aspect of production and sales. Among other areas concerned are design engineering, testing procedures, marketing procedures, advertising, record making and retention procedures, and packaging and labeling choices.

Most product liability litigation has little or no effect upon product or company reputation, but frequent large suits attacking a particular product or a particular company can affect public trust in that product or company. There are some who suspect, for example, that Chevrolet's decision not to continue production of the Corvair automobile might have been attributable at least in part to adverse publicity surrounding various Corvair suits, even though General Motors has been successful in defending most of those suits. As a result, management would do well to formulate a policy which would decrease the number of potential claims, as well as attempting to defeat as many of those claims as possible. Such a policy is emphasized by the unusually high cost of product liability litigation with all of its technical aspects, a fact which also tends to deter most experienced plaintiffs' counsel from pursuing such claims unless there are substantial damages. This chapter will review developments in the field of product liability, summarize the weapons and procedures of the claimant's lawyer, and highlight the areas upon which informed management decisions can be based.

The Governing Law

At the outset, it must be recognized that the legal principles involved are largely "court-made law," rather than legislative enactments. Since all of the 50 states and the District of Columbia have developed somewhat different rules of liability for manufacturers and suppliers, generalizations are not easily made in this area. Nevertheless, sufficient similarities can be found upon which to premise executive thinking. Moreover, managerial judgments usually should be based upon the legal rules of the states which impose the greatest obligation upon suppliers, since the law of those states may well control eventual litigation.

It is not enough for management to inquire about the rules applied in the state where they are situated or licensed, or even in the states where they do the greatest bulk of their business. When merchandise enters the stream of commerce it can be expected to pass into almost any state, and if it is defective it can be expected to cause damage in almost any state.

Courts differ markedly as to the choice of the state law which should govern a particular set of circumstances, and this is especially true for product liability. Some courts find that the law of the place of manufacture shall govern, others choose the law of the state where the injury was caused, and still others favor the law of the state where one or more of the sale transactions for that product occurred. A newer approach that has increasing support considers all the possible geographical aspects of the manufacture, the sale, the injury, and the injured person so as to determine which state has the greatest contact with the entire set of circumstances and the greatest legal interest in the rights involved.

It is not even possible to predict with any great degree of reliability where the potential lawsuit might be tried. For many years, a manufacturer could assume that he was subject to suit only where his company was incorporated, licensed, or engaged in substantial business. However, more recent decisions have expanded the term "doing business" to include situations where far fewer business activities are conducted. Further, more and more states are enacting so-called long-arm statutes which permit suits if the product caused damage in those states and the supplier derives substantial revenue from them, directly or through intermediaries. Therefore, manufacturers have little choice in the selection of the place where a lawsuit will be decided or the law which will determine the outcome of that suit. As suggested earlier, this means that executive decisions must take into account the law of virtually every American jurisdiction.

Historical Basis

In order to consider the broad scope of modern jurisprudence for product responsibility, the historical development of the various legal bases for such liability should first be reviewed.

REQUIREMENT OF PRIVITY

In 1842, an English court established the traditional common-law rule which has protected manufacturers from responsibility in varying degrees for more than 100 years. A contractor named Wright agreed to supply a mail coach for the English postmaster, with assurances in the sales contract that the coach would be proper, safe, and secure. The postmaster then contracted with another man to operate the coach, and he in turn hired a driver named Winterbottom. As Winterbottom was driving the coach, it broke and threw him from his seat, causing him to sustain injuries.

The court refused to permit an action by the driver Winterbottom against the coach supplier Wright, on the basis that there was no direct contractual relationship (known in law as "privity") between them. This meant that the manufacturer or supplier of any product was secure from any claim by the ultimate user or members of the general public, unless he sold the product directly to the person who was injured. Even the person who had purchased the object was extremely limited in early decisions by the ancient concept that a buyer must accept all defects in the product he acquires, without complaint, unless the seller expressly assured him that the merchandise was free from that specific defect. This rule of caveat emptor (let the buyer beware) combined with the privity doctrine to make the manufacturer or supplier virtually immune from most claims for damage which he caused.

Negligence Liability

The new era of manufacturing responsibility was signaled by Judge Cardozo's decision for the highest court of New York in *MacPherson* v. *Buick Motor Company* in 1916. MacPherson had purchased a Buick from a retail dealer and had no direct contractual relation with the Buick Motor Company. As he was driving his car, one of the wheels collapsed because of a defect in its construction, and MacPherson was thrown out of the car and injured. Evidence was presented that the defect could have been discovered by a reasonable inspection but that no such inspection had been performed by Buick.

Judge Cardozo rejected the old contractual-privity rule in that case on the basis that the product involved was inherently dangerous, so the manufacturer owed a duty of care to anyone who was likely to be injured by the manufacturer's negligence. Notice that even a mere bystander would seem to be protected by this decision. It is also interesting to note that Buick had not itself manufactured the wheel in the *MacPherson* case, but had rather purchased the defective wheel from another supplier and assembled it into its own automobile without adequate inspection. Thus this decision encompassed both the manufacturer and the subsequent assembler or supplier in its impact. After the *MacPherson* case, most courts insisted that drugs, food, and other products which come into direct intimate contact with their users are "inherently dangerous," so producers of such materials would be held responsible for damage from their negligence in production.

The rather broad term "negligence" began to have increasing meaning.

Traditionally it referred to a failure to exercise the same degree of care that other reasonable persons would exercise in the same or similar circumstances. But the courts did not accept the proposition that a manufacturer is safe in duplicating the mistakes his competitors make. Most or all of an industry could be said to be acting negligently if a reasonably prudent manufacturer would act in a different manner. Numerous forms of negligent conduct by producers and suppliers were recognized, including (1) negligent design of the product, (2) negligent inspection of component parts, (3) negligent assembly and packaging of the various parts, (4) negligent inspection of the finished product, and (5) negligent testing of the product both before and after production.

Recently an Illinois housewife recovered close to $1 million in damages from a drain cleaner producer because inadequate packaging caused it to explode in her face as she was trying to open it. Negligence took verbal as well as physical forms when the courts allowed claims for (1) negligent failure to warn about prospective dangers, (2) negligent failure to give adequate instructions for proper usage, (3) negligent failure to warn about new dangers which are discovered and reported after the product is in general usage, (4) negligent representations as to the effectiveness of the product, (5) negligent description of proper uses for the product, and (6) negligent packaging and labeling.

While these rules of negligence were initially limited to so-called inherently dangerous products and later expanded to products which are directly consumed or used on the individual's person, they rapidly became applicable to virtually any product. If harm could result in ordinary use, then the product was capable of being dangerous. The legal formula for responsibility was negligence plus damage which could conceivably have been anticipated or foreseen (legally described as damage which was proximately caused by that negligence).

The second half of this formula likewise underwent considerable development as our judicial system recognized that most harmful results can be anticipated. A federal court in North Carolina found, for example, that a furniture polish manufacturer should expect that children might drink furniture polish if there isn't sufficient warning on the bottle for untrained parents to realize that it is poisonous. And a Florida court held a hair-coloring manufacturer liable for inadequate warnings on the container since it was sold to a consumer in an ordinary retail store even though the manufacturer intended it only for professional beauticians with the necessary knowledge. In other words, it is not sufficient for a manufacturer to say that he never intended this particular use, if the use could be anticipated under normal circumstances, unless the manufacturer provides adequate warning and protection against that use.

EXPRESS WARRANTY

As the scope of liability for negligence broadened, other bases for responsibility were also developing. Legal philosophers frequently concluded that manufacturers and suppliers, instead of their individual consumers, should assume the burden of damage and loss caused by their products. First, the producer is typically a large corporate concern with considerable accumulated assets, while the consumer is typically dependent upon his own individual limited productivity. Second, the producer is in a position to spread the cost of such losses among the general public by adjusting his prices to include the expense of claims for product-caused injuries. Third, the producer can conveniently distribute that total cost among many producers by purchasing product liability insurance, the premiums for which would presumably be reflected in product sales prices. Fourth, the producer is usually in a better position than the uninformed and unsophisticated consumer to structure the product so that injury will not occur. These considerations and others led to the development of further grounds upon which the supplier could be held responsible for product-caused damage.

One prominent form of responsibility was liability for violation or breach of an express warranty. A warranty or guarantee is, of course, a contractual promise by a seller which the buyer has a right to rely on and to enforce. An express warranty is one which is expressly stated in writing, or even orally. A supplier can warrant that this product will serve a particular purpose, that it will last a specified time, that its elements will withstand identified stresses, or myriad other details. However, it is again to be noted that the typical consumer has not purchased the product directly from the producer or assembler. Modern merchandising procedures may well involve two or three intermediary sales between the manufacturer and the ultimate user. And, here again, the courts initially insisted upon a direct contractual relationship (privity) before the manufacturer could be held responsible to a claimant on the basis of his warranty.

Just as courts abandoned their insistence upon a direct contractual relationship to enforce negligence claims, they also began to relax their insistence upon such a direct relationship to enforce claims for breach of warranty. At first, some judges suggested that warranties made by the manufacturer to intermediary suppliers might constitute negligent misrepresentations, so as to use rules of negligence referred to earlier. Later, some simply withdrew their judicial decrees that there must be a direct contract between the claimant and the producer to enforce a warranty. The *Restatement of Torts* is a publication prepared by outstanding lawyers and law professors in an attempt to summarize court-made law and to point the direction in which modern trends are moving. The *Restatement (2d)* describes the express warranty rule as follows:

402 B.   Misrepresentation by Seller of Chattels to Consumer

> One engaged in the business of selling chattels who, by advertising, labels, or otherwise, makes to the public a misrepresentation of a material fact concerning the character or quality of a chattel sold by him is subject to liability for physical harm to a consumer of the chattel caused by justifiable reliance upon the misrepresentation, even though
>
> (*a*) it is not made fraudulently or negligently, and
> (*b*) the consumer has not bought the chattel from or entered into any contractual relation with the seller.

The authors of the *Restatement* do not specify whether their rule applies to injuries suffered by a bystander who is not a consumer.

As a result of this rule, the manufacturer of an industrial machine might well be held liable for breach of warranty if a safety device on his machine fails to operate as promised, even though the injured claimant is a factory employee who had nothing to do with the purchase of that machine. However, most courts are still unwilling to make the original producer liable for breach of warranty to an injured person who is a mere bystander and is not a purchaser, a subpurchaser, a subsequent purchaser, an employee of any of such purchasers, or a member of the family or social guest of any of such purchasers. Some courts place special emphasis upon the contractual nature of a warranty claim, with associated concepts of knowledge, agreement, and reliance. A woman who learns about a cosmetic manufacturer's warranties and who then agrees to buy that product at least partly because she believes and relies upon those statements can probably recover for any damage resulting to her from inaccuracy in those assurances. Indeed, courts are more frequently describing advertising claims as warranties, so that an ultimate consumer who buys a product because of that advertising may have a right to damages for injury caused by the failure of the product to live up to the advertising boasts.

IMPLIED WARRANTY

The first two general bases for legal responsibility (negligence and express warranty) have been supplemented in recent years by the doctrine of implied warranty. The law has assumed for many years that every seller promises the purchaser that the product is reasonably fit for the purpose for which it is ordinarily intended, at least unless the parties expressly agree that there is no such promise. This court-made rule was reinforced in almost every state by provisions of the Uniform Sales Act and its more modern successor, the Uniform Commercial Code. So the retailer has traditionally been responsible for damage which resulted when the product was not able to perform its intended usage without damage. This would be true despite the retailer's total lack of knowledge about the condition of the product and his total lack of any assurances to the purchaser about it. If the retailer could show that his technical legal responsibility was not a result of any fault on his part, he could generally recover from the negligent supplier any amount he was forced to pay. Thus, after the canned-goods customer recovers damages from the grocery man for swallowing a lead bolt in the canned peas, the grocery man could usually look to the canner for reimbursement.

Over the past 20 years, numerous courts have extended the doctrine of implied warranty to include in its scope the original manufacturer or supplier. They conclude that the supplier also warrants that the product is reasonably fit and that implied warranty can be enforced by the remote consumer. Since that rule eliminates any requirement of a direct contact between the claimant and the product manufacturer, some courts have extended implied warranty beyond the supplier-consumer situations. Some would say, for example, that the manufacturer makes that same implied warranty of fitness to anyone who might reasonably be expected to come into contact with the product. A workman on a construction project could well be injured by the collapse of a defective steel beam installed by a completely different contractor. If that happens, he may well have a right against the manufacturer of the steel beam for breach of implied warranty. An airplane passenger might well be able to claim breach of implied warranty by the manufacturer of the autopilot in the cockpit if a defect in that autopilot causes the plane to crash, with resulting injuries to the passenger. In those states applying the broad implied warranty doctrine, recovery is possible from the supplier if (1) the product was defective, (2) the defect was present when it left the supplier, (3) injury resulted from that defect, and

(4) the injured person was one within the general range of persons who might be expected to come into contact with the product.

STRICT LIABILITY

The last and most recent basis for manufacturer responsibility is the doctrine of strict liability. The name of that doctrine is unnecessarily frightening, since the rule does not impose responsibility on the manufacturer for all damage resulting from any use of his product. If a man cuts himself with a kitchen knife he cannot ordinarily expect to blame the knife manufacturer or supplier. The *Restatement of Torts (2d)* adopts the rule of strict liability in the following language:

402 A. Special Liability of Seller of Product for Physical Harm to User or Consumer

(1) One who sells any product in a defective condition unreasonably dangerous to the user or consumer or to his property is subject to liability for physical harm thereby caused to the ultimate user or consumer, or to his property, if

(*a*) the seller is engaged in the business of selling such a product, and

(*b*) it is expected to and does reach the user or consumer without substantial change in the condition in which it is sold.

(2) The rule stated in Subsection (1) applies although

(*a*) the seller has exercised all possible care in the preparation and sale of his product, and

(*b*) the user or consumer has not bought the product from or entered into any contractual relation with the seller.

It is clear that this rule is not greatly different from the broad form of implied warranty which was considered earlier. Because of these rules, California and Oregon courts have allowed recovery from the supplier of Sabin oral polio vaccine for polio contracted by users of the vaccine, even though the supplier had been as careful as possible and only a very small percentage of users had that reaction.

To prove a case of *strict* liability the claimant must show that there was a defect in the product at the time it left the supplier. To prove a case of *implied* warranty the claimant must show that the product was not reasonably fit for its intended purpose. The question might well be asked: What constitutes a defect? Similarly, one might wonder when a product is not reasonably fit for its intended use. What evidence is sufficient to show a defect or a failure to be reasonably fit for use? These are not easy questions, and they are often answered differently by different courts. Is a product defective or unfit simply because it causes injury? If an automobile driver turns the steering wheel so as to leave the road and strike a pole, no one could reasonably say that the auto manufacturer had produced a defective or unfit automobile. If the automobile left the road because the steering tie bar broke after a garage mechanic severely weakened it with a crowbar, the manufacturer should still be free from any responsibility. But suppose the car left the road because the steering tie bar was not designed to take ordinary road stresses in typical usage—that might well be a defect in design or a failure to make the automobile reasonably fit for use.

As is apparent, defects are not necessarily limited to errors in assembly or fabrication; they might well include errors of judgment in design or in any other part of the total production-sale procedure. Some counsel have argued that inadequate instructions for use of the product are manufacturing defects. Because the meaning of strict liability and the full meaning of implied warranty are subjects that are less than a decade old, it is very difficult to predict how far the courts may go. An Ohio federal court decided that the claimant failed to prove his case when he showed that the hood of his automobile flew up as he was driving, since this could result from his own failure to latch it securely as well as from a demonstrated error in design of the latch mechanism. By contrast, an Arizona court recently held that a claimant had presented sufficient evidence for a jury to find in his favor against a pogo stick supplier by simply showing that the pogo stick flew apart in usage. In the Arizona case, the court said the manufacturer or supplier may have the obligation to show that the unanticipated failure of the product did not result from a defect in the product.

LEGISLATIVE AND ADMINISTRATIVE REGULATION

The previous material has been concerned principally with judge-made laws, but the legislatures have been active in this area also. Almost every state has a false-advertising statute which might be a basis for a damage claim if a product falls below its advertised abilities. The Uniform Commercial Code (like its predecessor, the Uniform Sales Act) imposes obligations for violation of express warranties. The Commercial Code also creates implied warranties that the labeling is truthful, the goods are acceptable, the goods are uniform, the goods are in proper containers, and the merchandise is fit for its intended purpose. The public utilities commission and the industrial commission in most states have adopted industrial codes and safety codes, which may establish required standards for some machinery. On a national level, the Congress has enacted the Federal Hazardous Substance Labeling Act, the Flammable Fabrics Act, the Truth in Labeling Act, and numerous other regulatory provisions for product control. The Department of Transportation and the Federal Trade Commission issue regulations for minimum product standards.

Any of the legislative or administrative standards established by statutory regulations may be the basis for a civil damage action if the product falls below those standards. But compliance with these standards is not necessarily sufficient care. Recent New York and North Dakota cases upheld verdicts against manufacturers which did meet prescribed statutory or administrative standards. The governmental standards were considered as minimal requirements for the product.

Counsel's Weapons and Procedures

If a company is subjected to a products claim, management should consider the steps which the claimant's lawyer will take. Because these cases are relatively complicated, they tend to gravitate into the hands of the relatively few plaintiff's counsel who are particularly experienced and sophisticated in this legal area. Indeed, only a lawyer whose practice does involve a significant volume of product litigation is likely to recognize such claims when he learns the circumstances of an accidental injury. For example, when his client's car had been struck by another car which was violating the traffic laws, a resourceful and experienced New Jersey lawyer decided to sue the manufacturer of his client's own automobile, along with the offending driver of the other car. This lawyer was able to obtain a very substantial judgment against the auto manufacturer on the basis that the interior design of the car caused his client to sustain particularly serious injuries in the impact. Therefore, the plaintiff's lawyer can be expected to have a reasonably good grasp of his subject matter in most product liability cases.

Often, the claimant's attorney will begin his preparation by obtaining all available advertising literature for the allegedly defective product, as well as all available catalogues and advertising brochures for competitive products. In this manner, he can find the differences between the product in question and its equivalents on the market. Through such national organizations as the American Trial Lawyers Association, he may well be able to find the names of other attorneys who have been involved in cases which concern the same or similar products. This leads to a general exchange of information between such interested attorneys. Sometimes these counsel will even assemble an informal group to discuss the information which they have collectively gathered.

Generally, the plaintiff's counsel will retain an expert consultant at an early stage of his preparations. That consultant may be a university professor in an appropriate field or a trained engineer with knowledge about the type of product involved. He will then work intensively with the consultant to evaluate the available information about the allegedly defective product and to determine other avenues for investigation and research. This may mean independent testing of the product, and it may involve a review of all available technical literature describing the history and development of this type of product. Patent applications submitted for the particular product or similar products can be a fruitful source of such information. Many safety organizations and trade associations publish safety standards and related literature. Recently, certain governmental information centers have been created from which information can be obtained about product safety. Typically, governmental regulatory agencies maintain files of complaints or reported defects about products under their general supervision. All these potential sources, as well as many others, may be examined by the plaintiff's attorney before a formal lawsuit is filed.

The manufacturer usually learns about the injury long after it has occurred, sometimes when the lawsuit is filed. This means that the claimant's attorney may have a significant head start in investigating the accident itself and in securing some of the materials described here. However, the manufacturer has much greater knowledge about the history, production, and sales of the product involved.

After the lawsuit is filed, the two sides tend to equalize their respective knowledge about relevant materials through formal "discovery" procedures available in litigation. For example, each side may submit one or more sets of detailed questions (known in legal terminology as "interrogatories") which must be answered by the other side under oath. Each side can compel the other side to produce relevant documents and records. Each side can compel witnesses to appear for pretrial testimony (known in legal terminology as "deposition"). The claimant's attorney may obtain a court order authorizing him to enter the manufacturing plant, to inspect the manufacturing procedures, and to photograph significant areas and procedures. The company's attorney can usually obtain a court order requiring that the allegedly defective product be produced for inspection, examination, and testing. The company may be required to give opposing counsel most of its records dealing with the design, manufacture, assembly, and sale of a product. Key personnel may be subpoenaed to give pretrial testimony. In all these procedures, of course, company counsel will provide guidance and will be present during any visits to the factory or questioning of executive staff.

The defense of product claims also involves the use of attorneys who are specially trained and experienced. Indeed, until recent years the defense attorneys were quite generally better trained and more experienced for this type of litigation. However, activities by such organizations as the American Trial Lawyers Association have greatly enhanced the training of the plaintiff's bar, so there is now more nearly a parity between counsel for the two sides. The defense attorney will need to interview key personnel at the factory. He may well wish to take a guided tour of the production premises so that he can understand the intricacies of the production process. He will most certainly wish to review all records which are subpoenaed by opposing counsel before they are produced, as well as to discuss the testimony of all witnesses subpoenaed from the factory before they testify.

Some producers feel that a product liability case is an affront to their personal or professional integrity and are therefore reluctant to discuss the matter with anyone. As a result, some do not cooperate fully with their own counsel in explaining potential weaknesses in their position as well as their strengths. If the plaintiff's attorney is able to bring out weak portions of the defense and defense counsel has no prior knowledge of these weaknesses, the defendant's attorney is obviously at a substantial disadvantage. The phrase "forewarned is forearmed" applies to the defense counsel who must understand all aspects of the litigation in order to "soften the blow" for points on which the plaintiff may seek to capitalize. In addition, an understanding of both weaknesses and the strengths is critical for evaluation of settlement possibilities. All too often, the plaintiff's attorney must develop the details of his attack through the manufacturer's own records and witnesses before the defense counsel understands the justification for settlement. By that time, the defense counsel is in a poorer position to accomplish a favorable settlement. If plaintiff's counsel learns by subpoenaing company records or company witnesses that there have been 25 previously reported failures of the safety switch on the same model machine, he will be less interested in settlement on the defendant's terms.

Guidelines for Managerial Decision

Taking into consideration the rules of law that are developing in this area, as well as the typical procedures employed in such lawsuits, certain general recommendations can be made to management. Again, these recommendations would seek to minimize the number of these claims, while also attempting to give a solid basis for their eventual defense. The first suggestion, which is perhaps the simplest and most obvious, is to make a good product. High quality tends to produce a low litigation rate. Of course, this means careful attention to detail at every stage of product development, from the idea to the post-delivery follow-up. At each of these stages, the same emphasis must be given to safety for ultimate users that is given to economical production and effective selling.

Plant safety has become an accepted necessity in most companies, but many still do not pursue the safety of potential consumers with the same vigor. It must be kept in mind that the ultimate user is unsophisticated and untrained, with minimal understanding of the technical elements of the product. The user may well employ the merchandise in a bizarre manner, thus, the product has to be physically structured so that an incorrect or hazardous use is extremely difficult or even impossible. A walk through a modern factory building reveals the safety efforts that have been employed to prevent accidents which result from human failings. The same attention must be given to accidents from human failings in the use of the products assembled and produced in that factory.

Similar caution is appropriate in drafting instructions for the user, warnings to users, and general advertising. Plaintiffs' counsel delight in the fact that there is typically an internal war at the factory between the engineering staff and the sales staff. The sales staff wants to make the most extraordinary claims, which the engineering staff realizes are far beyond the abilities of the product. The sales staff is concerned that restrictive instructions or warnings will be harmful to merchandising, but the engineering staff realizes they are important for safety. If a product is described as "absolutely safe," "foolproof," or "harmless to any user," it can be sold more easily. At the same time, such labels may constitute warranties upon which a user can base his claim for subsequent damage.

When warnings are necessary, they should be clear and unequivocal. Certainly, technical descriptions of the chemical composition are meaningless to an average user. A Washington court held that even a label describing an insecticide as dangerous and poisonous was insufficient, since the manufacturer should have anticipated that the containers would be handled and used by illiterate field hands. The court said that the bags should have had a large skull and crossbones to denote their dangerous character. A Texas appellate court decided against a pharmaceutical producer when its medicine produced an adverse reaction in calves, on the ground that the drug label did not recommend an antidote to be given in the event of adverse reactions. And a West Coast federal court found against a fertilizer manufacturer and for a deliveryman who had some fall into his boot because the manufacturer had not warned against prolonged contact of the product with the skin. From a safety standpoint, instructions for use of the product should be (1) simple, (2) brief, (3) bold, (4) direct, and (5) glaringly obvious.

RECORD RETENTION POLICIES

As a practical matter, every manufacturer should anticipate the possibility that his product may be the subject of litigation. Products do cause injury. He may be able to defeat those claims if sufficient emphasis has been placed on safety through all the manufacturing steps (design, fabrication, assembly, testing, inspection, and so on), and if he has given sufficient warning and avoided unreasonable advertising claims. But, in order to meet and defeat such claims, proper records should be maintained and retained. Where safety tests are performed, careful records should be made of the nature of tests and the successful results obtained. Where defects are discovered before, during, or after production, careful records should be maintained of the affirmative steps which have been taken to eliminate dangers from those defects. Where a post-production problem is discovered, copies should be kept of all notices which are sent to distributors, retailers, or the public. Lists of all persons receiving such notices should also be maintained. Where the files show recommendations from company staff or others as to safety improvements, the files should also show that these recommendations were given careful consideration and accepted in appropriate form or rejected for justifiable safety reasons.

Although most of these ideas are no more than common sense, it is more difficult to decide how long the various safety records should be retained. The Statute of Limitations, which limits the number of years within which a lawsuit can be brought for personal injury or wrongful death, varies among states from one year to six years. In addition, many states have a provision that a claim for injuries to a minor can be brought within the prescribed number of years after the minor reaches age 21. This means that the lawsuit could conceivably be filed as long as 27 years after the injury. And, with many products, the injury may not occur until many years after it was sold by the producer or supplier. A hydraulic lift in a service station that exploded after 12 years of trouble-free use created liability for its seller in Ohio. In another decision, the supplier of an oil derrick was found responsible for its collapse 17 years after its sale. Therefore, as a practical matter, there is almost no limit on the time within which these safety records might be required in litigation.

This leads to conflicting views as to the most sensible record-retention procedure. Some counsel would suggest that all records relating to safety be kept indefinitely. Others recommend that safety records be treated like all other records and systematically discarded after a reasonable period of time (presumably no less than five years). If the safety records are discarded as part of a routine limitation on record retention, the claimant's attorney will have greater difficulty in arguing that they have been destroyed to eliminate damaging admissions. On the other hand, those safety records could be valuable aids to the defense attorney if they are still available to him. Perhaps the most sensible rule would be the indefinite retention of safety records only if they relate to a product which has already been challenged by some claims or has been reported to have caused some injuries. If there have already been some reported injuries or claims, there may be additional claims in the future.

Product Liability Insurance

Since the possibility of some product litigation cannot be ignored, realistic attitudes should be adopted toward their handling. Certainly, this means that product liability insurance should be purchased in sufficient amounts, unless the producer is large enough and anticipates enough overall claims to act as a self-insurer. When products can cause grievous injury or death, limits of no less than $500,000 per person injured are the minimum that should be maintained. Most manufacturers would be surprised to find that the premium difference between a $100,000 policy and a $500,000 policy is not substantial, since most claims are concluded for much less than either of those sums. Some larger manufacturers purchase policies that provide only for claims services and the costs of defense, without any payment of the actual settlement or judgment amount. These policies, which take various forms, utilize the expert services of trained insurance personnel and their selected counsel for companies that wish to run the risk of payment themselves. The risk of being forced to pay a major claim can be substantial and one which most smaller companies would be wise to avoid, when the overall level of production and sales cannot be counted on to produce a substantial number of claims. Of course, if the company's history demonstrates a likelihood that there will be many claims to defend, some of which will require payment, management may determine the actuarial risk of such claims and set aside sufficient funds to act as a self-insurer in order to avoid the profit which an independent insurer would have to make on carrying that risk.

CONTRACTUAL PROTECTION

Many companies are now attempting to shift these risks to other concerns with which they do business. This may be done by means of a provision in the contract with the manufacturer's supplier or with the company to which he sells the product. In that contract the component supplier or the wholesale purchaser agrees to indemnify or reimburse the manufacturer for any loss relating to that transaction or the product involved. These contractual attempts to shift the risk of loss to an earlier or later stage in the production-sales progression are sometimes done by language on the purchase order, sales order, invoice form, or other routine records. While these "indemnity" provisions may not be fully effective in every state, and while they are narrowly construed by most courts, every manufacturer and supplier should consult his own counsel to consider the drafting and use of such language on his routine business forms.

At the same time, he should recognize that he in turn may be accepting the risks of his component suppliers or the companies to which he sells products by reason of the language in their contracts or on their forms. Careful examination of the small print on the reverse of routine business forms may be worthwhile. Or the manufacturer and supplier might attempt to protect himself from undertaking any other firm's obligation for its own negligence or warranty breaches by inserting language on his own business forms that he has not accepted such obligations, despite any language to the contrary in any contract or business form relating to that transaction. Since most product liability insurance does not protect the insured company against obligations which are assumed by a contract with another company, the insured manufacturer and supplier cannot be certain that he is protected against product claims unless appropriate precautions are taken against having such obligations shifted to him by those with whom he deals.

Some manufacturers have attempted to limit their obligation by providing express disclaimers of responsibility together with the product. Thus they provide an express warranty that the product will be suitable for a specific period of time, that the warranty includes repair or replacement of the defective merchandise, and that there is no other express or implied warranty as to the product. While this has been held effective in some states, a New Jersey court began a trend to reject defense based on that kind of language. The New Jersey court said that the manufacturer and the ultimate consumer were not in an equal bargaining position, that the consumer did not realize he was supposedly precluded from exercising his other legal rights by the language, and that this would be an "unconscionable" contract provision which is rendered void by the Uniform Commercial Code. In California, an appeals court held that a warranty cannot provide only "illusory protection" where it in fact greatly reduces a consumer's rights. The Supreme Court of South Carolina would not enforce a restrictive warranty which the consumer had not bothered to read. Other decisions in Texas and California simply found that restrictive warranties were contractual and, therefore, irrelevant in strict-liability cases. While no real prediction can be made as to whether other states will follow New Jersey, manufacturers cannot rely with absolute certainty upon written statements in their literature or on the product itself that there is no assurance against injury from its use.

SETTLEMENT ATTITUDES

Finally, a realistic attitude should be taken with regard to settlement negotiations in pending product claims. This returns again to the determination by management to maintain product image. Within reason, this is an entirely sensible policy, but it can also lead to purposeless expense and eventual obligation in cases where there is a significant risk of loss. Therefore, it seems foolish for management to stand in the way of settlements where corporate counsel consider them to be reasonable and sensible. Yet some executives do precisely that. Perhaps they are motivated by pride of product or a simple unwillingness to admit that anyone in their company could possibly have made a mistake. Nevertheless, that approach can be foolhardy.

✦ ✦ ✦

Some executives may believe that these liability rules are unfair to industry. Some may accept them as part of the present-day cost of doing business. But, regardless of their philosophical orientation, today's executive must recognize that today's industry must live with the reality of product liability. The old maxim that the buyer must beware has been replaced by a newer social philosophy: Let the seller be wary.

The Law of Advertising

Felix H. Kent

W HEN ONE SPEAKS OF THE "LAW OF ADVERTISING" TO THE AVERAGE BUSINESS-
man or even the average lawyer, one can generally expect to draw a
quizzical expression. The law of advertising is not a clearly defined field
and is a relatively new area of specialization. In a society which seemingly
becomes more complex from decade to decade and in which means of
communication and media of advertising become more sophisticated from
year to year, new problems arise almost daily and old problems become
more refined. When we speak loosely of the law of advertising, we touch
upon many areas of law such as the law of copyright, the laws of libel,
slander, and invasion of privacy, the antitrust laws, and other laws relating
to trade regulations as well as the law of unfair competition, trademark
law, and so forth.

Undoubtedly, the greatest force which has led to the creation of new
controls and inhibitions on advertising through legislative, administrative,
and private control bodies has been the development of television. It is
superfluous to elaborate on the vast, unquestioned impact made upon the
public by this medium and by advertising through this medium. It is
perhaps significant to mention that where an advertising message today

FELIX H. KENT is a senior partner in the New York law firm of Lawler, Sterling &
Kent.

may be seen by some 30 or 40 million Americans, or even more, tomorrow's advertising message may well be seen by hundreds of millions of people around the globe, through the use of satellites for television transmission. Needless to say, where today we must concern ourselves, from a legal point of view, with the laws of the United States and of the individual states, tomorrow we may be faced with controls on a worldwide scale.

The legal problems relating to advertising perhaps can be broken down best into two categories: (1) problems of governmental and private controls; (2) problems relating to the rights of others.

Governmental and Private Controls

Advertising has come a long way from the day when patent medicines were peddled with the promise of curing everything from arthritis to zoonosis. No doubt, American industry has matured immeasurably since the days of P. T. Barnum, but, over the years, the Federal Government as well as state and local governments have nevertheless considered it necessary to step in to protect the consumer from "false, unfair or deceptive advertising."

Whether these actions are necessary and whether any of these governmental bodies has transgressed its powers can be subjects for lively discussion. The incontrovertible fact is that advertising has become a popular whipping boy in the halls of Congress and various state houses, to the point where in a few states we have even seen highly discriminatory taxes levied on advertising. Above all, we have seen the legislatures and regulatory bodies exercise control over the contents of advertising. Let us now examine the various regulatory bodies with which the industry must concern itself, as well as the areas of their activities.

THE FEDERAL TRADE COMMISSION

Of primary concern to all those engaged in advertising is the Federal Trade Commission, which is the principal arm of the Federal Government in controlling advertising. The specific authority of the Federal Trade Commission rests in Section 5 of the Federal Trade Commission Act, which, very broadly, outlaws "unfair or deceptive acts or practices in commerce." Over the years, the Commission has applied this statute to a great variety of situations. In the eyes of the Federal Trade Commission "deceptive advertising" can be a statement, claim, or pictorial demonstration which *may have the capacity or the tendency to deceive the average man on the street.* It should be noted at the outset that the Commission does not have to prove that anyone was deceived, it must prove only that there was a capacity to deceive [*U.S. Retail Credit Ass'n, Inc.* v. *F.T.C.*, 300 F.2d 212 (1962)]. Deceptive advertising can take in any number of things misrepresentation of the quality of a product or its efficacy; misrepresentation of the product's size, shape, weight, origin, or whatever; the use of an unauthorized or untrue "testimonial"; false disparagement of a competitor's product; or an ambiguous statement. In the last, the Commission has said that where a statement can be construed two ways, one truthful and one capable of being misleading, the Commission will construe the statement against the advertiser—that is, as misleading.

Deception can also be the *omission* of a statement. Every word the advertiser says can be literally true, but if he omits a material fact he may be misleading the public. For instance, cases in the Federal Trade Commission involving hearing-aid advertising were related to use of the words, "No buttons, wires or cords are attached to the hearing aid." The advertising omitted the fact that a plastic tube ran from the device to the ear. The Commission felt that this was a material omission and that the advertising without the statement of this fact constituted a deception.

It should be noted clearly that the advertiser is liable for all material used to advertise his product, including television commercials, even though the creation of the material may have been in the hands of its advertising agency or perhaps in the hands of other suppliers, such as film producers. In one case, the evidence was clear that the advertiser had no knowledge whatever of the fact that an independent film producing company, which had been engaged by its advertising agency, had used certain photographic techniques which were held to be deceptive. Even though neither the advertiser nor its agency knew that these techniques were being employed or had reason to suspect that any deceptive practice had been followed by the film producer, the advertiser was held in violation of Section 5 of the Federal Trade Commission Act.

Deceptive advertising can be a television demonstration using a mock-up that is not identified as such or a demonstration that is not truthful. Several years ago the Federal Trade Commission brought a proceeding against Colgate-Palmolive Co. and its advertising agency in connection with a television commercial advertising Colgate Rapid-Shave Cream, in which the advertiser demonstrated how easily even sandpaper could be shaved if it had been softened with Rapid-Shave. In fact, what purported to be sandpaper was a piece of plexiglas. The case went all the way to the U.S. Supreme Court and a decision was rendered by Chief Justice Warren [*Colgate-Palmolive Co.* v. *Federal Trade Commission,* 85 S.Ct. 1035 (1965)].

The decision has had wide import in the industry and can be said generally to have established the guidelines as to what may be done in the way of television demonstrations. Principally, the law established by this case is (1) that one may not use in television advertising any mock-up or any material which purports to be something else, without making disclosure thereof and (2) that any demonstration must be absolutely accurate and truthful. Although the Court's language is firm and uncompromising, there may still be exceptions to the generality of these requirements where the mock-up or substitute is not material to the principal point of the commercial and where the public is not asked to perceive something for themselves. Chief Justice Warren cited an example in his opinion: The advertiser may depict "happy actors delightedly eating ice cream that is in fact mashed potatoes or drinking a product appearing to be coffee but which is in fact some other substance," if he does not ask or invite the viewer explicitly or by implication to see for himself the truth of the claims about the ice cream's "rich texture and full color" or ask the public to perceive for itself anything about the product.

The Colgate case still leaves many questions unanswered; and, inevitably, there will be borderline cases in which bona fide questions will arise on the applicability of the rules established by this case. Undoubtedly, however, the U.S. Supreme Court gave the Federal Trade Commission a large vote of confidence in this case and strengthened immeasurably the Commission's powers in connection with the control of television advertising.

Deceptive advertising can also be the violation of specific rules issued by the FTC. For instance, the Commission has recently ruled that the advertiser may not use the word "new" in relation to a product unless there has been a material change in the formulation or some other material aspect of the product; and even then the use of "new" is limited to six months. The Commission also has issued rules on the use of the word "free" or other words denoting that advertisers are offering some free goods or services. Basically, this word may not be used unless the article is truly given away free and unless all qualifications or requirements, if any, are clearly set forth. Similarly, the Commission has ruled that an advertiser may not refer to "guarantees" in advertising unless all essential terms and conditions are spelled out.

It should be noted also that an advertising agency can be, and often is, named a co-respondent with the advertiser, in a false advertising proceeding in the Federal Trade Commission. In 1965 the Federal Trade Commission initiated a proceeding against Merck & Co., Inc., the manufacturer of Sucrets, and the advertising agency which had created certain advertising for this product. The Commission held the agency jointly liable with its client, stating:

> We believe that the agency should have been aware of the deceptive capacity of such advertising. The agency, *more so than its principal,* should have known whether the advertisements have the capacity to mislead or deceive the public. This is an area in which the agency has expertise. Its responsibility for *creating* advertising cannot be shifted to the principal who is liable in any event (italics supplied).

The effect of this and similar decisions seems to be that the only defense available to the agency in connection with false advertising is that it neither knew nor had reason to know of the falsity or the deceptive capacity of the advertising created by it. The cases clearly place an obligation on an agency to use due diligence in acquiring the necessary information or back-up material to substantiate advertising created by it.

In summary, the FTC has broad powers to regulate and review advertising in interstate commerce, and it is using and applying these powers to an unprecedented extent. The Commission has increased its staff substantially in recent years and has been given an increased budget. There is every reason to believe that the Commission's activities in this area will continue to expand, particularly in view of the evidently ever-increasing desire on the part of Congress to "protect" the consumer.

OTHER GOVERNMENTAL CONTROLS

Aside from the FTC, which claims jurisdiction over all types of advertising with very few exceptions, we are faced with governmental controls in specific industries or problems.

1. The Securities and Exchange Commission asserts jurisdiction over certain types of financial advertising. It is, of course, well known that "tombstone" advertising has to follow a certain pattern. Further, care must be taken that the company's product or institutional advertising does not recite such factors as growth, dividend record, increase of net worth, increase of the value of stock, and so on if the advertising is timed concurrently with or in anticipation of a public offering of stock or debentures.

2. The Alcohol and Tobacco Tax Division of the Internal Revenue Service concerns itself with liquor advertising. So do state liquor control boards in practically all the states where liquor is legally sold. Liquor control regulations range all the way from not being permitted to refer to the percentage of alcohol content to not being allowed to show a member of the fair sex holding a beer glass in a television commercial.

3. The Secret Service of the Treasury Department concerns itself with the use of reproductions of money, stamps, bonds, and so on in advertising. As a general rule, no obligation of the U.S. Government or of any foreign government may be reproduced in either print or film because the creation of engraving plates or negatives violates the counterfeiting statutes. An exception was recently created with the introduction of electronic tape: A tape reproduction of currency or other obligations may be made, since the tape with its electronic imprints does not constitute a counterfeit.

4. The Post Office Department, the Federal Trade Commission, the Justice Department, and just about every state government, are concerned with contests and sweepstakes. This is an area in which federal and state laws and regulations differ widely and in which uniformity would be highly desirable. As a general rule, under federal and most state laws and regulations, a contest or sweepstakes becomes a "lottery," and thus illegal, if the following three elements are present: consideration, chance, and prize.

Since a prize or prizes are always present in a contest or sweepstakes, the legality turns on whether both consideration and chance are involved. The element of chance has been held to be present whenever and wherever winners are selected either wholly or partially by chance. Consequently, the element of chance is always found in sweepstakes where the winners' names are drawn or in some other manner selected by random.

The element of chance can be eliminated if the contestants are asked to create jingles, write sentences about the product, or otherwise demonstrate their skills. The selection of winners must then be based on bona fide skill with bona fide selection by qualified judges. It should be noted that while years ago the spelling of "dog" may have been adjudged "skill," today the court decisions clearly require a showing of the kind of skill that can be objectively observed, compared, and judged.

Finally, in those cases where the winners are selected by chance, the question arises whether there was any "consideration" given by the participant. Basically, consideration is the giving by the participant of something of value; however, interpretations vary widely among the states as to what constitutes consideration. Obviously, the mailing of a boxtop or label from the product, which clearly requires a purchase, is consideration.

Some states assert that having to go into a store to pick up an entry blank is consideration, and others maintain that the making of a long-distance telephone call is consideration. At one time in New York State it was even held to be consideration to be required to send in a penny postcard with the participant's name and address on it. That decision has since been overruled. The differing definitions of consideration remain the most difficult aspect of contests and sweepstakes. Indeed, uniform lottery laws, federal and state, would be a great benefit.

In summary, the illegality of a lottery can be eliminated either if the consumer is not required to give or do anything of value or if the winners are selected purely on the basis of skill and not at all on the basis of chance.

5. State and even local governments have statutes on the subject of false advertising. Many states have put into force their own laws on false and deceptive advertising in an effort to proceed against those companies which are primarily involved in intrastate commerce or which are otherwise immune to FTC investigation. As recently as December 1967, the Massachusetts legislature passed a so-called little FTC Act. Other states either have passed or are considering various and sundry statutes on false and deceptive advertising. The Federal Trade Commission encourages the passage of legislation in the state legislatures.

In a recent speech, Chairman Paul Rand Dixon of the Federal Trade Commission dismissed the argument which had been made by some authorities that this type of legislation in the states would conflict with federal law. On the contrary, Mr. Dixon takes the position that Congress did not intend that its legislation in this field be exclusive, but that the Federal Government and the state governments should join in an endeavor to protect the consumers. To that effect, the FTC apparently has established liaison with the various state governments and has held seminars for state officials.

6. The Food and Drug Administration concerns itself primarily with the labeling of food and drug products and the consistency of advertising with labeling. The FDA and the FTC have entered into an agreement relating to their respective powers and responsibilities in connection with advertising; and, very generally, the FDA has jurisdiction over the advertising of prescription drugs while the FTC has jurisdiction over proprietary drugs.

7. It might be noted that the Federal Communications Commission also has involved itself in advertising, although indirectly, through the application of the so-called Fairness Doctrine. Under this doctrine, radio and television stations are required to make time available to both sides of any controversy. In June 1967, the FCC applied this doctrine to cigarette commercials, to the effect that stations which carry cigarette commercials are required to give free time to organizations which are opposed to smoking. This ruling may result in a reluctance on the part of stations to accept cigarette advertising.

Although the Commission has avowed that it will not apply this doctrine in connection with the advertising of other products, it seems difficult to understand by what logic the FCC can refuse to apply the Fairness Doctrine as relating to beer advertising or the advertising of fluoride products, such as some toothpastes, or any other products which are opposed by organized groups. It would appear that the FCC has opened a Pandora's box. Its ruling in connection with cigarette advertising is being contested in the courts. Presumably, the ultimate decision will shed some light on the extent to which the FCC, through the application of the Fairness Doctrine, may be expected to involve itself, though indirectly, in the inhibition of advertising of specific product categories.

8. Other administrative departments or agencies, such as the Agriculture Department, the Civil Aeronautics Board, the Farm Credit Administration, and the Federal Power Commission, also have certain powers to control advertising within their particular limited areas of competence. The types of advertising to which they apply, of course, are very special and limited in scope.

ORDERS

It is, of course, impossible in this space to review all the possible consequences of proceedings by governmental authorities for violations of the many different laws relating to the control of advertising. The result can range from a slap on the wrist by the Federal Trade Commission or another federal agency in exchange for a promise not to rerun a certain advertisement to criminal convictions and fines, as happened in a case involving the advertising of certain reducing tablets. Depending on the forum, different nonmonetary consequences can arise—such as, perhaps, the suspension or cancellation of a liquor wholesaler's or manufacturer's license or suspensions of other types of licenses.

It should also be noted that, although the analogy may be resented, a corporation can build up a "record" just like that of a criminal. Time and again, in issuing orders against well-known, large, and prestigious corporations, the FTC has made reference to the fact that the particular corporation had been before it on prior occasions and had built up an unfavorable record.

PRIVATE CONTROL BODIES

A summary of advertising problems, even in the limited space of this chapter, would be incomplete without mentioning that private control bodies exist which exercise a substantial amount of control over advertising. The exact extent of legal control of these bodies may be indefinite, but they do exist. They exercise powerful controls, and their rulings may have important consequences. Some of these organizations exist with the blessing of the appropriate governmental authority and presumably collaborate with it. It may be helpful to mention a few of the more important bodies:

The tobacco industry established the Cigarette Advertising Code, whose administrator is former New Jersey Governor Robert Meyner. All cigarette advertising of the companies adhering to this Code is cleared by the administrator's office. The national television networks, through departments called "continuity acceptance" or the like, screen all television advertising going out over their networks. Further, the networks and independent stations which are members of the National Association of Broadcasters, created the so-called Code Authority which fulfills substantially the same functions for all their subscribers as the continuity acceptance departments fulfill for the networks.

The New York Stock Exchange and the N.A.S.D. have rules relating to the advertising of their broker members. Miscellaneous trade associations will review and, to a certain extent, censor, the advertising of their members.

Of course, the purpose of these review activities of various private organizations or associations presumably derives from the theory that a certain amount of self-policing by an industry may prevent or reduce government interference or control. The difficulty from a legal point of view is that these private control bodies are not bound by rules of law or by any rules of legal procedure, such as the right to confront the party complaining of particular advertising or to examine the "experts" retained by some control bodies who determine the invalidity of a product claim. These rights of due process are, of course, inherent in our system of law, and a strong argument can be made that sometimes a fairer trial can be had in a court of law or in a federal administrative proceeding than in voluntary or industry control bodies.

Problems Relating to the Rights of Others

It is impossible to even attempt to cover all the multitudinous types of contracts which are entered into in connection with the business of creating and using advertising or to cite the many types of claims and actions which have arisen in the advertising business. The purpose here is to touch upon the more common problems with which an advertiser or an advertising agency can get involved.

CONTRACTS WITH ADVERTISING AGENCY

No discussion of advertising law would be complete without referring, at least briefly, to the relationship between the advertiser and his advertising agency or agencies. It is an amazing fact that each year many millions of dollars are committed by advertising agencies on behalf of their clients; the agencies become privy to the innermost workings and secrets of a company, and yet many companies are extremely casual about the contractual relationships between client and agency. Some years ago, the American Association of Advertising Agencies published the results of a survey which showed that about 50 percent of advertisers polled did not have any written agreement with their advertising agencies.

The reasons for this lack of written agreement are various and sundry. Some companies believe that trade practice is so common and so generally recognized that it is not necessary to have a written agreement. Others merely let the matter go by default even though they recognize that problems between agencies and advertisers can and do arise. Many companies let the matter slide since neither side wants to get into any discussion of potential differences when the agency is first appointed. In actuality, such problems as do arise between advertisers and agencies usually do not come up until the termination of the relationship; and, of course, at that time it is too late to enter into an agreement. The problems generally fall into two categories.

1. To what compensation is the outgoing agency entitled during the termination period? The trade practice is not entirely clear, although the tendency is that the outgoing agency is entitled to commissions on all

advertising placed in print media whose closing dates fall prior to the effective date of termination and on all broadcasting actually broadcast or telecast during that period. In certain rare cases, an agency may even continue to be entitled to compensation beyond the termination date. For instance, exceptions occur in connection with highly seasonal products. It would clearly be inequitable for an agency to spend all year working up a Christmas campaign and then be terminated before space or time is actually used and commissions are earned. There is some sentiment that an agency should continue to receive commissions so long as advertising created by it is still used; but, at present, such commitments are rare and certainly not established trade practice. Although there have been many disputes in this area, practically no court cases are reported, and it cannot be said that any legal precedent has been established.

2. Who owns advertising materials after termination? It is commonly recognized that any advertising material prepared for and used by the client during the term of the agreement, or paid for by the client, belongs to him and not to the agency. The questions that do arise usually relate to material prepared by the agency and not used or paid for by the advertiser. In a dispute, the agency will take the point of view that ideas are its stock in trade and that any ideas or creative material not used or paid for by the particular client should remain the agency's property.

There are many different views on the proper approach to this problem, and it cannot be said that there is an established, generally accepted trade practice. Some agreements provide that either party may use such material and that it belongs to the one which first reaches the marketplace with it. This would seem to be a somewhat impractical solution because one party may be spending time, money, and effort in developing the material—including, perhaps, even the expensive production of television commercials—and then, all of a sudden, may find itself foreclosed because the other party has begun using this material. To make such an approach effective and practical, each side would have to advise the other of its impending plans, which, obviously, they may not wish to do. It would seem more equitable and practical for the advertiser who switches agencies to seek to acquire those particular materials or ideas which it had not used but which it may desire to use in the future and to compensate the originating agency for these in some manner. Again, there is very little law in this area; such decisions as are available would indicate that the agency, in the absence of specific agreement, retains the rights in unused ideas or material for which the client did not pay.

There is some reason to believe that in recent years agencies and advertisers have become somewhat more conscious of the legal problems which might arise between them, and written agreements seem to have become more common. Aside from the awareness of potential legal problems, another reason for this greater attention to written contracts may have been the fact that new types of agency compensation have been introduced into the business, such as the fee basis, the fee against commission, or the guaranteed profit basis. Companies entering into these financial arrangements presumably consider it necessary to set them out in agreements, and it is likely that the parties then proceed to incorporate into their agreements various other clauses relating to their mutual rights and obligations, including provisions on the critical problems just mentioned.

Liability to Media

Is an advertiser liable directly to media for media costs? As a general rule, the advertising agency enters into contracts with the media; and the advertiser usually pays the agency and the agency then pays the media. What happens, however, if the advertiser has paid the agency and the agency refuses or is unable to pay the media?

For an understanding of this problem, a discussion of the legal status of an advertising agency is indicated. An advertising agency may be considered either an independent contractor or an agent for the advertiser. If the agency is an agent, then the third parties—the media—have a right to look for payment to either the agent or the principal. If, on the other hand, the agency is an independent contractor, and the media, when they enter into contracts with the agency, expect to look solely to the agency for payment, then presumably the advertiser cannot be held directly liable by the media.

There are many conflicting cases in various states. These conflicts are understandable because the legal status of the advertising agency is not clear historically. Originally, advertising agencies acted as agents for the media. In fact, the payment of a commission by media to their agents was the origin of the commission system as we know it today. As the business evolved, however, the function and status of the agency underwent continuing change. At one time, agencies bought and sold space and acted in the manner of space jobbers. At the present state of development it seems clear that agencies are deemed to act as agents for the advertisers. In small towns, however, and with respect to certain specialized media, there may still be some dual function, with the agency seeking to sell space or time on behalf of media.

Most of the recent court decisions dealing with this question indicate that the agency is considered the advertiser's agent. Consequently, if the agency becomes insolvent or for whatever reason does not pay the media, the media may and will look to the advertiser for payment. As a result, an advertiser may find himself paying twice for the same space or time. To protect against such a contingency, some advertisers have been known to demand that the agency submit receipted invoices from media before the agency will be paid by the advertiser. Such a demand, of course, works a hardship on the agency, not only because the agency in effect is asked to finance the client's advertising, but also because the agency then becomes exposed to the converse risk of the client's insolvency or refusal to pay after the client's advertising has already been run.

Another approach taken by certain advertisers has been to insist that each contract or order for space or time issued by their agencies contain a provision that the media will look *solely* to the agency for payment. Of course, if the agency is substantial enough, the media may accept this condition; similarly, if the client is of enough importance, the media may still accept this proviso even though the agency is financially insubstantial. If, however, the client's bargaining power is limited, the media may well refuse such an order from an agency whose credit is not established. The end result, of course, is that media may discriminate in favor of larger advertisers or agencies, or both, in deciding whether to grant such a request.

RIGHT OF PRIVACY

The right of privacy is a principle which has grown in the law in the past 20 to 30 years. In a number of states, including New York, there are specific statutes relating to this right. In some other states where there is no statute on the subject, courts have sometimes created a similar theory.

Basically, the right of privacy prevents the use of a person's name or likeness in advertising or for purposes of trade without his written permission. In New York and in the other states where this right is created by statute, it has been rigorously enforced. Yet various interpretations have tended to create exceptions to the statute. Most especially, the question has arisen whether any person in the public light or in the news has such a right of privacy, the argument being that the use of a newsworthy person's name or likeness is protected by the constitutional right of free speech.

Conflicting decisions exist relating to the use in advertising of newsworthy persons. For instance, in the case of *Flores* v. *Mosler Safe Company*, 196 N.Y.S. 2d 975 (1959), the Mosler Safe Company, in an advertisement for its fireproof safe, used a reprint of a news story and a news photo relating to a spectacular fire; the plaintiff's name and picture were contained in it. The news report mentioned that the fire allegedly had been started through the carelessness of the plaintiff or his companion. Mosler pleaded that the use of the news story was a constitutional right. The court held in favor of the plaintiff—that is, Mosler had infringed on his privacy. However, the court, in its decision, mentioned that at the particular time of the advertisement, the news of the fire had become somewhat stale. It is questionable whether the same decision would have been rendered had the fire been a very recent event.

An altogether different result was reached in an action brought by Shirley Booth against Curtis Publishing Co. [223 N.Y.S. 2d 737, aff'd 228 N.Y.S. 2d 468 (1962)]. Miss Booth's picture had appeared in some editorial material in *Holiday*. Subsequently, Curtis ran an advertisement for *Holiday*, using the page in which Miss Booth's picture had appeared, to demonstrate the type of content found in *Holiday*. The court decided that this use, even though it was for advertising purposes, was incidental to the dissemination of news and not a collateral advertising use. The distinction between these two cases is perhaps somewhat tenuous; however, recent U.S. Supreme Court decisions give additional weight to the Booth decision and tend to limit the right of privacy in its application to newsworthy or famous persons. It appears that the application of this right to well-known persons is limited to situations where the person's name or likeness is used in a presentation which is "infected with material and substantial falsification" or with "reckless disregard for the truth." [See *Time, Inc.* v. *Hill,* 385 U.S. 374 (1967)]

Although the U.S. Supreme Court may show a tendency to limit the application of the right of privacy doctrine, the courts of New York and other states are still applying this doctrine quite rigorously. There is no reason to relax the requirement that any person whose name or picture is used in an advertisement must give his written consent.

It should also be noted that the use of a name or likeness in a house organ or a sales brochure is also covered by this statute. Some companies occasionally will show pictures of their employees in annual reports or in their house organs. There are cases of disgruntled or former employees successfully bringing suit as a result of such uses. The mere fact of employment, without any additional written consent, does not give the employer the right to use the employees' names or likenesses in advertising or promotion materials, even though their circulation may be quite limited.

DEFAMATION

The laws of defamation, of course, apply to advertising as they do to every other form of public communication. A common definition of defamation is that "a communication is defamatory if it tends so to harm the reputation of another as to lower him in the estimation of the community or to deter third persons from associating or dealing with him."

On the whole, cases of defamation arising out of advertising are quite rare. On occasion, a libel suit may arise from situations peculiar to the industry and not along the historical lines of libel. For instance, an advertiser used a model in a print advertisement. She had signed a release form and had been properly compensated. The advertisement used some risqué language in the copy. The model sued on the basis that the use of her picture in conjunction with the copy impugned her character and reputation. The advertiser's defense was that she had signed a full release which gave him the right to use her photograph in any manner. The court disagreed, holding that the release did not give the advertiser the right to juxtapose the picture against writing which could affect the model's reputation.

In another case [*Bert Lahr* v. *Adell Chemical Co., Inc.,* 300 F. 2d 256 (1962)], Mr. Lahr, a prominent entertainer, sued Adell Chemical Co. because of television commercials using an imitation of his voice. Among other theories, Mr. Lahr claimed that he had been libeled because his reputation had been injured by indicating to the public that he was reduced to making anonymous television commercials. The case was decided on other grounds, but the court held that he might have an action in libel. It should be noted that Mr. Lahr probably would not have succeeded had it been made clear that someone was mimicking his voice rather than trying to make the listeners believe they were hearing Mr. Lahr.

Conversely, an advertiser may also be on the receiving end of a libel. For instance, Arthur Godfrey, on a television program, mentioned that the manufacturer of ukuleles selling for $2.98 ought to go to jail. Only one such manufacturer existed: He sued Mr. Godfrey as well as Columbia Broadcasting System, Inc., and prevailed. (*Smith* v. *Godfrey et al.,* 102 N.Y.S. 2d 251; 1951.)

COMMERCIAL DISPARAGEMENT

The phrase "commercial disparagement" encompasses false statements concerning the quality of the services or product of a business, which are intended to cause business or financial harm and which in fact do so. Other names have been used for this type of legal violation, such as "trade libel," "disparagement of quality," and "injurious falsehood." The law in this area is most unsettled,* and in some jurisdictions a remedy can be had only if proof can be adduced that specific damages were suffered as the result of a competitor's disparaging or defamatory statement. In other jurisdictions, no specific damages need be shown if the statement was clearly defamatory of the product's manufacturer.

As a general rule, it is difficult for a competitor to recover damages for misleading or deceptive statements contained in advertising unless the advertising served to confuse the public and attempted to palm off the advertiser's goods for his competitor's. In one case, *Remington Products Corp.* v. *American Aerovap, Inc.,* 97 F. Supp. 644 (1951), a U.S. District Judge enjoined competitive advertising which was considered deceptive although there was no showing of a "palming off," but the case must be deemed an isolated one.

The principal remedy available to an advertiser for a competitor's deceptive advertising appears to be a complaint to the Federal Trade Commission, which may then initiate its own proceeding.

COPYRIGHT INFRINGEMENTS AND OTHER UNAUTHORIZED USES

It is, of course, not permissible to include in advertisements any copyrighted materials, although in certain circumstances very brief excerpts may be used. Special care should be taken in connection with the use of musical jingles on radio and television which may infringe somebody's property rights. For instance in the case of *Robertson* v. *Batten, Barton, Durstine & Osborne, Inc., et al.,* 146 F. Supp. 795 (1956), two bars in a

---

* An excellent discussion of this entire problem may be found in 77 *Harvard Law Review* 888 (1964).

commercial were found to be substantially similar to the key theme of a song, and the songwriter prevailed in an action against the advertising agency and the client.

Advertisements should not use, without specific permission, book, magazine, play, or movie titles or column headings. Although titles are not copyrightable, recoveries have been had for the unauthorized use of titles under theories of law other than copyright infringement, such as "unfair competition" or "unjust enrichment." If a title has achieved a "secondary meaning" with the public—that is, if it creates a particular association in the minds of the public—it should not be used. Of course, if a title is merely the use—not in a fanciful manner—of some generic words, the owner of the title would have no basis for a lawsuit.

For example, an advertiser should not say "My Fair Lady smokes XYZ cigarettes." "My Fair Lady" is obviously a fanciful phrase which, as a result of the Broadway play and motion picture by that title, has received wide publicity and achieved a secondary meaning. On the other hand, one may say "Beautiful girls smoke XYZ cigarettes" even though "Beautiful Girls" may have been the title of a play or motion picture. It should be noted, however, that if use is made in a normal, colloquial manner of generic words which also happen to be the title of a play or other literary work, then it should be done in such a manner that no intention is shown to capitalize on the fact that the words are the title of such a work. For instance, in the example cited, the words "beautiful girls" should not be in any kind of special script or written in any other manner to set them apart from the balance of the sentence. No indication should be given that the advertiser seeks to profit in any way from the goodwill which the particular literary work using such title may have achieved with the public.

Unsolicited Submissions

One of the ever-recurring problems facing advertising agencies and advertisers is the receipt of submissions from members of the public of ideas and suggestions for advertisements. Most companies have a policy that they will not consider any unsolicited submissions under any circumstances. From the legal point of view, this is by far the safest course to follow, as unsolicited submissions can bring about annoying claims and lawsuits. It might also be mentioned that, although probably the vast majority of these submissions are transmitted by bona fide members of the public who feel that they have created some idea which should be of some value to an advertiser, it also seems clear that there are habitual submitters who have managed to make a business out of submissions. Some of these submitters have been known to send the same submissions to different companies under different names, and some submissions have been known to be predated and to incorporate ideas contained in television commercials which are then on the air. These submitters seem to count on confusion and delay which, particularly in very large corporations, may follow receipt of their submissions; and, eventually, they hope to receive some sort of nuisance settlement.

Most companies which have made it a practice not to consider any unsolicited submissions do so not only because of the potential legal consequences but also as a result of finding that out of a multitude of submissions they receive, only an infinitesimal number have any value whatsoever.

There are still some companies which will consider unsolicited submissions as a result of the feeling that adverse consumer reaction would follow the refusal to read a submission, although most companies which belong to this school of thought would at least require a signed release form. The rationale of these companies seems difficult to follow: If, indeed, the company agrees to consider the suggestion or idea submitted to it, then, sooner or later, in practically all cases, it will have to follow up with a letter of rejection. It would seem logical that the rejection would bring on at least the same measure of resentment that an initial refusal to consider the submission might have brought about.

Unsolicited submissions have been the basis for many lawsuits, and in many of them the submitters prevailed. Generally, the courts have said that where an idea is novel and unique and reduced to concrete form and where it is submitted under such circumstances that it is clear that the submitter expects to be paid, a contract will be implied. For instance, in *Healy* v. *R. H. Macy,* 297 N.Y.S. 165 (1937), the submitter offered the slogan "A Macy Christmas and a Happy New Year," as well as some other similar slogans. Although the company brought evidence that it had used similar slogans created by its own advertising department, the plaintiff succeeded in the action.

It would seem quite evident that the best way to avoid this type of problem is to flatly refuse the consideration of any unsolicited submissions. It should also be mentioned that signed release forms are not necessarily an absolute protection. In some cases, these release forms have been considered invalid; in other cases, courts seem to have been intent on limiting their effect.

It is often said by copywriters, art directors, and others in the creative areas that restraints are being put in their way by "the lawyers" and that lawyers were inhibiting creativity. No doubt, as advertising has grown, so have the restrictions on it. Where once the advertiser was practically unlimited in his ability to exaggerate, or even deceive the public, and the principle of *caveat emptor* ruled unchallenged, today the advertiser is limited to expounding the true virtues of his product; he may merely indulge in "puffery"—and the interpretation of puffery continuously becomes more circumscribed, in relation both to third parties and the government.

It seems to this writer that strict adherence to truthful advertising should be considered not an inhibition but a challenge, not only to create good advertising but to introduce better products. Let it also be said that while we may smart under some controls, and under the inevitable occasional abuses of power by those who administer the controls, we are still—and, hopefully, always shall be—a long way from the ultimate control: the absolute censorship of advertising which some countries have imposed, using the excuse of "protection for the public," the traditional rationale of tyranny.

The Law of Packaging and Labeling

Peter Barton Hutt

THE PROPER PACKAGING AND LABELING OF ANY PRODUCT MUST TAKE INTO consideration both voluntary standards adopted by the industry and mandatory requirements imposed by federal and state statutes and regulations. Today it is the rare exception, rather than the rule, when no pertinent guidelines or legal requirements are found.

This chapter provides a broad view of the legal aspects of packaging and labeling in order that a company executive may understand the nature and importance of the questions that arise and establish an internal system to handle these matters. It will not enumerate all existing guidelines and requirements, or all products subject to such requirements, or even the sources where all applicable requirements may be found. The guidelines and requirements are so diverse, and the questions they raise are often so complex, that any detailed consideration of proper packaging and labeling must be handled on an individual product basis.

PETER BARTON HUTT is a partner in the law firm of Covington & Burling in Washington, D. C.

Voluntary Industry Standards and Guidelines

A recent Department of Commerce publication lists 486 American organizations that consider standardization to be a major or important part of their work. It has been estimated that more than 13,600 standards now exist and that more than 3,000 new and revised standards are adopted every year. Many of these standards deal directly with product packaging and labeling. Others, concerned with product specifications, affect packaging and labeling indirectly.

The vast majority of voluntary standards have been adopted by industry without statutory prodding or even authorization. The benefits of standard labeling terminology and standard container sizes, both to the industry and to the public, are obvious. Indeed, if industry did not voluntarily undertake standardization in such areas it is likely that it would be imposed by statutory requirements.

Although standardization necessarily limits competition, the Department of Justice and the courts have generally concluded that voluntary industry standardization activities are in the public interest and therefore not in violation of the antitrust laws. Only use of standardization activities for unreasonable purposes—to exclude competitors, eliminate product options, or agree upon prices—has been held illegal. In short, standardization of packaging and labeling is vulnerable to antitrust challenge only when it is used to attain illegal objectives.

Guidelines and standards adopted by industry usually do not carry enforcement provisions with them. Only rarely has an industry trade association attempted to establish its own sanctions to penalize noncompliance with published standards.

Voluntary industry guidelines can, however, be enforced indirectly by government agencies. The Federal Trade Commission would clearly consider it an unfair trade practice, in violation of the Federal Trade Commission Act, for a company to label its product "Grade A" if the product did not meet the voluntary industry standard for "Grade A." Although not all industry guidelines can be policed in this manner, many have far greater legal authority behind them than may originally have been intended. Thus voluntary industry standards, and even generally accepted industry practices that are not reduced to writing, can readily become mandatory.

Since 1901, the National Bureau of Standards, now part of the Department of Commerce, has had statutory authorization to cooperate with private organizations in the establishment of standard practices. The Bureau's present procedures for the development of voluntary product standards provide that such standards may cover terms, classes, sizes (including body sizes for wearing apparel), dimensions, capacities, quality levels, performance criteria, testing equipment, and test procedures. The packaging and labeling of many products are affected by more than 400 voluntary standards adopted under these regulations.

Use of the National Bureau of Standards' voluntary standardization procedures has been given new impetus by the enactment of the Fair Packaging and Labeling Act (FPLA) of 1967. The FPLA was the result of Congress' conclusion that the number of package sizes in which consumer commodities were available sometimes made it difficult for consumers to make value comparisons among different sizes. Early versions of the FPLA would have imposed mandatory standardization of package sizes rather than voluntary standardization. Congress was persuaded, however, that industry should be given an opportunity to reduce the number of package sizes voluntarily. The Secretary of Commerce was therefore authorized to request industrial participation in the development of a voluntary product standard whose purpose would be to reduce the number of available package sizes for any consumer commodity for which it is determined that an undue proliferation of sizes impairs the reasonable ability of consumers to make value comparisons.

It is hoped that industry will take the initiative in alleviating the problems that prompted enactment of the package standardization provisions of the FPLA. If this does not happen, the Department of Commerce must report to Congress that voluntary efforts have failed and must recommend whether Congress should enact legislation providing regulatory authority to deal with the situation. Industry's failure to respond voluntarily could therefore lead to restrictive new packaging legislation.

Legal Requirements

Congress and the states have enacted an enormous number of regulatory statutes controlling various aspects of product packaging and labeling. The agencies established under these statutes have, in turn, promulgated detailed regulations to administer and enforce the law.

Most federal statutes apply only to products that are shipped across state lines. In many instances, however, states have enacted virtually identical provisions that are applicable to products made and distributed wholly within a state. Thus it cannot be assumed that the manufacture and sale of a product within a single state provides exemption from the type of requirements that are contained in federal statutes.

In most instances, however, a company is justified in assuming that compliance with all federal legal requirements for packaging and labeling will also result in compliance with the requirements of all 50 states. The vast majority of state packaging and labeling statutes are directly patterned after federal statutes or are so interpreted. Instances even exist in which state statutory requirements inconsistent with federal statutes have been openly ignored by state officials.

Thus most companies distributing products nationally comply with all federal packaging and labeling laws, together with pertinent voluntary industry standards and guidelines, and then deal on an ad hoc basis with whatever state questions may arise. They find it impossible to maintain a current file on the statutes, regulations, interpretations, informal attitudes, and court decisions in all states, counties, and cities throughout the country. Only where certain states are widely known to have unusual packaging or labeling requirements—such as Pennsylvania's requirement that certain food labels show that the product is registered by the State Department of Agriculture—are those requirements consistently met in the first instance.

The volume and complexity of the federal legal requirements alone can be bewildering, particularly in sensitive industries that are heavily regulated. These requirements sometimes leave the manufacturer virtually no discretion in packaging and labeling. Thus the importance of understanding and correctly applying these legal requirements cannot be overemphasized. Failure to comply with the law can have severe consequences.

The complexity of the statutory requirements as elaborated by governmental regulations requires continuous detailed checking for compliance with all legal requirements. No one should trust his memory about these requirements or rely upon an old copy of the law or regulations. The consequences are too important.

Even for those most familiar with a given product field, the period of expertise is uncomfortably short. Checking for the latest information in the *Federal Register* and in the multitude of press releases, speeches, bulletins, and reports published by federal agencies is a necessary daily routine. One can no longer rely even upon the *Code of Federal Regulations*, printed once a year, because of the swift and crucial changes that take place in the applicable legal requirements almost daily.

Statutes with Specific Product Application

Many federal and state statutes have been enacted to meet ad hoc problems related to the packaging and labeling of specific products. For the most part, these statutes are well known in the affected industries. It is unlikely that a radio manufacturer would be unaware of the labeling requirements established by the Federal Communications Commission, or that a seed distributor would not have heard of the Federal Seed Act of 1939, or that an importer would be ignorant of the labeling requirements of the Tariff Act of 1930.

Each of these statutes is highly technical and detailed. Some are the subject of multivolume legal treatises. It is therefore impractical to do more in this chapter than to provide the reader with a general understanding of the types of requirements imposed by these statutes.

Statutes with General Product Application

Congress and the states have also enacted laws of wider application that deal generally with packaging and labeling of commodities. Although they are perhaps less well known, they are of equal importance to industry.

The Mail Fraud Act of 1909, for example, prohibits the use of the mails for any fraudulent scheme, and other statutes permit the Post Office Department to refuse to send fraudulent labeling through the mails if it is part of a scheme for obtaining money or property by means of false pretenses or lotteries. The Federal Trade Commission Act of 1914 prohibits misleading packaging or labeling of any product shipped in interstate commerce, and the Fair Packaging and Labeling Act of 1967 provides new federal controls for the packaging and labeling of all consumer commodities distributed in interstate commerce. There are few, if indeed any, products that do not fall under one or more of these general statutes.

The Consequences of Noncompliance

Each federal and state statute embodies its own unique sanctions. It is therefore impossible to make any general statement about the penalties that may attach to noncompliance.

It must be assumed, however, that failure to comply with a regulatory statute is a very serious matter. The economic costs alone may be overwhelming. One pharmaceutical manufacturer reportedly spent $385,000 on telegrams alone in recalling a defective product from the market. The time, effort, and expense required to correct illegal packaging and labeling should be sufficient incentive for the establishment of internal company procedures that will prevent noncompliance.

Many federal regulatory statutes authorize use of confiscation or injunction procedures to enforce the law. Failure to comply can therefore result in the manufacturer's being shut down until the problem is corrected.

Many of these statutes also authorize criminal proceedings against the officers of the company as well as the company itself. Both the regulatory agencies charged with bringing enforcement action under these laws and the courts that determine the appropriate penalties have not hesitated to impose jail sentences where the facts show a willful or fraudulent violation of the law.

In many of these regulatory statutes, moreover, Congress has provided for what lawyers call "strict criminal liability." The fact that the manufacturer did not intend to package or label his product illegally is of no relevance. Mere noncompliance is sufficient to establish criminal liability for the violation. Thus the plant manager for a food company may be found criminally liable for packaging or labeling that violates the Federal Food, Drug, and Cosmetic Act of 1938, whether or not he was aware of the problem which caused the violation. Fortunately, however, regulatory agencies usually impose criminal penalties only in cases of willful violation of the law or of inexcusable negligence.

The consequences of regulatory problems may have even more adverse effects than the regulatory action itself. For example, the courts have generally concluded that regulatory agencies may properly advise the public when action is taken against a company for a violation of the law. Agencies protecting the public health have even broader authority to warn the public about improperly packaged or labeled articles that may endanger health. Adverse publicity of this type can damage both the good name of the company and the brand name of the product in question. Not long ago one of the nation's largest corporations decided to abandon completely one of its leading brand names because of nationwide publicity that the product was contaminated by salmonella and therefore dangerous to health. In other cases, the Federal Trade Commission has required products to abandon well-established brand names that are potentially misleading to the public if clarifying language will not be sufficient to preclude consumer confusion. Although these examples are rare, they illustrate the very practical and extremely important business consequences that can result from regulatory action by a government agency.

It therefore makes good business sense to take the extra precautions that will insure the satisfaction of all legal requirements for packaging and labeling. The amount of time and expense required is relatively small compared with the enormous problems that can result from a violation.

Regulated Aspects of Packaging and Labeling

There is virtually no part of packaging and labeling that is not affected by at least one statute, regulation, or voluntary standard. The following discussion summarizes the more important aspects of packaging and labeling that are regulated under current voluntary guidelines and legal requirements.

PRODUCT CLAIMS

Packaging and labeling are frequently used to make product claims. These claims include the quantity of the contents of the package, the product specifications, and representations for the product's quality, performance, and usefulness.

General policing. All product claims are subject to policing under the general powers granted to the Federal Trade Commission. The Federal Trade Commission Act of 1914, as amended by the Wheeler-Lea Act of 1938, broadly prohibits "unfair methods of competition" and "unfair or deceptive acts or practices," and the courts have held that this includes misleading labeling claims. Thus a statement that the product contains a specified amount of an item when it does not, or any other false or misleading statement in the labeling, is subject to regulatory action by the Commission.

It is most important to understand that the Federal Trade Commission possesses only general policing authority. The manufacturer is free to package and label his product as he believes proper. Prior approval by the Commission is not required, although advisory opinions can be obtained upon request. If the Commission concludes that a given package or label violates the law, it then institutes informal or formal action to bring it into compliance.

In addition to this authority granted to the Federal Trade Commission over labeling for all products, Congress has enacted a number of statutes granting similar policing authority to other governmental agencies over labeling claims for specific products. The Federal Food, Drug, and Cosmetic Act of 1938 prohibits false or misleading statements in the labeling of foods, drugs, cosmetics, and medical devices. Other examples of federal statutes granting regulatory authority over labeling claims are the Federal Alcohol Administration Act of 1935, the Federal Stamping Act of 1961, and the Indian Arts and Crafts Act of 1935 which protects purchasers against misrepresentation about Indian and Eskimo arts and crafts.

Preclearance. In a few situations, because of the important public interest involved, Congress has also granted preclearance authority over product claims to regulatory agencies. Under these statutes, certain products may not legally be marketed until the regulatory agency specifically approves the labeling claims (and usually other aspects of the product as well). The most accurate and truthful claim will be illegal unless the required prior approval has been obtained.

The Alcohol and Tobacco Tax Division requires preclearance of all labels for alcoholic beverages. Similar preclearance is required under the Federal Meat Inspection Act of 1907 as recently amended by the Wholesome Meat Act of 1967, the Federal Poultry Products Inspection Act of 1957, the Federal Insecticide, Fungicide, and Rodenticide Act of 1947 as strengthened in 1964, and for new drugs under the Federal Food, Drug, and Cosmetic Act. These statutes are, however, the exception rather than the rule. Most product claims are subject only to general policing authority and not to preclearance.

Truthfulness of claims. Entire books have been written about the legal and factual standards used to judge the truthfulness or falsity of product claims. Suffice it to say here that the same standards are applicable to labeling claims as to advertising claims. The preceding chapter of this book contains a fine summary of the guiding principles that underlie these standards.

REQUIRED INFORMATION ON LABELING

Explanatory information is frequently required to appear on product labeling either directly by federal statute or indirectly through interpretative regulations promulgated by the enforcing government agency. In most instances these affirmative labeling requirements can be found in the published statutes and regulations.

Such requirements have also been imposed on an ad hoc basis in specific situations where a need is demonstrated. The Federal Trade Commission Act provides that promotional material may be judged misleading because of a failure to reveal material facts, as well as because of a false representation. When the Federal Trade Commission or other regulatory agencies conclude that confusion or misrepresentation can be prevented only by an affirmative label disclosure, it does not hesitate to impose this requirement wholly outside any specific provision in the applicable statute or regulations.

Product identity. Many regulatory statutes have been enacted solely for the purpose of establishing and emphasizing the identity of the product. The Oleomargarine Act of 1950, for example, was intended by Congress to require margarine manufacturers to emphasize the name of the product in all labeling and to preclude any labeling that would confuse the product with dairy products.

The Fair Packaging and Labeling Act of 1967 requires the identity of all consumer commodities to be specified on the label. Regulations recently promulgated under that Act by the Federal Trade Commission and the Food and Drug Administration stipulate that this statement appear conspicuously on the principal display panel of the consumer package.

Product composition. A number of regulatory statutes have also been enacted as a result of confusion about the composition of products available in the marketplace. The Federal Trade Commission has long had general authority to police misrepresentation with respect to product composition, but this after-the-fact policing was thought insufficient to meet the problems adequately in several specific areas. Thus Congress enacted the Wool Products Labeling Act of 1940, the Fur Products Labeling Act of 1951, and the Textile Fiber Products Identification Act of 1958, all three of which require affirmative disclosure of the nature and composition of the product covered. The Federal Stamping Act of 1961 similarly governs the labeling of articles made in whole or in part of gold, silver, or any alloy of those metals.

The Food and Drug Administration and the United States Department of Agriculture enforce the statutory requirements of a specific label declaration of each of the ingredients in all food products except those for which standards of identity have been promulgated. The Federal

Seed Act of 1939 similarly requires detailed information about composition to be stated on the label.

The Fair Packaging and Labeling Act opened the possibility that specific ingredient declaration will be extended beyond foods. Discretionary authority was given to the Federal Trade Commission and the Food and Drug Administration to promulgate regulations requiring such a declaration for any consumer commodity if it is necessary to prevent consumer deception or to facilitate value comparisons.

Product quality. Statutory regulation of product quality has occurred almost exclusively in the area of foods and drugs. Congress has granted wide authority to several governmental agencies to prohibit impure and unsafe foods and drugs from the marketplace. Such statutes include the Tea Importation Act of 1883, the Federal Import Milk Act of 1927, the Federal Animal Virus, Serum, and Toxin Act of 1913, and the Public Health Service Amendments of 1944, as well as the more widely known regulatory statutes covering foods and drugs. The basic Federal Food, Drug, and Cosmetic Act of 1938 has frequently been amended to add new regulatory controls, under such statutes as the Durham-Humphrey Prescription Drug Amendments of 1951, the Miller Pesticide Amendments of 1954, the Food Additives Amendment of 1958, the Color Additives Amendments of 1960, the Drug Amendments of 1962, and the Drug Abuse Control Amendments of 1965. Congress has also regulated so-called inferior products under the tax authority in statutes such as the Renovated Butter Act of 1902 and the Filled Cheese Act of 1896. However, in only one statute—the Filled Milk Act of 1923—has Congress gone so far as to prohibit an unadulterated product from interstate commerce completely.

Standards of quality ranging from high to low have been authorized for foods of all kinds under the Federal Food, Drug, and Cosmetic Act, and specifically for meat and poultry under the Federal Meat Inspection Act and the Federal Poultry Products Inspection Act. Failure to abide by these quality standards involves a direct violation of law.

Although the Perishable Agricultural Commodities Act of 1930 is concerned basically with economic regulation, quality labeling standards are essential to the controls that it establishes. The Department of Agriculture has also promulgated voluntary standards of quality for agricultural products under the Agricultural Marketing Act of 1946. This statute includes no direct enforcement provisions, but any misleading labeling with respect to the quality of an agricultural product would unquestionably violate the Federal Trade Commission Act.

For products other than foods and drugs, voluntary quality standards adopted by industry have usually prevailed in the marketplace. Packaging and labeling based upon these standards will generally meet all legal requirements.

Quality standards for all products purchased by the Federal Government as established by the General Services Administration under the Federal Property and Administrative Services Act of 1949 have also had a substantial impact on private industry. It is estimated that over 50,000 standards and specifications for government purchasing have been established under the 1949 Act. Although these quality standards are mandatory only for Federal Government purchases, their impact upon private industry is obvious. Requirements of the General Services Administration have frequently become accepted practice throughout industry.

Net quantity of contents. The Fair Packaging and Labeling Act of 1967 requires, for all consumer commodities shipped in interstate commerce, that the net quantity of contents be separately and accurately stated in a uniform location on the principal display panel of the product label in terms of weight, measure, or numerical count. For packages containing less than four pounds or one gallon, but at least one pound or one pint, and labeled in terms of weight or fluid measure, the statement of contents must be expressed alternatively, in both ounces and pounds. Pursuant to this statutory authority the Federal Trade Commission and the Food and Drug Administration have issued regulations requiring the use of minimum type sizes for the net quantity statement in relation to the area of the principal display panel, in order to make certain that it is sufficiently conspicuous and legible.

The FPLA explicitly prohibits the use of any term to qualify the net contents declaration, such as "giant quart." In addition, it grants to the Federal Trade Commission and the Food and Drug Administration discretionary authority to establish and define standards for characterizing the sizes of packages. Congress was concerned that, in some instances, such package descriptions as "large economy size" or "king size" might be deceptive, and therefore authorized standards for specific consumer commodities where they were necessary to prevent consumer deception or to facilitate value comparisons.

Long before the enactment of the Fair Packaging and Labeling Act, the National Conference on Weights and Measures (sponsored by the National Bureau of Standards) adopted a model state law on weights and measures, along with regulations to implement it. The FPLA requirements are patterned basically after the model law and regulations. Although most states adopted the model law and regulations, Congress decided that these requirements should be made mandatory throughout the country. Consequently the FPLA not only wrote the requirements into a federal law, but also prohibited different state requirements with respect to net quantity of contents.

The United States Constitution provides for the establishment of weights and measures by the Federal Government. The present statute governing weights and measures, enacted in 1901, authorizes the Secretary of Commerce to maintain national standards of measurement. In exercising this authority, the National Bureau of Standards has also established uniform specifications, tolerances, and other technical requirements for commercial weighing and measuring devices. Label declarations of net contents that fail to meet the uniform weights and measures specified by the National Bureau of Standards violate both federal and state law.

Manufacturer's identity. The new Fair Packaging and Labeling Act also requires, as does the model state law on weights and measures, that the label specify the name and place of business of the manufacturer, packer, or distributor of a consumer commodity. This requirement was previously imposed upon specific commodities under other federal regulatory legislation, as well as under the model state weights and measures law, and is now applicable to all consumer commodities shipped in interstate commerce.

Congress and the state legislatures have generally thought it necessary that labeling identify the manufacturer of an item in order to permit a consumer to have recourse against any product that fails to meet his satisfaction. Thus the regulations promulgated under the FPLA provide that the full address of the manufacturer must appear conspicuously and prominently on the label, with the exception of the street address if it appears in the city telephone book or business directory.

Product hazards. Perhaps the single most important cause of federal regulation of packaging and labeling is the existence of product hazards. Most federal statutes deal with this problem, either directly or indirectly.

The food and drug laws (particularly the Drug Amendments of 1962 that greatly increased the authority of the Food and Drug Administration over new drug products) are the most obvious examples of federal regulation of labeling for safety purposes. There are, however, numerous other examples of federal control of labeling to protect the public from potential harm.

The Interstate Commerce Commission has long regulated the labeling of dangerous articles shipped by railroads and truckers. In 1927 Congress enacted the Caustic Poison Act requiring strong warning language and appropriate symbols for a limited number of household articles that might be dangerous if misused. The Federal Hazardous Substances Act of 1960, which was further strengthened by the Child Protection Act of 1966, expanded the 1927 Act and largely displaced it. The FHSA controls the labeling of all products used in or around the house that may cause substantial personal injury as a result of any reasonably foreseeable handling or use. It requires strong warning language for toxic, corrosive, irritant, sensitizing, flammable, and other dangerous products. Similarly, the Cigarette Labeling and Advertising Act of 1965 requires the well-known health warning to appear on every cigarette package.

In cases where the hazard is so substantial that informative labeling is insufficient to protect the public, products have been banned completely. The Flammable Fabrics Act of 1953 prohibits the sale of any fabric that is so highly flammable as to be dangerous when worn. The Child Protection Act of 1966 amended the Federal Hazardous Substances Act of 1960 to give the Food and Drug Administration authority to ban the marketing of toys, children's articles, and other substances so dangerous that cautionary labeling is not adequate.

In November 1967 Congress created a National Commission on Product Safety to determine whether additional regulation, perhaps in the form of protective packaging, informative labeling, or product specifications, is necessary to protect the public from potentially dangerous household products. This Commission is required to report its findings and recommendations to the President and Congress within two years. It is anticipated that the new Commission will examine all products for which no regulatory legislation currently requires affirmative disclosures or warnings of potential hazards to users.

PRODUCT PACKAGING

Relatively few federal or state statutes deal directly with the proper packaging of products. This is for the most part left to voluntary standards established by industry and to specifications maintained by the General Services Administration under the Federal Property and Administrative Services Act of 1949. Nevertheless, the form of product packaging has been regulated by legislation whenever it was considered necessary to prevent deception or to assure safety.

Misleading packaging. Since 1914, the Federal Trade Commission has possessed the authority to proceed against misleading packaging of any product as a violation of the Federal Trade Commission Act prohibiting deceptive acts or practices. Similarly, the Food and Drug Administration has been authorized since 1938 to proceed against misleading containers for foods, drugs, cosmetics, and medical devices.

Neither of these agencies (especially not the latter) has expended extensive resources on enforcement in this area. In 1967 Congress decided that the general policing authority granted to the agency was insufficient to protect the public interest. In the Fair Packaging and Labeling Act it gave the Federal Trade Commission and the Food and Drug Administration discretionary authority to promulgate regulations prohibiting nonfunctional slack fill of packages containing consumer commodities. The FPLA defines a package as nonfunctionally slack filled if it is filled to substantially less than capacity for reasons other than protection of its contents or the requirements of the machines that fill and seal it. This definition is substantially the same as the approach that was followed by the courts in the earlier cases brought by the Food and Drug Administration. Regulations have not, in fact, yet been issued under this statutory authority.

The National Bureau of Standards has also spent substantial effort working on the problem of slack fill. The Bureau maintains a manual for weights and measures officials to use in checking prepackaged commodities.

Statutory regulation of packaging has also been undertaken to distinguish different types of competing commodities. Many states specify the type of package in which margarine must be sold at retail in order to prevent the use of the traditional one-pound butter carton. Because of the inability of the states to agree on a specific package form, margarine must be marketed in different types of packages in different parts of the country.

Unsafe packaging. Packaging may be potentially harmful in a number of ways. It may fail to protect the product as intended, it may contaminate the product, or it may contain a defect that will harm the person who handles it. The standards voluntarily adopted by the packaging industry largely control the safety aspects of packaging. Packages that are unsafe or that render their contents unsafe are, of course, subject to private product liability lawsuits even though they are not regulated under federal or state statutes. Nevertheless, Congress has enacted some statutes directly controlling the safety of packaging for which a need has been demonstrated.

The federal statutes prohibiting the marketing of adulterated foods and drugs have been interpreted and applied to forbid the use of a container that fails to protect the product from contamination. Thus a sterile medical device must be packaged so that the device will be sterile upon opening the package at the hospital.

Similarly, the various food and drug laws prohibit the use of containers or other packaging material that may result in the product becoming adulterated. The Food and Drug Administration has established, pursuant to the Food Additives Amendment of 1958, an elaborate regulatory preclearance program requiring the testing of all packaging material that may transfer from package to food. Although similar preclearance requirements have not been established for many drugs or for cosmetics or medical devices, the very existence of the food packaging requirements has undoubtedly made the entire packaging industry far more conscious of potential problems.

Several federal statutes directly regulate packaging that, if improperly made or used, could harm the user. The Interstate Commerce Commission has established, in addition to its labeling requirements, extensive packaging rules for the shipment of dangerous articles. The Federal Plant Pest Act of 1957 controls the packing of dangerous plant pests when shipped in interstate commerce. It can be anticipated that the National Commission on Product Safety will generally review product packaging as part of its task.

A Suggested Company Approach

A busy company executive cannot be expected to carry in his head the details of all the voluntary guidelines and legal requirements applicable to even one product, much less to a series of items manufactured or marketed by his company. He should, of course, be generally aware of the purpose of those regulations and of the important bearing they have upon his daily production and marketing decisions. But the detailed application of those provisions should properly be handled by company staff personnel responsible for ascertaining that all packaging and labeling requirements have been satisfied.

Many companies have found that the proper packaging and labeling of a product requires the expertise of personnel in at least three different fields: (1) technical personnel who understand the structural aspects of packaging and the scientific basis for label statements about the product, (2) sales personnel who are responsible for marketing the product and therefore understand the role of packaging and labeling in making a sale, and (3) legal personnel who can locate, interpret, and apply the pertinent voluntary guidelines and legal requirements. It is readily apparent that members of each of these groups will view packaging and labeling from a different perspective, with a different objective in mind. The company's ultimate decision will undoubtedly represent a blend of all three approaches.

For this reason, it seems advisable to adopt a committee approach to packaging and labeling within the company. A scientist may use terminology that is inappropriate under the applicable laws and regulations. A lawyer undoubtedly would not write effective sales copy. A marketing man's enthusiasm may require tempering by both technical and legal personnel. A joint decision is more likely to reflect a proper balance among these three competing considerations.

A joint meeting of representatives of all three fields is, moreover, often the best way to resolve whatever questions arise. Only when the objectives and considerations of all three groups are placed on the table at once can they readily be sorted out and the best decision made.

Legal Problems
of Executive Compensation

Walter S. Rothschild

A GREAT NUMBER OF PROBLEMS ARISE IN CONNECTION WITH COMPENSATING corporate executives. These include the corporate power to hire and compensate executives, the mutual obligations of executives and the employers they serve, and the relationship between the executives and the corporation following retirement or other termination of service. Such problems, however, arise in relatively few instances. The legal questions most frequently raised concerning the relationship between executives and their corporations are tax questions. This chapter will therefore consider the tax consequences to the executive and to the employer corporation of various kinds of executive compensation.

THE CORPORATE DEDUCTION: REASONABLE COMPENSATION

In order to be deductible for tax purposes, compensation paid by a corporation to its executives must be reasonable in amount. The question

WALTER S. ROTHSCHILD is a partner in the New York law firm of Cleary, Gottlieb, Steen & Hamilton.

of reasonableness arises primarily in the case of closely held corporations in which the executive or his family is a principal or, perhaps, the sole shareholder. In such instances it is not unusual for the Internal Revenue Service to claim that a portion of the compensation paid by a corporation to its executive is unreasonable, with the result that the corporation is denied a deduction for tax purposes.

The question of the reasonableness of compensation paid by a corporation to its executives depends upon all the relevant facts. Among those which are considered important under the regulations and the cases in which rulings have been made are the absolute amount of compensation paid (particularly in relation to comparable companies); the manner in which compensation was determined; the education, ability, and experience of the executive; the results achieved by the corporation and the effort which the executive contributed. In addition, the relationship between the compensation paid and the stockholdings of the several executives and their family groups may indicate that the payment is to be considered a dividend rather than compensation.

Reasonable compensation is most frequently questioned where contingent compensation is involved. There are a number of factors which make this area troublesome. For example, it is widely recognized that in a closely held corporation, results will necessarily affect the amount of compensation. Of course, this is also true in the case of widely held corporations, but it is characteristic of the closely held firm that the stockholder-employees will receive more compensation in years when the company does better and will receive less when it does worse. To the extent that compensation rises and falls with the fortunes of the company, it resembles a dividend. On the other hand, the management group in a small corporation often consists of only one or a few employees. Where good results are directly attributable to the services of these individuals, the argument is frequently expounded and upheld that since the results are attributable to the hard work, special talents, or long experience of the individuals involved, they are entitled to more compensation than would ordinarily be the case.

Under these circumstances, the closely held corporation should take steps to initiate a reasonable *method* of determining compensation. If a fair, equitable, and reasonable compensation arrangement is adopted when the absolute amount of compensation is modest, large payments in later years often can be justified.

Although the majority of cases have upheld contingent compensation contracts which provided relatively modest amounts in early years, this has not always been so. On occasion the court has recognized that the power to alter an existing arrangement lies with the shareholder-employees. In most situations, however, a contract which is reasonable when executed will be recognized by the Service as the regulations provide.

In certain instances, the question of reasonable compensation concerns minimum, not maximum, compensation. Corporations which have chosen to be taxed under Internal Revenue Code Section 1372, as "electing small business corporations," appear to be required to pay not less than the value of services to shareholder-employees. Section 1375(c) of the Code provides:

> Any dividend received by a shareholder from an electing small business corporation (including any amount treated as a dividend under section 1373(b)) may be apportioned or allocated by the Secretary or his delegate between or among holders of such corporation who are members of such shareholder's family (as defined in section 704(e)(3)), if he determines that such apportionment or allocation is necessary in order to reflect the value of services rendered to the corporation by such shareholders.

This permits the commissioner to allocate the value of services to employees who are members of the same family as the shareholders. These corporations are taxed like partnerships, with the result that failure to compensate certain family stockholder-employees adequately will result in an assignment of income from the employee to his family members. Thus, for example, if a father and each of his three sons own one-quarter of the stock of a small business corporation of which the father is principal executive, failure of the corporation to pay salary to the father will increase the income of the sons. Since they may have little other income, the total tax paid by the family is thereby reduced. The regulations permit allocation of reasonable compensation to the father under these circumstances.

WHEN MAY COMPENSATION BE DEDUCTED?

The deductibility of deferred compensation is governed by Internal Revenue Code Section 404(a)(5). It provides that compensation which otherwise would be accruable is not accruable for tax purposes until paid. In other words, a corporate employer which keeps its books on the accrual basis cannot deduct deferred compensation until such compensation actually is paid. This principle applies to all deferred compensation, even if the liability is fixed in time and amount, and there are no contingencies attached to it. Moreover, while Section 404(a)(5) refers to a "plan" of deferred compensation, the regulations are clear that a plan can apply to a single deferred compensation arrangement.

The most important form of executive compensation always has been and continues to be fixed cash compensation. While this statement is quite obvious, it has several important implications. The types of deferred compensation which make up the "compensation package" will be discussed later in this chapter and may be considered amounts which otherwise would have been payable in cash. This is particularly true in the case of arrangements under which the executive has the right to elect to defer income or to receive it currently. Where there is such an election, the executive may be taxed on amounts which he has elected to defer and which, therefore, he does not receive during the year involved. This tax is based on the doctrine of constructive receipt under which the executive is considered to have received amounts which he could have had but which he did not in fact receive. The Internal Revenue Code and the relevant regulations do not permit the executive to "turn his back" on income for tax purposes.

The question of constructive receipt in executive compensation has been the subject of numerous court cases, Internal Revenue Service rulings, and comments by various authorities in the field. The avoidance of the application of the doctrine of constructive receipt is the heart of any deferred executive compensation, since no executive arrangement is acceptable if the executive is taxed currently on amounts which he will not receive until later years.

Income is considered to be constructively received if the taxpayer has, at any time, the right to receive it simply by stretching out his hand. The deferral of income at the request of the taxpayer does not defer the tax on it. However, the application of this principle to deferred compensation has been limited. In Revenue Ruling 60-31, the Treasury has indicated that it will not go behind the contract or plan which sets forth a deferred compensation arrangement to determine whether the deferral was at the request of the employer. It states that "the statute cannot be administered by speculating whether the payor would have been willing to agree to an earlier payment," citing a case in which it is almost certain that gross income was deferred at the payee's request.

This does not mean that the doctrine of constructive receipt is dead. It can and does have application in many important cases. It is reasonably clear that the deferral of income which already has been earned by the taxpayer and which presently is due him unconditionally cannot ordinarily be deferred for tax purposes, but even this principle may have its exceptions. In two cases involving the same executive—*Howard Veit*, 8 T.C. 809 (1943) and 8 T.C.M. 909 (1949)—the further deferral of previously deferred income was recognized for tax purposes as part of an overall compensation arrangement. Thus it would seem that an executive may defer income from year to year under contract, at least if there are additional economic benefits (other than tax savings) to him under the deferral arrangement.

Permissible Revision of Compensation Arrangements

The doctrine of constructive receipt does not prevent the revision of compensation arrangements in order to stretch out payments, even when the income is fully earned. In the case of *James F. Oates*, 18 T.C. 570, aff'd 207 F. 2d 711, the taxpayer, an insurance agent, was entitled to renewal commissions. Under the standard form of renewal arrangement, aggregate commissions are larger in earlier years and gradually decline. The employer permitted its agents to elect to spread commissions evenly, rather than to receive them as earned, an arrangement which the court upheld. In Revenue Ruling 60-31, the Treasury accepted the principle of the *Oates* case.

One aspect of the arrangements approved in Revenue Ruling 60-31 that is not frequently noted is that they are in writing. This may be more important than has been generally assumed, since a written plan or contract for deferral of compensation is legally binding in and of itself. No further evidence is required to establish the facts. Deferral of income pursuant to oral arrangements is another matter, however, since difficulty in establishing the facts may jeopardize the principle of deferral.

Another important aspect of fixed cash compensation is that, in many cases, all other deferred and noncash compensation is based on the amount of fixed compensation. Many, if not most, corporate pension plans provide that the salary which is used as a basis for the pension be fixed compensation without regard to deferred or bonus compensation. Similarly, profit-sharing plans often provide that deferred compensation and even current contingent compensation not be included. The coverage under various types of group insurance arrangements such as group life insurance, medical insurance, and the like may frequently be based on the amount of the executive's fixed compensation. Accordingly, the deferral of what otherwise would be paid as fixed current compensation can be viewed as the executive's sacrifice of a portion of the other rights which are built upon fixed compensation.

STRAIGHT DEFERRAL AND ITS CONSEQUENCES

The most common form of deferred compensation is the mere deferral of compensation which otherwise might have been paid currently. Thus, for example, under an arrangement between the executive and his company, compensation in the annual amount of $10,000 may be deferred until the executive's employment is terminated when he leaves the company for whatever reason or when he dies.

The contract may provide that at that time the amount of accrued deferred compensation will be paid out to him in equal installments over a fixed period of years—for example, 10 or 15 years. Alternatively, it may provide that the accrued executive compensation will be paid in annual installments of a fixed amount (let us say, $7,500), which will continue until the accrued amount has been exhausted. This includes not only the amount accrued in the first year of the contract but all further amounts which have been accrued by the executive under subsequent arrangements with his corporate employer.

Straight deferred compensation arrangements generally do not provide for any forfeiture for cause or for any earning-out period. Whether they do is generally dependent on the basis upon which the deferred arrangement was reached. If, as a practical matter, the deferral was at the request of the executive, the corporation would have been required to pay the amount currently if the executive had not requested deferral. Under these circumstances, it is not reasonable to provide for any earning-out period, a noncompete provision, forfeiture for any cause, a posttermination consultation obligation, or any other contingency, since the executive could have received the compensation in cash currently had he wished.

If, on the other hand, the compensation arrangement was one which was arrived at by other means than the executive's own request, it is not unusual to find a period of earning-out of the forfeiture in the event of posttermination competition, or an obligation on the part of the executive to consult with the employer after his services have terminated.

The tax consequences of straight deferred compensation, whether or not there are any contingencies, are quite simple. The compensation is taxed, to the executive when received and to the employer when paid, in the amount of the payment. If all or a portion of the compensation which otherwise would have been paid to the executive during his lifetime has not been paid and is therefore payable to his estate or to a beneficiary named by him, the estate or the beneficiary is required to include in its income the amount of the payment just as the executive would have had to do. Moreover, the value of the payments, offset by the appropriate discount, is subject to federal tax against the executive's estate. In this case, the estate or the beneficiary is allowed to deduct from the income received the amount of the tax attributable to the inclusion of the payments in the estate.

EARNINGS ON DEFERRED COMPENSATION

It is possible for deferred compensation arrangements to have the additional feature of providing the executive with some earnings on the amount of the compensation which has been deferred. Thus Revenue Ruling 60-31, the principal authority in the deferred compensation field, clearly provides that some form of interest or earnings may be allowed on the deferred amount in accordance with the contract between the executive and his employer.

The Ruling considers a situation in which the earnings on an amount which the employer has placed in reserve would be credited to the account of the executive. It does not make clear whether the corporation would be *required* to set aside any amounts. Nonetheless, it is now reasonably clear that the crediting of actual earnings realized by the employer on reserves attributable to deferred compensation will not result in either the principal amount or the earnings being subject to tax in the hands of the executive until actually received by him.

It is unclear, however, to what extent the executive can exercise control over funds whose earnings are to be credited to his account and whose principal is based on his deferred compensation. For example, the compensation contract might provide that the corporate employer would pay $10,000 annually into a brokerage account, and the executive would have the full right to invest and reinvest both proceeds and earnings during the period of his employment, with the amounts in question paid to him in ten annual installments beginning upon his termination of employment (for any reason) but not subject to any contingencies or earning-out requirements. Would the doctrine of constructive receipt then apply?

While the doctrine of constructive receipt would not technically appear applicable, it is also not certain that the arrangement would be upheld for tax purposes. Since the executive has full power over the income except the right to possess it currently, the arrangement might be considered a sham which would not be recognized for tax purposes. While such a doctrine has not generally been applied in the case of executive compensation, the same reasoning has been applied in *Clifford* v. *United States*, 309 U.S. 331 (1940), which dealt with the attempt by grantors of trusts to reduce income taxes through devices for spreading income among family members.

ALTERNATIVE FORMS OF EXECUTIVE COMPENSATION

In many instances, a plan or contract embodying a mere deferral of compensation is not considered suitable. Rather, the company, the executives, or both wish to utilize other forms of compensation which may have advantages for them. Among the advantages sought by the company from such forms of compensation is the ability to retain the executive in its employ and to motivate him to greater performance. The executive, on the other hand, wishes to make sure that his compensation is as great as possible, and that, if possible, it is paid to him in a form taxable as long-term capital gains rather than as ordinary income.

In order to satisfy the varying objectives of employers and employees, a number of different types of compensation have been developed. The greatest variety of arrangements is possible in the large, publicly held company. This is because such a company has stock which is publicly traded and its compensation arrangements can be keyed to issuing stock to the employees or to providing them with compensation whose amount is determined by the market price of the underlying shares of the corporate employer. Companies which do not have publicly held stock are more limited in the compensation arrangements which they can provide. Even in such cases, however, there are a number of possible plans which permit management to attract, retain, and motivate competent executives.

The most attractive forms of compensation for both executive and corporate employer are those paid under qualified arrangements. Thus compensation paid into a qualified pension, profit-sharing, stock bonus, or thrift plan has the advantage of providing the executive with the possibility of (*a*) deferring the amount paid into the plan by the company from ordinary income and (*b*) having the amount (when eventually paid) treated as a long-term capital gain. The corporation benefits from an immediate tax deduction. However, under such arrangements the coverage of the plan must be established on a broad basis; that is, coverage and benefits cannot discriminate in favor of highly paid employees. Accordingly, these plans are not really executive plans but companywide plans covering a majority or at least a substantial body of corporate employees. They are not, therefore, extensively considered here.

Similarly, an employee stock purchase plan established under IRC Section 423 is an attractive means of compensating executives. However, such a plan must cover most employees of the company, with the result that it, too, is not truly an executive arrangement but, rather, a compensation arrangement for employees in general.

The following discussion will concentrate on selective arrangements under which the corporate employer can freely choose which employees will participate, exclude those employees whom he does not wish to participate, and determine the basis of participation in the plan. All these arrangements, therefore, can apply to one executive or to many and need not be related in any way to any other form of compensation. They can be applied exclusively to attract new employees or to compensate existing employees. In short, there is no limit on the persons benefited or the manner in which these arrangements can be used.

THE QUALIFIED STOCK OPTION

The most popular form of deferred executive compensation probably is the qualified stock option. While the Internal Revenue Service Code was amended in 1964 to make the qualified option (formerly known as the restricted stock option) less attractive to the executive than it formerly had been, it still remains a highly effective means of attracting new executives and retaining old ones. Its principal feature is that it permits the executive to realize the benefits of the market appreciation of the employer's stock optioned to him in the form of a long-term capital gain.

By definition, a qualified stock option is an option granted by a corporate employer to its employees or to the employees of a subsidiary corporation which meets the following requirements:

1. The option price of the stock must be not less than the fair market value of the stock on the date the option is granted.
2. The option must be exercised within five years from the date of grant.

3. Immediately after the grant, the optionee may not own as much as 5 percent of the granting corporation or its parent.

4. The option must not be assignable by the executive or transferable during his lifetime but may be exercised by his estate or beneficiary after his death.

5. The option must be issued under a plan which specifies the employees who may benefit from the plan by class or other description and the aggregate number of shares which may be issued under the plan.

6. The option must be granted within ten years of the date when such a plan is adopted or the date on which it is approved by the shareholders, whichever is earlier.

7. The option cannot be exercisable while there is unexercised any previously granted qualified or restricted option on any class of the employer's stock—except, however, for a previously granted, lower-price option on the same class of stock.

The option is qualified if these requirements are met. If, at all times after the grant of the qualified option until no more than three months before exercise, the executive is employed by the optioner corporation, its parent, or a subsidiary of it, and if he holds the stock for more than three years after exercising the option, he qualifies for favorable tax treatment.

Under this favorable treatment, no income is realized by the executive on the grant of the option or on its exercise. Upon sale of the stock (after the three-year holding period), the difference between the amount he received on sale and the price he paid on exercise is treated as long-term capital gain. In other words, the entire appreciation in the market price of his employer's stock from the date the option is granted until the option stock is sold is long-term capital gain, and the executive never realizes any ordinary income from the transaction. Similarly, the corporation which granted the option never gets a tax deduction.

If the executive exercises a qualified option but sells the option stock before the required three-year holding period has elapsed, he has made what is known as a disqualifying disposition. In this case, he realizes as ordinary income the difference between the fair market value of the stock on the date when he exercised his option or, if less, the fair market value on the date of sale, reduced in each case by the option price. If the fair market value of the stock on the date of sale exceeds the value on the date when the option is exercised, the balance of the gain is capital gain.

The regulations cite the example of a qualified stock option exercised at $100 per share (the fair market value on the date of grant). The stock is valued on exercise at $200 per share, but before the three-year holding period it is sold at $250 per share. The executive realizes ordinary income on the date of sale in the amount of $100 ($200 less $100) and a capital gain of $50.

If the executive makes a disqualifying disposition, the corporate employer is entitled to a deduction in the same amount when the executive realizes his ordinary income. Corporations sometimes fail to realize that this sort of deduction is available; rather, steps should be taken to ascertain whether stock acquired by each exercise of a qualified stock option has been transferred under a disqualifying disposition.

If the executive dies before exercising the option, and if the stock option plan provides for exercise by his estate or a beneficiary (as generally is the case), the option of course has a value in the executive's estate. This value is generally the excess, if any, of the fair market value of the stock subject to the option over the option price on the date of the executive's death. If the estate or the beneficiary then exercises the option, its basis for purposes of later gain or loss is the value of the option in the executive's estate plus the option price paid by him. If there has been no change in the value of the option stock between the time of the executive's death and its exercise by the estate, the estate will have a basis equivalent to the fair market value of the stock on the date of exercise. The estate can then sell the stock without realizing any gain or loss. In this instance, no capital gains tax is ever paid, either by the executive or by his estate.

If the executive has exercised his option prior to his death, the option stock is included in his estate at the fair market value. In this case, the three-year holding period requirement is inapplicable, and the estate can sell the stock immediately without causing ordinary income to be realized.

A difficult problem in connection with stock options is providing the executive with sufficient funds to pay for option stock. Under present rules of the Federal Reserve Board, loans by banks, brokerage houses, the corporation itself, or nonbank or brokerage-house lenders of an amount in excess of 80 percent (as of July 1, 1968) of the value of the stock for the purpose of buying marketable securities are prohibited. This means that the executive must have cash approximating 80 percent of the market price of the stock on the date when he exercises the option. If the stock has appreciated greatly in value, 80 percent of the current market price may be a much smaller percentage of the option price, and he will be able to borrow all or most of the option price. If, however, the appreciation has been more modest, the executive may be required to produce a relatively larger amount of cash in order to exercise his option.

While the qualified stock option is attractive to executives because of the possibility it offers of long-term capital gains, it also is attractive to corporations interested in retaining their key executives. The qualified option can be utilized for this purpose by providing for staggered exercise of the option. Thus, for example, an executive given the chance of acquiring 500 shares may be allowed to exercise the option on 100 shares during the first year after grant, with options on succeeding lots of 100 shares becoming exercisable on the first, second, third, and fourth anniversaries of the date of grant. Under this type of plan, the executive must remain in the corporation's employ for at least four years in order to exercise all the options allotted to him under the plan.

Sometimes this form of plan provides for cumulative exercise of option. Thus, for example, options not exercised during the first year remain exercisable for the remaining four. In other plans, an unexercised option expires, with the result that executives are forced to exercise the option or to lose it.

Restricted Stock Plan or Nonstatutory Stock Option

While the qualified stock option is probably the most prevalent form of incentive compensation tailored specifically for executives, the 1964 amendments to the Internal Revenue Code have made these options considerably less attractive than they previously were. In view of the tax changes made in 1964 with respect to qualified options, other forms of executive compensation which were available prior to 1964 have since become relatively more attractive. One of these is the so-called restricted stock plan or, if options are utilized, the nonstatutory stock option plan.

The basis of a restricted stock plan or nonstatutory stock option is Regulation 1.421-6. Under this regulation, the issuance to an employee of stock which is subject to restrictions significantly affecting its fair market value does not result in taxable income. The employee to whom such stock is issued will have no income until the restriction expires. If the so-called restricted stock is purchased by an option, neither the issuance of the option nor its exercise will be taxable until the restrictions expire.

What sort of restrictions are there, under Regulation 1.421-6, which significantly affect the fair market value of the stock offered? There might, for example, be a requirement that the employee who owned the stock sell it to his corporate employer at its cost in the event that he terminated his employment prior to a specified date. A similar restriction would be an option on the part of the corporate employer to purchase the stock at its book value (or at some price other than fair market value) at any time. Also, an absolute prohibition on the sale of the stock by the employee during his employment would appear to be a restriction significantly affecting fair market value.

Under a stock bonus plan, the employee has taxable income at the time the restriction expires. The amount of the taxable income (provided he has not paid for the stock) is the stock's fair market value on the date when he took title to it, valued without regard to the restriction, or its value on the date the restriction expires, whichever is less. The corporate employer has an equivalent tax deduction at the same time that the employee realizes the income.

To take a concrete example, let us assume that Executive E received as a bonus on January 1, 1965, 100 shares of stock which on that date was selling at $30 per share. At the time he received the stock, he was required to reconvey it to the company if he left its employ at any time prior to January 1, 1970. In fact, E does not leave the employ of the company until after January 1, 1970, on which date the stock is selling at $50 per share. E realizes taxable income in the amount of $3,000 on January 1, 1970. His basis in the stock for purposes of later sale is $3,000. Since E acquired title to the stock on January 1, 1965, at which time his holding period began, he has held the stock for five years on January 1, 1970, and can sell it on January 2, 1970, for $5,000, thereby realizing a long-term capital gain of $2,000. The corporation has a tax deduction of $3,000 on January 1, 1970.

If E had left the employ of the corporation prior to January 1, 1970 and pursuant to its employment agreement had reconveyed the stock to the corporation without receipt of consideration, E would realize no taxable income and the corporation no deduction from the arrangement.

After E acquires the stock on January 1, 1965, he has all the rights of a shareholder. He receives dividends, copies of the annual report, and all other statements sent to shareholders and has a right to vote at meetings. If the corporation merges into another corporation, he will receive stock of the other corporation. Whether such stock is similarly restricted depends upon the terms of E's employment contract.

Differences between restricted stock plan and qualified stock opinion. A restricted stock plan under which bonus stock is issued to executives has several features which distinguish it from a qualified stock option. These features may make the plan more or less desirable than a qualified stock option plan:

1. No investment by the executive in stock of the corporation is required. His only investment is, in effect, the taxable income that he is required to realize at the time the restrictions expire.
2. E has all the rights of a shareholder, immediately upon acquiring stock, except the right to sell it. Under a qualified stock option, on the other hand, the optionee has no shareholder rights until the exercise of his option.
3. When the restrictions expire, the executive can immediately sell his stock and realize his long-term capital gain, whereas under a qualified stock option plan he must hold the stock for three years in order to receive long-term capital gains.
4. There are no limitations with respect to the type of restrictions which may be imposed on the option period, so long as they have a significant effect on the fair market value. Under a qualified stock option plan, however, the option cannot be exercisable more than five years after the date of grant.

Differences between restricted stock plans and nonstatutory stock options. The principles applicable to restricted stock plans involving bonus stock also apply to nonstatutory stock options. In a nonstatutory stock option plan, however, the restricted stock is purchased by the executive, whereas in the restricted stock plan it is transferred to him in lieu of a cash bonus.

The provisions of a nonstatutory stock option depend solely upon the discretion of the corporation establishing the plan. As a result, the option price (as related to market value on date of grant), the option period, the existence of prior options, and other matters can be decided by the employer corporation without regard to any rules of the Internal Revenue Code applicable to qualified options. Under a nonstatutory plan, Executive E might be granted an option on January 1, 1968, to purchase 500 shares of his employer's stock at $25 per share, which, as of that date, is selling at $30 per share. The option is exercisable at any time within the next ten years. Upon exercise, E holds the stock subject to the contractual commitment to resell it to his employer, which is obligated to purchase it, at $25 per share under the following conditions: If he leaves the company during the first year after purchase, he must sell all of it; if he leaves during the second year, he must sell 80 percent of it; and so forth until, at the end of five years, the stock is vested in him fully. The tax consequences of this transaction are as follows: On the date when each restriction expires— that is, at the end of the first, second, third, fourth, and fifth years follow- ing exercise of the option—*E* realizes taxable income from the stock on which the restrictions have expired. The amount of the income realized on each lot is the difference between the fair market value on the date when he acquired the stock and the fair market value on the date when the restrictions expire, whichever is less, reduced in either case by the option price. If he leaves the company before he has exercised his option, or after he has exercised his option and before some or all of his stock becomes vested, the stock which he is required to reconvey to the company results in no taxable income or loss to him.

Differences between nonstatutory and qualified stock options. The obvi- ous disadvantage of this program as compared to a qualified stock option program is that the appreciation in the value of the stock, subject to option, between the date of grant and the date of exercise eventually may result in ordinary income to the executive, whereas in a qualified program such appreciation ordinarily will be realized as long-term capital gain.

The advantages of a nonstatutory stock option may outweigh the disadvantages in many cases. First, the option price can be a bargain even when measured by the market on date of grant. Second, a nonstatutory option can be issued even if there are previously issued, higher-priced non- statutory or statutory options outstanding. This is not the case for qualified stock options; so that, in the case of a qualified stock option, once a high- priced statutory option has been issued and is exercisable, no subsequent option can be exercisable during the period in which the higher-priced option remains outstanding. Third, the employee is in a position to sell the stock immediately following the expiration of the restriction. Thus, when he realizes the income and pays tax on the compensation involved (which tax is, in effect, a part of his investment in the stock), he can immediately sell it, realizing a long-term gain; whereas in a qualified program he must hold the stock for three years after making his investment before he can sell it and so realize the capital-gains benefits of a qualified stock option program.

Another benefit of the nonstatutory stock option to the corporation is its ability to hold executives through the operation of the restrictions. Once an executive has exercised a qualified stock option, he can leave the company without affecting his plan rights. While he must hold his stock for three years after exercise of the option, he need not remain an employee in order to realize his tax benefit. On the other hand, in a non-qualified program the restrictions which are imposed are the heart of the program, and they can be used to bind executives to the company as a condition to realization of some or all of the benefits of the program. Thus the benefits of a nonstatutory stock option program can be restricted to those employees who serve the company not only throughout the option period but throughout the period of the restriction; whereas in a qualified program, once the executive has exercised his option, he is free to leave the company.

A further advantage of a restricted stock plan or a nonstatutory stock option plan is, of course, that the corporate employer receives a tax deduction. Since the aggregate state and federal corporate income tax rates are in excess of 50 percent, the deduction for a part of the benefits provided to the employees under such a program is important and should permit the corporation to make greater benefits available than would a qualified plan where no tax deduction ever is available. For this reason, the non-statutory stock option program and restricted stock plan, which are just now coming into favor, should become even more popular in the future.

Finally, it should be noted that the nonstatutory stock option plan or restricted stock plan can be used to compensate directors and persons other than employees who render service to the company. While qualified stock options are limited to employees, compensation to directors and independent contractors can be paid in the form of restricted stock or nonstatutory stock options. A number of companies have decided that paying a director's fees in cash is not satisfactory; that, instead, the director should have a long-term interest in the company, with the tax on his fees perhaps deferred until he retires from his principal business connection. A restricted stock plan for directors accomplishes this purpose.

SHADOW-STOCK OR STOCK-UNIT PLAN

Another compensation arrangement which may be attractive is the so-called shadow-stock or stock-unit plan. This arrangement is really a form of deferred compensation, with the amount of the compensation based upon the changes in the market value of the employer company's stock and, if so provided, upon the dividends distributed on such stock during the period in which the executive has an interest in the plan. In the case of a closely held corporation whose stock has no market value—

or, for that matter, in the case of a publicly held corporation—book value rather than market value can be substituted as a base upon which the amount of the compensation is determined.

Under a shadow-stock plan, a portion of the executive's compensation is paid to him in "stock units." Each stock unit is equivalent to one share of stock of the employer corporation. However, the value of the unit is not paid to the executive currently, but is credited to his account in the plan. For example, if the executive were awarded a bonus of $5,000 in stock units and the stock of the company were then selling at $50 per share, the equivalent would be 100 stock units. When a dividend is paid on company stock, an equivalent amount is credited to the executive's account on the basis of the number of units held. Thus, in the preceding example, the executive with 100 units would receive a $100 credit in the event that a dividend of $1 per share were paid. The $100 would then be converted into units. At the then current value of $50 per share, this would be two units, and the executive's account in the plan would therefore be increased by 102 stock units and so on for each year in which there are further awards under the plan to the executive. The executive's account also may be credited with dividend equivalents.

How the plans operate. Shadow-stock plans almost always provide for distributions beginning not later than the executive's retirement. They also may provide for distribution after a stated number of years—for example, ten. In most shadow-stock plans, the amount of the distribution is based upon the full value of the executive's account in the plan. However, this is not necessarily the case. It is possible to provide only for increases in the market value of units and to distribute dividend equivalents, so that the basic dollar awards do not result in any cost to the employer. Under this arrangement, the executive benefits from the awards only to the extent that shareholders benefit—that is, from increases in market value and from dividends distributed.

Accounts in a plan need not be fully vested—in fact, they usually are not. Rather, the plan will provide for an earning-out period, and the executive will forfeit part or all of his account if his employment terminates before his account is fully vested. Instead of a period in which the account vests over a period of years, the plan can provide that the units attributable to each year's service will vest after further service—for example, after five years. By so providing, the company insures that whenever the executive leaves the company's employ he will be sacrificing some amounts under the plan that otherwise would, in time, be paid to him. In all plans, of course, benefits ordinarily vest on retirement or death.

The plan can impose further conditions on the receipt of benefits, such as a noncompete clause. Similarly, it can require post-termination consultation or some similar commitment.

Awards under the plan can be based upon individual employment contracts or may represent a fixed percentage of fixed compensation. Usually, however, they are based upon the decision of a committee appointed by and responsible to the board of directors or the top management of the corporation.

Distributions generally are made in cash, not stock. They begin no later than retirement (or retirement age in the case of executives who leave the company with vested rights before retirement) or death. It is advisable to give the executive the choice, exercisable at or shortly before distributions are to begin, to convert his account from stock units to dollars. This permits him to make sure of the amount of his postretirement distributions, thus permitting him to plan his postretirement income and style of life.

The corporation can fund the plan through the purchase of stock at the time when the stock units are awarded. Under such an arrangement, the corporation purchases its own stock in the open market up to the amount of the units awarded and the dividend equivalents credited under the plan. By so doing, it fixes the cost of the plan at the time of the award and any dividend credits, and no increase in market value can affect that cost. As a matter of fact, under these circumstances an increase in the market value of the stock reduces the cost to the company, since the tax deduction which the company eventually gets from the plan is based upon the amounts distributed. If, when distributing the value of each unit, the company were to sell the underlying stock in the market, the plan would cost the company nothing (other than lost use of the money invested in the plan) if the stock had doubled while held by the company for purposes of the plan. This is because each dollar invested in stock under that plan would have doubled; the tax deduction would be based on the doubled value; and, at a 50 percent tax rate, the company would recover its original dollar invested.

In the case of a closely held company, it may be difficult to establish a plan based on stock-market values. In this case, stock can be assigned a book value and the plan operated accordingly. Such a plan has the merit of compensating executives in proportion to the profits which they produce for the company rather than the market price of stock over which they have only indirect control.

The stock-unit plan really is a deferred compensation arrangement. Its rules and tax consequences are not provided by statute; they are based on the general tax principle that an employee has no income until he receives cash or its equivalent. Thus distributions from the plan are taxable to the employee when received and deductible by the company when paid.

Advantages and disadvantages. Compared to other compensation programs discussed here, these plans have the prime disadvantage from the executive's point of view of not having any capital-gains potential—all distributions are ordinary income. On the other hand, the full amount committed by the employer is deductible, which, of course, is not the case with plans (other than qualified pension and profit-sharing plans) which provide capital gains. The shadow-stock plan has great flexibility, moreover. Eligibility, amount of award, vesting, forfeiture, and distribution provisions are within the complete control of the company. Since cash is distributed, there is no such problem of violating property law with respect to the suspension of ownership as might arise in the case of restricted stock or nonstatutory stock option plans. In addition nonemployee directors, as well as employees, may be included.

However, shadow-stock plans are not very popular. First, they do not provide any capital-gains possibilities, and executives, as noted previously, are interested primarily in such possibilities. Second, shadow-stock plans do not provide any actual stock ownership, which has a psychological advantage for many executives that transcends its financial advantages and is provided by qualified stock option plans, restricted stock plans, and nonstatutory stock option plans. In other words, shadow-stock plans provide many of the financial advantages of stock but not stock ownership itself. Finally, shadow-stock plans are complicated, and the concept of the stock unit is not familiar to most people.

IN CASE OF MERGER OR ACQUISITION

Corporations adopting executive compensation programs which provide a potential tax deduction should be aware of certain problems which could arise in connection with that deduction in the event of a change in the form of doing business. The deduction for payment of deferred compensation is available only to the corporation when it makes the payment. If, however, the assets of that corporation are sold to another corporation in a taxable transaction, the buying corporation will generally assume the liability to make the payment as well as all other liabilities of the business. No tax deduction for this assumed liability is usually available to the buyer, and the selling corporation also gets no deduction when it sells the assets. As a result, the deduction is lost—neither the buyer nor the seller ever gets it.

If the assets of the corporate employer which owes the compensation are acquired by another corporation in a tax-free transaction, the deduction may not be available. Section 381(c)(16) provides that the deduction is available unless the amount of the consideration paid by the acquiring corporation for the assets of the selling corporation took into account the deferred-compensation liability. If, for example, the transaction was negotiated on the basis of the approximate market value of the outstanding stock of the two corporations involved, the deferred compensation liability would not have been taken into account and would be deductible by the acquiring corporation. If, on the other hand, the acquired corporation's business was valued on the basis of book value and, in making the valuation, the deferred compensation liability was taken into account, the eventual payment of that compensation by the acquiring corporation probably would not entitle it to a deduction.

Most cases are not so simple, of course. However, these two will serve to illustrate the principles which govern the availability of the deduction for deferred executive compensation.

Legal Aspects of
Employment Practices

Eugene F. Rowan

EQUAL EMPLOYMENT OPPORTUNITY IS REGULATED ON THE FEDERAL LEVEL BY
Title VII of the Civil Rights Act of 1964; Executive Orders 11246
and 11375, which set forth the equal opportunity obligations of those who
do business with the Federal Government; prohibitions against discrimination on account of age in the Employment Act of 1967; and the equal
pay for women amendments to the Fair Labor Standards Act.

The social conscience of the United States has been aroused, and, as
a consequence, much legislation and regulation prohibiting discrimination
in employment is on the books. The fact that this is federal rather than
local is important since traditionally, with few exceptions, enforcement is
considerably more effective when undertaken by a federal agency than
when left in the hands of authorities on the state or local level.

The thrust of this chapter will be aimed at discrimination on account
of race, color, religion, sex, or national origin and its effect on some of
the more traditional employment practices. A brief review of the prohibi-

EUGENE F. ROWAN is personnel relations manager at the J. C. Penney Company in
New York City, and is admitted to the New York and District of Columbia bars. The
author wishes to acknowledge the assistance of L. Adlerstein, who did some of the research
for this chapter.

tions against discrimination on account of age, which went into effect on June 12, 1968, is also included.

The reader should be aware that enforcement policy and philosophy are in a great state of flux and that specific problems should be discussed with a practitioner who is experienced in these areas. An understanding of the authorities' unswerving intention to see that discrimination in employment is eliminated from the American industrial scene and an understanding that these authorities are *results*-oriented may be all the guidance needed to determine whether a particular employment practice will survive the scrutiny of an enforcement agency.

The enormous scope of the problem which management faces and the newness of the federal effort in the area tend at times to result in an enforcement policy that appears to be more reflective of the personality of the enforcer than of the empowering statute. This should change as the problems reduce themselves to manageable proportions and the enforcement agencies develop an expertise in the relatively new field of equal employment opportunity.

This chapter seeks to assist the executive who genuinely wants to comply with the requirements for equal opportunity, but who occasionally thinks himself the victim of novel legal theories or unjustified charges of discrimination.

Equal Employment Agencies at a Glance

Equal Employment Opportunity Commission

EEOC is a creation of Title VII of the Civil Rights Act of 1964. It is composed of five commissioners appointed by the President and approved by the Senate. EEOC sees its responsibility as insuring that all Americans will be considered for hiring and promotion on the basis of their ability and qualifications without regard to race, color, religion, sex, or national origin.

The Commission's jurisdiction extends to four major groups: employers, public and private employment agencies, labor organizations, and joint labor-management apprenticeship programs. All such employers of 25 or more people became subject to the provisions of Title VII on July 2, 1968.

Armed with computers, publicity, and enthusiasm, EEOC has become quite effective despite the fact that Title VII does not grant enforcement powers to the Commission. EEOC has developed techniques to fashion broad remedies and not limit itself to case-by-case determinations based on individual charges of discrimination. And pending legislation which would bestow upon EEOC powers to issue cease and desist orders will add additional strength to a determined and not ineffective agency.

Although an EEOC charge can reach the courts upon a finding of probable cause by the Commission, most often the charge is resolved in a conciliation process. The Commission claims that one-half of these meetings results in a satisfactory conciliation agreement.

Employers that employ more than 100 workers are required to fill out EEOC's EEO-1 reporting forms which are analyzed extensively by computer. These reports give the total employment picture for minority groups and women in reporting companies. The analysis of the 1966 employment data submitted by employers in 1967 gave rise to hearings in New York City, in January 1968, concerning discrimination among white-collar workers. It is reasonable to expect more such investigations and adverse publicity whenever the computer so indicates. Under the chairmanship of Clifford L. Alexander, Jr., the budget of EEOC continues to increase and, with it, so does the staff of investigators.

EEOC has a limited power of subpoena which permits it to demand records and depositions. After such a demand is made, an employer who objects to the demand is given 20 days in which to appeal directly to a court.

EEOC does not require any particular kinds of records, but it relies on those records which are essential for an on-going business or are necessary for the preparation of the EEO-1 reporting form. The Commission has suggested that post-employment records of racial or ethnic identification of employees be kept separate from basic personnel records.

THE DEPARTMENT OF JUSTICE

The function of the Department of Justice is to prosecute those cases where the Attorney General believes there is a "pattern or practice of intentional resistance to the full enjoyment" of the rights granted under Title VII. Suits brought by the Civil Rights Division have been on the increase, and increased resort to these remedies may be expected. In such proceedings, for which the statute requires expedition, the attorney general may request a three-judge court if the matter is one of public importance.

Investigations of cases of this type have employed agents of the Federal Bureau of Investigation and are characterized by a high degree of thoroughness.

A survey of the complaints filed against defendant companies is useful in determining which patterns and practices are sufficiently discriminatory to invoke the action of the Attorney General. A recent complaint in one of these proceedings alleged the following discriminatory practices.

a. Preferential hiring, referral, transfer, and assignment procedures and by hiring, referring, transferring, and assigning whites for employment without regard to qualifications while placing stringent requirements on Negroes. . . .

b. Administering and rating tests for assignment to jobs in the mechanical and electrical departments of the . . . plant in a manner so as to give preferential treatment to white applicants and to exclude Negro applicants similarly qualified.

c. Assigning Negroes to less desirable positions . . . while assigning more desirable jobs to white persons with similar or lower qualifications.

d. Failing to provide opportunities for advancement to Negroes on the same basis as opportunities for advancement are provided to white persons.

e. Failing to provide for advancement opportunities in the lines of progression and to supervisory positions to Negroes equal to those opportunities provided for white persons.

The Attorney General asked that the defendant be enjoined from committing further discriminatory acts.

Another recent complaint cites the following policies and practices: certain departments were "white only"; Negro departments were for menial labor; advancement was for white people; and finally, the company made no effort to correct and offset discrimination policies.

A complaint against a metal-working company and the union with which it deals alleged that the company excluded Negroes from higher-paying jobs by classifying its rolling mill employees artificially into two separate departments called "mill tonnage" and "mill auxiliary" so as to exclude Negro employees from the higher-paying rolling mill jobs. This distinction allegedly allowed the company to discriminate against Negroes in jobs similar to those held by whites. The complaint also alleged that the distinction allowed testing of Negroes but not their white counterparts; that Negroes would be paid less and Negro transfers to new departments would be without seniority; and that Negroes were excluded from apprenticeship opportunities. This complaint demonstrates that the Department of Justice will look behind mere departmental or job labels in ferreting out discriminatory practices.

OFFICE OF FEDERAL CONTRACT COMPLIANCE

The Office of Federal Contract Compliance is responsible for co-ordinating and developing federal policies applicable to those who do business with the government. OFCC is a product of Executive Orders 11246 and 11375, which superseded the earlier executive orders creating the President's Committee on Equal Employment Opportunity. This Office, through coordination with enforcement officers in the other federal agencies, enforces the government's nondiscrimination clauses not only in its contracts with private employers but also in contracts under which the government has provided financial assistance in the form of grants, loans, insurance, or guarantees. Its investigatory powers and the compliance checks by so-called predominant-interest agencies conducted under OFCC standards are thorough and impressive, particularly since no complaint is necessary to initiate such actions.

Generally, OFCC and EEOC agree as to what constitutes discrimination. However, their enforcement powers differ. OFCC not only requires that government contractors not discriminate, but requires as well that they take affirmative action to correct past discrimination. The emphasis is upon affirmative action. Just what affirmative action is evolves on an ad hoc basis and changes as circumstances change. Affirmative action is action which is devised to overcome obstacles to equal opportunity and which will result in the full and effective utilization of minority group manpower. There is no formula or prescription, no set of steps or actions to achieve the desired results. Action undertaken must be geared to the particular situation at hand and may include matters as diverse as specific minority recruiting, rearrangement of seniority lines, or elimination of de facto segregated facilities. The compliance officer sees his role as one of enforcement rather than education, conciliation, or consultation.

In addition to the other obligations undertaken by the prime contractor, he assumes the additional responsibility of requiring an equal opportunity pledge from his subcontractors.

Although not included in the original orders, an amendment, effective October 13, 1968, includes sex as a prohibited basis of discrimination.

The range of sanctions available to OFCC is wide, but most impressive is its ability to suspend or cancel federal contracts. Inasmuch as government contractors account for an estimated one-half of the civilian labor force, it is obvious that the power and prestige of OFCC is extensive.

NATIONAL LABOR RELATIONS BOARD

At the same time that the Civil Rights Act of 1964 established a new agency to challenge employment discrimination, an older agency, the National Labor Relations Board, was implementing a new doctrine to extend its jurisdiction to encompass discriminatory practices based on race. In the *Hughes Tool* case, NLRB held that a union's failure to process minority members' grievances on the basis of race constituted a violation of the union's duty to represent all workers fairly. The Board held further that such a breach of duty was an unfair labor practice within the Board's administrative enforcement powers. Under the *Hughes Tool* theory, a member of a minority race may now receive administrative relief directly against the union that fails to represent him fairly and against an employer who, for example, the union encourages to commit an unfair labor practice by discriminating in hiring or seniority.

The use of this forum has particular advantages to minority groups. The Board tends to be faster than EEOC and the courts in processing complaints and reaching final decisions. Furthermore, the Board has enforcement powers which EEOC lacks at present. It can hold hearings, issue cease and desist orders, grant back pay awards, and decertify a union. Nevertheless, its powers to proceed are limited to cases which grow out of a collective bargaining relationship.

Last and most important, an NLRB proceeding relieves the aggrieved person of the heavy financial burden of vindicating his rights through the courts. Under the statute, the general counsel has sole and independent responsibility for investigating charges of unfair labor practices, issuing complaints, and prosecuting cases where his investigations find evidence of violations of the Act.

STATE AND LOCAL LAWS

The role of the states in providing fair employment legislation has not entirely escaped the social revolution which has resulted in so much federal legislation. Since 1945, the year in which New York enacted the first state law on this subject, most of the states have enacted prohibitions of varying severity against discrimination. No such legislation has been enacted in the Deep South.

Thirty-two of the states provide for hearings, orders, and court enforcement. Four states make discrimination a misdemeanor but do not provide any particular administrative machinery for enforcement, and three states have "voluntary" provisions without enforcement procedures.

The states that provide for hearings, orders, and court enforcement are:

Alaska	Indiana	Missouri	Oregon
Arizona	Iowa	Nebraska	Pennsylvania
California	Kansas	Nevada	Rhode Island
Colorado	Kentucky	New Hampshire	Utah
Connecticut	Maryland	New Jersey	Washington
Delaware	Massachusetts	New Mexico	West Virginia
Hawaii	Michigan	New York	Wisconsin
Illinois	Minnesota	Ohio	Wyoming

(Similar statutes are in effect in the District of Columbia and in Puerto Rico.)

Statutes that make discrimination a misdemeanor but provide no particular machinery for enforcement are in effect in:

Idaho	Maine	Montana	Vermont

Statutes that have voluntary provisions with no enforcement procedures exist in:

Arizona	Oklahoma	Tennessee

In view of the relatively few employees a company need employ to be covered by Title VII, one may wonder about the significance of state statutes. Under Title VII, EEOC is required to defer to states in which a practice has occurred and in which there is a "local law prohibiting the practice alleged and establishing or authorizing a state or local authority to grant or seek relief from such practice or to institute criminal proceedings with respect thereto upon receiving notice thereof." EEOC has negotiated a series of deferral agreements with 21 states, the city of Philadelphia, and the District of Columbia. Others will undoubtedly follow as EEOC is assured that the jurisdictions involved have the resources to enforce the law.

It is also significant to note that law enforcement tends to have a cumulative effect, in that state and local activities increase and enforcement becomes more vigorous as federal activities begin or are stepped up.

WAGE AND HOUR DIVISION, U. S. DEPARTMENT OF LABOR

The Age Discrimination in Employment Act of 1967 was approved by Congress on December 6, 1967, and became effective on June 12, 1968. Although no regulations or interpretations have been issued as yet, indications are that the investigators from the Wage-Hour Division will routinely search for violations of this act as they conduct investigations to determine compliance with the Fair Labor Standards Act and its so-called equal pay amendments.

The protections of this act extend directly only to individuals of age 40 but less than 65. Employers may not fail or refuse to hire and may not discharge or otherwise discriminate against any individual with respect to his compensation, terms, conditions, or privileges of employment because of his age within the stated range. Employers are also prohibited from using age as a ground for limiting, segregating, or classifying an employee in any way which would deprive him of employment opportunities or adversely affect his status as an employee. Wages may not be reduced to comply with the law. Advertisements which indicate any preference, specification, or discrimination based on age are also prohibited.

The statute recognizes a number of exceptions to the prohibitions. Their precise meaning, where any doubt exists, will have to await interpretations by the Division and the courts. Exceptions are:

1. Where age is a bona fide occupational qualification that is reasonably necessary to the particular business.
2. Where differentiation is based on reasonable factors other than age.
3. To comply with the terms of any bona fide seniority system or employee benefit plan which is not a subterfuge to evade the purposes of this act, except that no employee benefit plan shall excuse the failure to hire an individual.
4. To discharge or otherwise discipline an individual for good cause.

As is the case with all the statutes discussed, appropriate notices and posters will be or have been issued by the agencies involved (excluding NLRB) which must be prominently posted in places accessible to employees and applicants and where such notices ordinarily are placed.

Discrimination on the Basis of Sex

The legal, political, and social status of women is in a great state of ferment. Today, women comprise the majority of voters, although not many years ago the suffragettes fought for the vote. With the change in status has come increasing responsibilities for employers. Many American women find it necessary to support themselves and often families as well.

The amendment to Title VII prohibiting discrimination on the basis of sex came about in a curious fashion. While this legislation was under consideration in the House, one of its most ardent opponents, Congressman Howard W. Smith, appeared on the television program "Meet the Press" and, when asked by newswoman May Craig whether the pending legislation would protect the rights of women, responded in his most courtly fashion, "Why, no, ma'am. But I think I'll introduce that myself." Introduce it he did, on the ground that he wanted to protect the "minority sex." And with virtually no debate—and thus little or no legislative history—it passed both houses of Congress and became part of the law.

Today's women are educated; today's women head households. Many of the traditional bases for disparate treatment between women and men will not stand up under close scrutiny.

Generally, the controversies center around two areas: (1) the working conditions and benefits derived by female employees and (2) the jobs available to either sex.

EQUAL PAY LAW

A precursor of the sex-discrimination amendment of Title VII was the Equal Pay Act of 1963, which provided:

> No employer . . . shall discriminate . . . on the basis of sex by paying wages to employees . . . at a rate less than the rate he pays to employees of the opposite sex . . . for equal work on jobs, the performance of which requires equal skill, effort, and responsibility, and which are performed under similar working conditions, except where such payment is made pursuant to: 1. a seniority system; 2. a merit system; 3. a system which measures earnings by quantity or quality of production; or 4. a differential based on any other factor other than sex. . . .

This legislation was enacted as an amendment to the Fair Labor Standards Act, which exempts from coverage executive, administrative, and professional employees and outside salesmen. Despite an amendment to Title VII to carry over these exemptions under Title VII, it is the position of EEOC that the amendment failed of its purpose and that it will take jurisdiction over pay questions concerning those exempted from coverage under the above-quoted legislation. This question has yet to be litigated. In other respects, EEOC defers to the Wage-Hour Division and honors their interpretations of this language.

Among the distinctions seen as discriminatory is allowing pensions to women at age 60 and to men at age 65.

STATE LEGISLATION PROTECTIVE OF WOMEN

A number of difficult questions have arisen with respect to state legislation which limits conditions under which women may be employed.

The EEOC has separated these laws into two categories:

1. Those which confer a benefit on women, such as premium pay, rest periods, seating facilities, and the like.
2. Those which prohibit the employment of women in certain occupations or during certain hours or which limit tasks they may perform.

In describing its enforcement policies with respect to the effect of such legislation on Title VII obligations, EEOC stated the following:

> . . . in cases where the effect of state protective legislation appears to be discriminatory rather than protective, the Commission will decide whether that state legislation is superseded by the Civil Rights Act. Where state law limits the employment of women in certain jobs, employers refusing to employ women in such jobs will not be found in violation of the Act, provided that:
> 1. They act in good faith and seek to obtain administrative exception where possible under the legislation and
> 2. the effect of the legislation itself is protective rather than discriminatory.
> Employers may not refuse to hire women, however, merely because state law requires certain conditions of employment such as minimum wages, overtime pay, rest periods, or prescribed physical facilities.

In fact, EEOC has held that benefits conferred under state protective legislation are required by Title VII to be extended to similarly situated members of the opposite sex.

Title VII allows exceptions where there exists a "bona fide occupational qualification reasonably necessary to the normal operation of that particular business or enterprise." This exception has been and will continue to be tightly construed regarding sex discrimination. For example, because the duties of airplane cabin attendants can be performed satisfactorily by both sexes, EEOC rejected the airlines' practice of hiring only women for stewardesses. The agency also criticized a practice by which married women were not allowed these jobs where no such restriction was placed on any male employees. Therefore, if a job can be performed adequately well by both sexes, discrimination in hiring one or the other will not be allowed. The Commission has exhibited little patience with some of the traditional generalizations, such as "They get married and quit," or "They have babies," or "They won't accept transfers to other sections of the country."

"Male" and "Female" Advertising

EEOC has reversed its ruling permitting employees to continue advertising in separate "Male," "Female," and "Male and Female" columns in newspapers and other publications provided the column headed "Male and Female" is used in the case of jobs where sex is not a bona fide occupational qualification. Effective December 1, 1968, Commission guidelines hold that the listing of jobs in columns segregated by sex is an expression of preference not permitted under Title VII, unless sex is a bona fide occupational qualification necessary for the performance of the particular job involved.

Testing

Section 703(h) of Title VII specifically provides that it is not an unlawful employment practice for an employer to give and act upon the results of any professionally developed ability or psychological test, provided that such test, its administration, and the actions based upon the results are not designed, intended, or used to discriminate because of race, color, religion, sex, or national origin.

In dealing with this subject, both EEOC and OFCC find themselves on the horns of a dilemma. Both agencies prefer the inherent objectivity of testing as a selection device, yet are confronted with complaints of case after case of poor test results. The official response to this takes a number of forms. It shifts to the employer the burden of proving that the test is nondiscriminatory by asking that he show a validation which includes appropriate representation of minority groups and that its relevance to the job in question be demonstrated.

Somewhat related to this is the matter of educational requirements for the job in question. Both agencies view with skepticism generalized educational requirements, such as "high school graduate," "eight years of schooling," and the like, unless specific relevance to the job to be performed can be shown.

These postures have proved difficult for employers whose hiring into entry-level jobs is predicated on a career progression into higher and more responsible jobs. Such employers seek a potential in the applicant to move up into progressively more responsible positions beyond the entry level and frequently employ elaborate tests to identify this potential.

A mutually satisfactory solution to these conflicts has yet to evolve, and resolution may have to await litigation. For the moment, a number of practical proposals have emanated from a variety of sources. One of the more useful suggestions appeared in *The Manager's Letter* of March 25, 1968, in which Lawrence J. Hassel, director of personnel and industrial relations at W. F. Hall Printing Company, stated:

+ Apply the "total man" approach, using all available objective predictors—evaluation of the application form, interviews, reference checks, psychological tests—and weighting them with regard to their effectiveness in predicting job performance.
+ Review present tests or test batteries in the light of carefully conducted job analyses, discarding those that do not conform with job conditions, requirements, or performance.
+ Select standardized tests with care, using as a criterion the amount and kind of evidence the author or publisher can present concerning what the test measures and how its scores can be interpreted.
+ Perform validation studies and attempt to establish your own range of optimal scores for your own local situation; obtain professional help if necessary.
+ Upgrade the personnel who administer and interpret tests; provide professional training on and off the job.
+ Audit your testing program annually and make adjustments where necessary.

✦ Establish a firm written policy that will assure the maintenance of high ethical standards and the professional handling of all aspects of the testing program.

Testing, particularly personality testing, may be in for further troubles if one may deduce a trend from comments on Capitol Hill. From time to time over the past three years, House and Senate hearings have been conducted concerning the use of personality testing in government agencies. Members of Congress have been highly critical of some of the questions asked and have been quick to label them invasions of privacy. Although their inquiries have been limited for the most part to abuses in the public sector, the overtones of these hearings sound a warning to the private sector.

The upshot of the foregoing is that care must be exercised in the use of tests, that they must be used by experts who are aware of all of their limitations, that they must be valid predictors of what they are claimed to be used for, and that they must be relevant.

Getting into Compliance

EEOC offers a folder called "Seven Steps to Equal Employment Opportunity," which is helpful in developing an affirmative action program. The first step is the formulation of a policy. It calls for a written public statement to supervisory personnel, employees, employment agencies, unions, and the community at large concerning the company's position on equal employment opportunity. It calls for systematic review of staffing patterns to insure that the policy is being implemented, and it also requires nondiscrimination clauses in contracts with unions.

The next step is recruitment. The employer is advised to broaden his recruiting sources by such methods as employing minority groups in the personnel division; encouraging minority groups to refer friends for job vacancies; conducting plant tours for students, teachers, and counselors from minority groups; and making known the company's employment needs to the churches, schools, and organizations of such groups. It also recommends that statements such as "All qualified applicants welcome" or "Equal opportunity employer" be used in job advertising.

Oftentimes an employer believes that he can avoid a discrimination problem by informing only certain groups of his placement needs. For instance, he may only inform placement counselors at high schools in which are enrolled few—if any—members of those minorities that he has vacancies for typists or clerks. Even though he simply avoids having to consider or discriminate against students from the other high schools, such limited recruitment could be interpreted as contrary to the spirit, if not the letter, of the Act.

Although the Commission puts emphasis on the affirmative obligation to recruit minority groups, it is obvious that one employer cannot recruit everybody; as long as his efforts are related to his business needs, and he has a reasonable mix of employees at all levels, he will not have to worry unduly about sweeping charges. Consequently, he need not send his recruiters to a distant school or college if his requirements can be met by a school more convenient to his plant.

The attempt of employers to recruit minorities has at times proved fruitless when the employer has traditionally recruited only through union sources. If the union refuses membership on the basis of race, color, religion, national origin, or sex, the employer should go beyond his union to obtain the omitted groups. The agencies are aware of the strife that may result, but they have nevertheless insisted upon this course of action.

The third step is hiring. Look at the whole person. EEOC and OFCC recommend that employers not treat all arrest records as an absolute disqualification and that they be realistic as to standards and hiring qualifications. Also, display the equal employment poster where applicants will be able to see it.

Educational standards that are unrealistically high in respect to the job for which they are a qualification may be regarded as discriminatory whether they are intentionally so or not. It is common knowledge that minority racial groups have not had educational opportunities or have not been able to take advantage of them, and an employer who sets unduly high educational requirements for unskilled jobs may be regarded as discouraging applicants from minority groups.

Although there are no restrictions under Title VII upon questions that can be asked on application blanks, several states have fair employment practice laws or regulations which do limit such questions. (An excellent guide has been published by the New York State Commission on Human Rights.) Under federal law, the Commission is inclined to look at the individual case and determine whether the questions asked are discriminatory.

Carefully drawn questionnaires should avoid seeking responses that would reveal the applicant's national origin, religion, or race. (Sex is ordinarily revealed by name.) But if there is a legitimate purpose for certain questions such as address and prior schooling, they will not be regarded as discriminatory—even though such questions may inadvertently offer information as to national origin, religion, or race.

The fourth step is testing. The folder says "not to let test scores become a mechanical substitute for an overall personal judgment based on the applicant's experience and performance and your actual job needs."

After testing, consideration should be given to training. The fifth step: Encourage employees from minority groups to participate in educational and training courses and also review the composition of these classes to insure fair integration. Training can be an apprenticeship program or management development program, on-the-job training, or even a brief orientation.

The Commission next addresses itself to promotion—the sixth step: "Maintain a roster of those minority workers whose skills and experience qualify them for upgrading. Before going outside and filling promotional vacancies, give prior consideration to workers on the roster."

The seventh, last, and possibly most important step is the follow-through. Supervisors should be made to understand that conscientious living-up to equal opportunity responsibility is essential to the company's reputation in the community and is equally essential to their own advancement. Management should show that it means business in company policy statements and that such statements are meant to be effective.

Religious Discrimination

The ban on religious discrimination in Title VII has not received the publicity which has surrounded the prohibitions against discrimination based on sex and race in that act. Nevertheless, EEOC has made it plain that it will deal as severely with religious discrimination as with other discrimination. However, the statute contains some exceptions that do not apply in the case of race; moreover, EEOC has recognized that there are certain unusual situations with respect to religious practices that require special handling.

BONA FIDE OCCUPATIONAL QUALIFICATIONS

As is the case with discrimination on account of sex, EEOC will narrowly construe any exceptions relating to religion as a bona fide occupational qualification. For example, religion may be a bona fide occupational qualification if the position is in an educational institution run by a particular religious association or society or if the curriculum of the institution is directed toward the propagation of a particular religion. Nor would it violate the act for a fund-raising organization of a particular religion to require that its fund raisers be members of the religion. On the other hand, the preferences of fellow employees would not justify discriminating in favor of or against a person of a particular religion.

RELIGIOUS HOLIDAYS

Employers have customarily recognized certain holidays, which, although observed as public holidays, are religious holidays as well. The most common of these is Christmas, with Good Friday also being observed more widely in recent years. EEOC has held that an employer who closes his business on Christmas or Good Friday is not thereby obligated to give time off with pay to Jewish employees for Rosh Hashanah or Yom Kippur. The Commission goes on to suggest that an employer make a reasonable accommodation to the needs of his employees in these matters where he can do so without serious inconvenience to the conduct of his business.

A related question arises in connection with Sabbath observance. In such situations, EEOC declares that an employer who is closed for business on Sunday does not discriminate merely because he requires that all his employees be available for work on Saturday.

Where an employee has previously been employed on a schedule not in conflict with his religious obligations and changes in schedule now become necessary, the Commission urges that reasonable attempts be made to avoid a conflict. However, the Commission adds that an employer is not obligated to make such accommodations if they cause serious inconvenience to the conduct of his business or a disproportionate allocation of unfavorable work assignments to other employees.

Applicants who accept a job knowing that its requirements will conflict with their religious obligations are not entitled to demand any changes to accommodate their religious needs.

Seniority

Seniority provisions are contained in approximately 90 percent of all labor contracts. Under the spotlight of recent investigations, seniority has been viewed in many cases as an institution to inhibit the advancement of members of minority groups.

In a number of instances, mainly in the South, Negroes and Caucasians have been assigned to separate departments, each with its own seniority list. Often, the better jobs and better opportunities were "for whites only," and the jobs were filled from the white seniority lists. Not only were Negroes commonly assigned the lower-paid jobs in these situations, but they were also the first to be laid off during plant cutbacks and the last to be rehired.

The elimination of racially separate seniority lists and their consolidation into a single integrated list have raised some of the most difficult problems in the field of equal employment opportunity.

Such problems take a variety of forms, one of which is the assignment of minority groups to segregated departments—generally those involving lower skills, lower pay, and a higher risk of layoff. In other cases, it may assume the form of somewhat parallel skills in racially separate lines of progression, with an earlier cutoff or promotional dead end for the minority line. The variations on this theme can be endless.

Integration of seniority lines usually assumes the status of a three-way negotiation, with the government in one corner, whether EEOC or OFCC; the employer in another (or just as often in the middle); and the union in still another.

Such seniority-line mergers vary from case to case; in general, the solution is an attempt to do justice to all employees, majority or minority, with some recognition of the employer's need for specific skills.

The government has not been willing to settle for seniority as of the effective date of Title VII or coverage under OFCC orders, with minorities being added to the end of the majority seniority list. Nor, on the other hand, has it insisted on total retroactivity for minorities involving wholesale bumping and job elimination of the majority, without regard to employer skills needs. Instead, some of the injustices resulting from the system are righted retroactively—usually by negotiation and sometimes with an assist from a federal court, by painstaking examination of length of service, skills, job experience, and training opportunities. With the aid of this knowledge, the seniority lists are combined.

Conclusion

A word of warning concerning the foregoing material is appropriate. Virtually all of the federal legislation referred to is less than five years old. There has been very little litigation involving these acts; hence there is very little interpretative material to rely on other than the views of the agencies charged with enforcement—a not always steady barometer. In fact, there may be very little litigation in the long run, given the sometimes emotional nature of the subject matter and the employer's reluctance to face up to the publicity surrounding a court trial.

Thus employers are confronted with the challenge of coming into "compliance"—whatever that means—with rather new and untried legislation in a rapidly and radically changing sociological atmosphere. Where common sense won't do, seek expert advice.

There is a curious paradox in this situation. Owing to the size of our population and many of our businesses, we tend to search for generalizations, for ways of sorting out people so that we may reduce the "traffic" to manageable proportions. At the same time, legislation and regulation are limiting the freedom of employers and others to generalize and, indeed, are forcing them to look at separate individuals in arriving at conclusions regarding the employment relationship.

Fast disappearing is the old idea of judging a man by "the cut of his jib." There are those who claim that this new system has resulted in a depersonalized employment relationship. Can this be true when it is the *individual* who must be measured by objective standards? Rather than depersonalizing the employment relationship, haven't we "desubjectivized" it? Time will tell.

The Complexities
of Labor Relations Law

William R. Linke

A PHILADELPHIA ATTORNEY, WELL RESPECTED FOR HIS ABILITY, LIKES TO TELL
people upon first meeting: "I am not a lawyer. I am a labor lawyer."
That there is a difference, even in jest, stresses to labor and management practitioners alike the high degree of specialty involved in dealing
with labor-management affairs. Moreover, the remark points to the unusual
nature of labor law, not only in its origins, but in the actions at law, the
decisions, and the *modus operandi* of the agencies that govern the law.

The law of labor relations is involved in human processes and reflects,
in its terms, the daily impacts of human activity in the collective bargaining relationship between management and labor. It is a complex subject,
covering the gamut of industrial life and strife, yielding almost daily to
the social and economic pressures of the participants, the public, and
governmental bodies.

Today's law is rooted in the individual, his rights, his protection, and
his association with unions, employers, and government. It moves—and is
constantly under review—owing to changes in the world of collective

WILLIAM R. LINKE is Director–Personnel for The Curtis Publishing Company in
Philadelphia and a lecturer in labor legislation at Rider College.

bargaining and in the application of the law by the administrative body chartered to put into effect the purposes of the law: the National Labor Relations Board. The Board's actions are further subject to judicial enforcement or review by the federal court system, thus creating a two-headed instrument of activity. Add to this the third-party determinations made by arbitrators sought out by the signatories to labor-management agreements, and the result is a welter of decisions affecting daily life in the plant and at the bargaining table.

To take us through this maze of legislation, decisions, and practices, it may be well to seek a base of understanding by reviewing the substance of the law in effect today. This excursion may prove a bit confusing to the average layman owing to our present-day political and social environment, the constant need for amendments to the law, and the Board's habit of ruling on a case basis. Be that as it may, let us consider first the law itself, then the agencies involved, and, finally, some practical approaches to labor-law problems—keeping in mind that our subject deals with human conflict and the complexities of human relationships under stress in the face of governmental involvement and, sometimes, accusations of political motivation.

Statutory Provisions

The most important federal statutes covering labor-management relations as these affect interstate commerce are:

+ The Wagner Act (National Labor Relations Act, or NLRA) of 1935. It was the first complete piece of legislation to grant freedom of choice of representation to employees. The law, born of New Deal philosophy, defined what was to be considered unfair practice on the part of employers. It was amended by—
+ The Taft-Hartley Act (Labor-Management Relations Act, or LMRA) of 1947. The LMRA attempted, by amendment to NLRA, to equalize the responsibilities of labor unions with those previously set forth for management. The law sought to have the parties recognize each other's rights. It was amended by—
+ The Landrum-Griffin Act (Labor Management Reporting and Disclosure Act, or LMRDA) of 1959. The LMRDA only slightly amended the LMRA. In the main, it established a bill

of rights for individuals in their relations with labor unions and spelled out reporting requirements with respect to financial and administrative dealings of labor organizations and employers.

PROVISIONS OF NLRA AND LMRA

The National Labor Relations Board, originated by the 1935 Act as an agency of the United States, was revised in 1947 to consist of five members, appointed by the President. Located in Washington, D.C., it is empowered to make such rules and regulations as may be necessary to carry out the meaning of the law—and herein lies its strength. It has regional offices, and its powers include delegation to the regional directors in employee representation cases. The general counsel has final Board authority in respect to charges and issuance of complaints in unfair labor practice cases.

The rights of employees include the basic right to self-organization: to form, join, or assist labor organizations, to bargain collectively through representatives of their own choosing, and to engage in other concerted activities for collective bargaining purposes or to refrain from any or all such activities except where this right is affected by a union-shop agreement.

Unfair labor practices were established for employers in the 1935 Act and for unions in the 1947 Act (as added to by the 1959 Act). Here they are in brief:

+ It shall be an unfair labor practice for an EMPLOYER—

    1. To interfere with, restrain, or coerce employees in the exercise of their rights under law.
    2. To dominate or interfere with the formation or administration of any labor organization or to contribute financial or other support to it.
    3. To discriminate in regard to hire or tenure of employment or any term or condition of employment to encourage or discourage membership in any labor organization. However, employees are allowed to bargain for union-shop agreements requiring union membership of employees as a condition of employment.
    4. To discharge or discriminate against an employee because he has filed charges or given testimony under the law.

5. To refuse to bargain collectively with bona fide representatives of employees.

6. To enter into any contract or agreement whereby the employer ceases or refrains from handling, using, or transporting the products of any other employer or to cease doing business with any other person. Any such contracts shall be to this extent unenforceable and void. (This refers to so-called "hot cargo" clauses.)

✦ It shall be an unfair labor practice for a UNION—

1. To restrain or coerce employees in their exercise of rights as established by law.

2. To cause or attempt to cause an employer to discriminate against an employee in regard to tenure of employment or any term or condition of employment; to encourage or discourage membership in any labor organization (with same proviso as for employers in union-shop agreements).

3. To refuse to bargain collectively with an employer.

4. To engage in or to induce or encourage any individual to strike or refuse to handle or transport goods where the object is to force any employer to join a union or cease using or handling any goods, or to recognize an uncertified union, or to recognize a union other than one already certified, or to assign work to employees where another union has been certified for such work.

5. To require of employees under a union-shop agreement the payment of excessive dues or initiation fees.

6. To cause or attempt to cause an employer to pay or deliver any money for services not performed.

7. To picket an employer where the object is to require the employer to recognize or bargain with a labor organization not certified as the representative of its employees where another union is recognized or where an election has been held within the preceding 12 months or where a petition has not been filed within 30 days of the start of the picketing.

8. To enter into any contract or agreement whereby the employer ceases or refrains from handling, using, or transporting the products of any other employer or to cease doing

business with any other person. Any such contracts shall be to this extent unenforceable and void. (This refers, again, to hot-cargo clauses.)

The Board is empowered to prevent unfair labor practices; it may issue a complaint and petition district courts for temporary relief, restraining orders, or enforcement of a Board order. In case of a jurisdictional conflict, where an attempt is made to force an employer to assign work to one union rather than another, the Board may issue subpoenas requiring the attendance and testimony of witnesses.

Free-speech provisions allow the expression of any view, argument, or opinion or its dissemination—written, printed, or visual—by both labor and management. This proviso is not applicable in representation-election proceedings.

The duty to bargain is a mutual responsibility of employer and employee representatives. It requires them to meet at reasonable times and in good faith with respect to wages, hours, and other terms and conditions of employment and to execute a written contract if either party so desires. Timely notice of termination or modification of an existing contract must be delivered by either party to the other and to the Federal Mediation and Conciliation Service.

Petitions for representation, decertification of representation, or deauthorization of a union shop may be filed before the National Labor Relations Board by the employees themselves, a group of employees, or any individual or organization operating in behalf of the employees. An employer may submit a petition in his own behalf. The Board investigates each such petition and provides for the necessary hearings.

The bargaining unit is the group of employees appropriate for collective bargaining. It may be an employer unit, a craft unit, a plant unit, or a subdivision of any of these.

Elections by secret ballot are conducted by the Board. They may be consent elections, stipulated elections, or Board-ordered elections.

Representatives who are elected by a majority of the employees are to be considered the exclusive representatives of the employees.

The right of strike is upheld by the law.

Supervisors are employees having authority in the interest of the employer to hire or discharge other employees, to direct them, to adjust their grievances, or to effectively recommend such action. Supervisors may not join unions of other employee groups.

Union-security agreements requiring membership in a labor organization as a condition of employment are not authorized by federal law in any state or territory in which such application is prohibited by state or territorial law.

Mediation of labor disputes is made available through the Federal Mediation and Conciliation Service, which was set up to aid and encourage employers and representatives of their employees to reach and maintain agreement in the event of disputes.

National emergencies, imperiling the health or safety of the country, which are the result of labor disputes allow the President to appoint a board of inquiry to inquire into the issues at stake, to conduct hearings, and to make written reports. The President may direct the Attorney General to enjoin strikes or lockouts and to provide an 80-day period to allow the parties to reach a settlement.

Suits for violation of contracts between labor and management or between labor organizations may be brought into district court. Judgments are enforceable only against organizations as entities and against assets.

Restrictions on payments to employee representatives include payments or loans to representatives, officers, or employees of labor organizations who are employees of another employer; also, payments to any employee or union officer for the purpose of influencing other employees in the exercise of their right to organize and bargain collectively.

Restrictions on political contributions are imposed upon corporations, which cannot make expenditures in connection with any elections to political office, and upon labor organizations, which cannot make contributions in connection with elections at which presidential and vice-presidential electors, senators, or representatives are to be voted for.

LANDRUM-GRIFFIN ACT PROVISIONS

The LMRDA provides for the reporting and disclosure of certain financial transactions and administrative practices of labor organizations and employers. In addition, it establishes standards of responsibility and ethical conduct.

Title I of the Act sets forth the bill of rights for members of labor organizations. It assures equal rights to nominate candidates, to vote in elections and referendums, to attend meetings, and to participate in the business of those meetings.

Freedom of speech is guaranteed to union members. It is understood that they may assemble freely to express any views, arguments, or opinions.

Dues, initiation fees, and assessments are not to be increased except where, in local labor organizations, a majority of the members so vote by secret ballot.

The right to sue a union is afforded by the Act to members of labor organizations.

Safeguards against improper disciplinary action are guaranteed to members, who must be served with specific written charges in any disciplinary case. Reasonable time must be granted for defense, and the member shall be permitted a full and fair hearing.

Civil enforcement is offered any member injured by violation of this bill of rights by civil action in district court.

The right to copies of agreements is assured members.

Title II requires reporting by labor organizations and employers.

Labor organizations are to adopt a constitution and bylaws and file copies with the Secretary of Labor (Office of Labor-Management and Welfare-Pension Reports). They are also to file a report giving names of officers, dues structure, assessments, benefit plans, and financial reports in detail. Such reports are made available to members for examination.

Reports are required of officers and employees of labor organizations. They must state any securities held in companies with which the labor organization has agreements and transactions.

Employer reports are to include any payments or loans to any labor organizations or officers or payments to employees or any group for persuading others to exercise or not exercise their rights of organization and collective bargaining. Agreements with labor relations consultants to attempt to influence employees' decisions are to be covered. Reports are due 90 days after the end of the fiscal year.

Title III requires that trusteeships or any method of supervision or control whereby a labor organization suspends the autonomy otherwise available to a subordinate body must be reported within 30 days after takeover and semiannually thereafter. Such trusteeship is to be in strict conformance with the constitution and bylaws of the parent body. Its purpose is to correct corruption or financial malpractice.

Title IV. The election of officers on both national and international levels shall take place not less than every five years. On the local level, elections must be held not less than every three years, by secret ballot. Removal of officers should be provided for by constitution and bylaws; where this is not the case, they may be removed by secret ballot if they are guilty of serious misconduct.

Bonding is required of all officers, agents, and shop stewards, and the fiscal responsibility of officers is established.

Members of the Communist Party, as well as persons who have been convicted of or who have served prison terms for major crimes, are not to serve as officers during or for five years after the period of party membership or conviction.

Anti-Injunction Act (Norris-LaGuardia Act) of 1932

The Norris-LaGuardia Act has not yet been mentioned. Passed in 1932, it provides that no court of the United States shall have any jurisdiction to issue any restraining order or temporary or permanent injunction in a case growing out of a labor dispute except in strict conformity to this Act.

Norris-LaGuardia spells out the rights of employees to self-organization and bargaining. Under this Act, no contract between an employee and an employer is held to be legal whereby either party agrees not to join or remain a member of a labor or employer organization or the employee agrees that he will withdraw from employment if he joins such organization. (This provision was directed at "yellow dog" contracts.)

To obtain labor injunctions, the testimony of witnesses is required in support of allegations:

1. That unlawful acts have been threatened and will be committed unless restrained or will be continued unless restrained.
2. That substantial and irreparable injury to the complainant's property will follow.
3. That greater injury will be inflicted upon the complainant by the denial of relief than will be inflicted upon defendants by the granting of the relief.
4. That the complainant has no adequate remedy at law.
5. That the public officers charged with the duty to protect the complainant's property are unable or unwilling to furnish adequate protection.

No injunction is to be granted to any complainant who has failed to comply with his obligations under the law or who has failed to make every reasonable effort to settle the dispute by negotiation or mediation.

Other Pertinent Labor Legislation

Worthy of brief mention are other statutes which deal with labor-management affairs.

The Anti-Petrillo Act (1946) is an amendment to the Communications Act of 1934. It pertains to the broadcasting industry and prohibits "featherbedding"—that is, the employment of persons in excess of those employees needed to perform actual services or the payment of money in lieu of employment in excess of need.

The Hobbs Anti-Racketeering Act (1946) protects trade and commerce against interference by violence, threats, coercion, or intimidation.

The Fair Labor Standards Act (1938) is the national wage and hour law. It sets forth restrictions on child labor, minimum wages (currently $1.60 per hour for employees in commerce), territorial minimum wages, maximum hours and overtime, exemptions from overtime, and rate of overtime.

The Portal-to-Portal Act (1947) establishes definitions of payments due employees who perform work and noncompensable activities related to nonworking time.

The Welfare and Pension Plans Disclosure Act (1958) requires the reporting of the financial operations of employee welfare and pension plans if interstate commerce is involved. Such plans include group life insurance, hospitalization, accidental death and dismemberment, wage continuation, savings, sick pay, severance payments, and similar employee benefit programs.

The Equal Pay Act (1963) provides for nondiscrimination in wages between sexes for like work performed.

The Civil Rights Act of 1964, in its Title VII, forbids employers to discriminate on the basis of race, religion, sex, or national origin in the hiring or firing of employees and in setting compensation and terms, conditions, and privileges of employment.

The Sherman Anti-Trust Act (1890) and the *Clayton Anti-Trust Act (1914)* are applicable in labor relations situations only where unions join with employees to establish illegal monopolistic activities or restraint of trade.

State Labor Relations Acts were made effective as "little Wagner Acts" after passage of the NLRA in 1935. These deal with employee rights of organization; with collective bargaining, mediation, representation, and unfair labor practices; and with arbitration panels and review boards. In many cases, they are as stringent as federal legislation—or more so. Such statutes are pre-empted by federal labor law where interstate commerce is involved.

The Railway Labor Act (1926) establishes machinery to resolve disputes in the transportation field. A permanent body of three members sits on the

National Mediation Board, weighing disputes, deciding on appropriate units, and holding elections. The National Railroad Adjustment Board, also set up by the Act, considers issues of collective-bargaining interpretation. Equal numbers of employers and union representatives make up the Board. The peculiar history and traditions of railroad bargaining, together with the close involvement of the Federal Government, have resulted in so unusual a situation, as compared with industrial relations in general, as to make detailed discussion impractical here.

The government bodies charged with administering labor law include both independent agencies, such as the important NLRB and FMCS, and the U.S. Department of Labor.

The Agencies

THE NATIONAL LABOR RELATIONS BOARD

NLRB was specifically created by the NLRA to administer federal labor law. Some say it is prosecuting attorney, jury, and court for labor disputes; others claim it shows political bias in its decisions. The court system is used by the Board when seeking judicial review of its rulings, but ordinarily courts rely on Board decisions, conceding that it possesses highly specialized ability and expertise. Thus NLRB actions in "effectuating the purposes of the Act" are pretty close to being accepted as rulings on law.

Organization of NLRB. As stated, NLRB consists of its members in Washington, the general counsel, and regional offices headed by regional directors in major cities. The Washington board operates as a reviewing authority for actions beginning at the regional level, delegating to field offices authority to determine appropriate bargaining units and issue orders following hearings, including direction and certification of representation elections.

The general counsel exercises general supervision over the officers and employees in regional offices.

Duties of the Board. The Board members are charged with the prevention of unfair labor practices, the designation of appropriate units of employees for bargaining, and the conduct of secret ballots to determine (1) exclusive representatives of employees, (2) deauthorization of union-shop status, and (3) employee votes in national-emergency situations. The Board (under Section 10(k) of the LMRA) is directed to resolve jurisdictional disputes by determining which of the competing groups of workers is to be assigned the work task involved.

Powers of the Board. The Board's powers allow the issuance of orders against unions, employers, or their agents to cease and desist from any of the specified unfair labor practices or to take affirmative actions, including reinstatement of discharged employees with or without pay. NLRB can order and conduct hearings and investigations, issue subpoenas, administer oaths, petition any U.S. court of appeals for enforcement of its orders, and petition U.S. district courts for temporary injunctions to prevent continuation of an unfair labor practice.

In representation cases other than consent elections, appeal from regional directors' findings may be presented to the Board for review. In unfair labor practice cases where the regional board has failed to issue a complaint, appeals may be taken to the general counsel. Board procedures allow for certain appeals to the Board itself, and review of the Board's orders may be obtained in a U.S. court of appeals.

Jurisdiction of the Board. The Board has no rights as to mediation or arbitration and cannot rule on wage disputes, nor can it set any terms of a collective bargaining pact. The Board's jurisdiction is defined in the Act to determine representation and prevent unfair labor practices in cases affecting interstate commerce, which term is delineated in the Act. The Board has set up specific standards of dollar flow—for example, for non-retail establishments, a $50,000 outflow or inflow of business, direct or indirect (referring to goods or services shipped or furnished outside the state or receipt of goods and services furnished to the employer from outside the state). Other dollar standards of volume of business can be found in NLRB statements of procedure.

NLRB procedure in representation cases. A petition for certification may be filed by an individual employee or group, by a union, or by an employer. A petition for *de*certification may be filed only by employees, by a group, or by a union. The certification petition must, among other pertinent statements, declare the appropriate unit sought and the number of employees. The petition, if sought by the union, must be accompanied by authorization cards representing 30 percent of the employees in the alleged appropriate unit.

Where a union currently represents a group of employees, the existing contract operates as a bar to any representation petition. The Board, however, allows petitions from rival unions during the period between 60 and 90 days prior to the termination of the contract. No election shall be held in any case where a valid election has been held in the prior 12-month period. Contracts beyond three years, or those prematurely extended, do not act as bars.

Regional directors will set formal hearing dates but will seek, in advance of any such hearing, to determine whether a consent election agreement is available from the union and employer. The Board proce- dure here is to help the parties set the time and place of the election, provide notices, and conduct the election. Results of consent elections are certified by the regional director, and any rulings are final. As a result of the Board's decision in *Excelsior Underwear, Inc.,* 156 NLRB No. 111 (1966), lists of names and addresses of unit employees must be furnished to the Board for transmission to the union.

If no consent election agreement is forthcoming, the regional board conducts a hearing into the question of representation, and makes an intial determination. The Washington Board, upon appeal, is given the hearing record and facts for determination as to an election or other disposition.

The NLRB election. In consent-election situations, the Board specifies during a meeting with the parties the payroll cutoff date of employee eligibility to vote. Permanently laid-off employees are not eligible to vote, but probationary employees and some part-time workers may be eligible. Generally, strikers may vote, but their replacements in unfair labor practice cases are not eligible.

The employer and the union involved have the right to appoint an equal number of observers at the polls, and these observers may challenge a voter's eligibility to cast a ballot. After the polls are closed, ballots are counted, and an official tally of ballots cast is given to the parties. Objec- tions to the conduct of the election may be filed within five days after receiving the tally. Any objections are investigated by the Board; and, if no issue is raised, the Board certifies the results of the election. If objec- tions are sustained, the Board sets the election aside.

One of the Board rules to be aware of is that campaign speeches are forbidden 24 hours before an election. Conduct prior to the date the elec- tion petition is filed will not be considered as an objection to an election.

Unfair labor practices. The Act is not self-enforcing—that is, the Board cannot take action on its own unless a charge is filed. This charge is filed with the regional director, provided the action leading to it occurred no longer than six months previous. The person against whom a complaint is issued has the right to file an answer to the Board within ten days.

A Board agent is assigned to investigate the case and talk with the aggrieved party and the defendant in an attempt to resolve the problem. The Board may conduct a hearing, presided over by a trial examiner, in which witnesses may be heard and subpoenaed. The Board case is represented by an NLRB attorney, and rules of evidence apply.

The trial examiner prepares and files a report with his recommendations, including findings of fact and action to be taken. The parties may file exceptions to this report. If there are no exceptions, the recommended order becomes the Board's final order, enforceable by a court but not by the Board itself. As previously indicated, the Board may, upon issuance of a complaint, seek injunctive relief to prevent injury to any party.

Jurisdictional disputes. The Board must hear the jurisdictional disputes which develop over unfair labor practices—such as secondary boycotts—and coercion of employees to force assignment of work to those in a particular group as opposed to another group.

If the dispute is settled, or a method of voluntary adjustment is agreed upon within ten days after the filing of the unfair labor practice charge, the Board is relieved of the hearing requirement. The Board will accept arbitration awards as final in Section 10(k) cases where certain standards of the arbitration process are met.

The Board may also petition for restraining orders in jurisdictional disputes.

FEDERAL MEDIATION AND CONCILIATION SERVICE

FMCS was established by the Taft-Hartley Act to assist labor and management in the settlement of disputes. The Service has no law-enforcement authority. Section 8(d) of LMRA, however, requires employers and unions to file with FMCS 60 days prior to the impending termination or modification of an existing contract which has an effect upon interstate commerce. An additional notice is required 30 days later if the contract dispute is not yet settled.

Offices of FMCS are located in major industrial cities. Mediators use persuasive methods of conciliation and mediation in an attempt to bring the parties to settlement on a voluntary basis. The Service offers its facilities upon its own motion or upon the request of one of the parties to the dispute.

Where interstate commerce is only minor in its effect on a case, state mediation agencies are available.

U.S. DEPARTMENT OF LABOR

The Department of Labor has a widespread organization dealing with a broad spectrum of matters related to labor, but it is not primarily engaged in dispute settlement although such peacemaker roles often fall to the Secretary and Undersecretary in national health and security cases. The Department has no direct responsibility for performance under the Taft-Hartley Act, but performs research and policy studies under its Office of Labor-Management Policy Development.

The Office of Labor-Management and Welfare Pension Reports is an organization under the direction of the Assistant Secretary for Labor-Management Relations in the Department of Labor. Its function is to administer and enforce the provisions of the Welfare and Pension Plans Disclosure Act and the LMRDA. The director receives, analyzes, and makes available for public disclosure the reports submitted by groups covered by the law. These duties are handled by a national Washington office and regional and area offices.

Practical Approaches

The state of apparent bliss enjoyed by the nonunionized company generally is achieved, in part, by an excellent understanding of laws affecting employee rights.

Should a company desire to maintain a nonunion status, the best advice it can follow is to treat its employees fully in accord with law—to know and recognize the representation processes of employees, unions, and NLRB. Remember, collective bargaining simply means the representation of two or more employees by another person or organization. The word "collective" is the key; employees are protected in their activities as individuals and as groups.

Management is free to communicate with employees and maintain free speech, but it cannot offer *promise of benefit* or *threaten reprisal* to any employees who seek representation. The company cannot deal with its employees in a group, with a leader, or with a "sounding board" if grievances are adjusted or matters of wages, bonuses, or working conditions are discussed and negotiated. Any such dealings may establish a "history of bargaining" under Board doctrine and result in an "instant union."

THE UNION ORGANIZING DRIVE (BEFORE THE PETITION)

The union organizer seeks issues between the employee and his employer and, having found them, expounds and publicizes them in propaganda leaflets, speeches, and mailings.

An employer's knowledge of union organizing activity puts the employer under the law, and he must thereafter be careful to act in a precise manner. For example, he can be charged with an unfair labor practice (possibly only for union rallying purposes). Thus any employee discharge during the union campaign should be for "just cause" and well documented. The employer should also avoid "captive audience" meetings at which he talks to employees without mentioning that their attendance is voluntary. Likewise on the "forbidden" list for the employer is any attempt at bargaining with the employees. Supervisors are allowed to offer opinions, however, and to listen to employee viewpoints. Employees are allowed to solicit for union purposes during nonworking hours on company property.

The union will seek to gain recognition from the employer in the easiest way possible; and recent Board opinions seem to allow "quickie" recognitions that may or may not reflect the employer's true intent. The authorization cards, signed by the employee and signifying his intention to become a union member, are the normal instrument used. It is not necessary to appeal to the Board for a representation election and certification. The company may willingly recognize the union, provided it believes in good faith that the majority of company employees desire to be represented by the union in question. The problem is that the innocent-looking authorization card may become a tool to gain recognition even from unwilling and unwitting employers.

Here is what can happen: A union demands recognition of an employer (a statutory requirement prior to the filing of a representation petition with NLRB), basing its request upon an authorization-card majority. The employer, under the *Joy Silk Mills* doctrine, must so recognize the union unless, in good faith, he doubts the union's majority status. Any doubt on his part allows him to request a Board election. If, however, his refusal of recognition is merely to gain time to undercut the union majority, or to avoid collective bargaining, he may be guilty of an unfair labor practice. The decision in the case of *Aaron Brothers Company of California* established in 1966 that employer action in such cases could be reviewed in light of all the relevant facts before an election could be denied the employer and an order to recognize and bargain could be issued.

Bargaining orders, issued by the Board in card-majority cases, are used when the employer's conduct makes a fair election impossible or when an election is lost by the union owing to the employer's actions.

The Board established in the *Bernel Foam Products Company* 146 NLRB No. 1277 (1964) case that a union which has had a demand for recognition on the basis of authorization cards denied by an employer could proceed to an election without waiving its right to file a refusal-to-bargain charge. Also, a union which possesses a card majority can, under certain conditions, file an unfair labor practice charge [Sec. 8(a)5] and petition the Board to order recognition on the basis of its card majority.

If the cards clearly show an election petition as the main purpose of the employee authorization, the card is not valid for the purpose of obtaining recognition without that election. Nor is the card valid if the organizer orally misrepresented the card's sole purpose.

Behavior at the Bargaining Table

There are no specifics in the law which relate to the parties' behavior, at the bargaining table or during a contract term, except the requirement to bargain in good faith, sign a written agreement if requested, give proper notice of termination, and allow suits for nonperformance under Sec. 301 of the Taft-Hartley Act.

Little similarity exists between a commercial contract at law and labor agreement. Moreover, this area of legal activity is left to the parties themselves or to parties appointed by them. However, a few guidelines are suggested here for those who may have to negotiate a labor agreement.

The legalistic approach at the bargaining table on the part of union or company representatives is not recommended. There is much to be gained by both parties if a problem-solving attitude can be created. Notwithstanding, the negotiator should possess an alert awareness of what the law says and what the parties' liabilities, limits, and rights are. Add to this the need for exhaustive preparation—and plenty of it! The good negotiator is not only prepared—he *knows* his counterpart and is not surprised by any action at the table.

Bargaining in good faith. Bargaining in good faith is just that—the making of offers and proposals and counteroffers and counterproposals that bear in the direction of attempts at settlement. Offers without intent, of course, are meaningless.

What is bargainable? Almost anything can be—work rules, safety rules, management decisions having significant or material effect on or relationship to wages, hours, or other conditions of employment. For example, more and more cases are being decided as to the duty to bargain where employee security is involved. Further, management for many years has had to determine policy in the interest of business in many areas of activity where decisions may eliminate jobs, close or move plants, or sub-contract work. The duty to bargain in these areas naturally occasions a deep conflict with unions, which wish to protect worker security.

The decision to subcontract work, the Board has held, is a mandatory subject of bargaining. There is, of course, no obligation to yield to the union position, but history has proved that the compromises attendant on bar-gaining benefit both parties.* NLRB, in the *Fibreboard* case, required the employer to notify the union prior to decisions to subcontract work of the bargaining unit in full or in part. If an employer unilaterally subcontracts such work without first bargaining with the union, it is a violation of the law. The far-reaching effects of *Fibreboard* can involve extra company work transfers, sale and merger decisions, mechanization, plant relocation, closing or partial closing, and even reorganization of operations.

Bargaining does not cease upon the signing of a contract. A continuing legal duty to operate and interpret the agreement is placed on both parties.

See your lawyer. It is not suggested here that this broad-brush treatment represents, in all cases, the facts of the law—rather, the purpose has been to alert management to possible Board decisions in these areas, where particular circumstances may invite ruling. Check with counsel on these areas before acting. Matters appropriate for discussion with him include the impact of the management decision on employees, the management rights clause, union attitude, past practice, notice, surprise, economic need, and the general conduct of the employer.

Information to unions. This is an area of bargaining duty stemming from case rulings of NLRB. It includes meeting union requests for em-ployee benefit plan data, or for time study data, where the purpose stated by the union relates to "a need to know" in order to bargain intelligently. Where "inability to pay" is a plea of management across the bargaining table, the company may find itself required to show its accounting books to union representatives.

---

* The principles involved here can be found in the *Town and Country* decision (*Town and Country Mfg Company v. NLRB* 316 F. 2d 846, 1963), the *Darlington* decision (*NLRB v. Darlington Mfg. Company* 380 US 263, 1965), and the *Fibreboard* decision (*Fibreboard Paper Products Corp. v. NLRB* 379 US 203, 1964)—all landmark cases.

POINTERS ON CONTRACT LANGUAGE

Although there is no specific law about the words you may put in your labor contract, it may be well to reflect that since written agreements cover "wages, hours, and working conditions," contract clauses should be composed in the light of current law.

Union security. The union security clause should be written in conformance with Board interpretations to provide language that on the surface, at least, does not fly in the face of law. A poorly written union shop clause could allow a rival union representation opportunity during a contract term. NLRB has suggested a model clause for the parties to labor pacts.

Recognition. The union should be recognized in the contract as the exclusive representative of the employees in the appropriate unit, which should be spelled out in detailed terms. One successful method is to incorporate the NLRB certification wording as to the unit in the clause. A poorly written clause might allow questions from the union as to the expansion of the unit or from management, which might feel the unit is too broad in its inclusions. A listing of inclusions and exclusions, by specific job title, is often helpful.

Management rights. Companies and unions are often in conflict over this clause's language. Management generally opposes any dilution of its rights by contract clauses, whereas unions seek to regulate management actions or become vocal partners by mutual-agreement provisos. What is written in this clause is important to both parties because it could affect the basic question of what is or is not bargainable during the term of the contract.

Checkoff. An employer must bargain with a union over the checkoff of dues and initiation fees. Many employees object, however, to checkoff of assessments. The checkoff authorization must be in conformance with Sec. 302 of the Taft-Hartley Act. It requires the signature of the employee, and it may not be irrevocable for more than one year or the duration of the contract, whichever is shorter.

Seniority. A question of law that might arise in the language of the seniority clause (together with the recognition clause) would be the continuance of employee rights under the contract in the event the plant is moved to a new location.

"No strike." The no-strike clause is essential in the labor pact to assure management its hoped-for objective—uninterrupted production—and to in-

sure fair treatment for union members in settling problems. Responsibility
for not striking is often placed upon union members, representatives, and
officers at every level. Unions, however, balk at no-strike clauses because
the strike is a significant union weapon. Many times unions agree to
a no-strike clause on certain issues or only until the grievance procedure
is exhausted.

Arbitration. Arbitration clauses are regarded as quid pro quo for no-
strike clauses, thus offering unions an opportunity to redress grievances
unsettled by contract machinery. (The written grievance procedure many
times limits grievances to disputes involving the interpretation, application,
or alleged violation of the specific provisions of the written agreement.)
The arbitration-clause language often embodies the authority of the arbitrator to hear cases dealing with specific matters, the arbitrator's authority
to amend or add to the contract, the rules of arbitration set forth by
appropriate state statutes, and voluntary arbitration agencies.

Termination. The termination clause, which may include rules for
change and amendment, should be carefully written to specify dates and
duties of the parties during the term and notice procedures. The law requires 60 days' notice in reopening provisions or in termination procedures.

The Process of Arbitration

When problem-solution methods fail the parties in a labor dispute,
arbitrators can make a positive contribution to settling the problem and
thus insuring the continuation of peaceful relationships. They can also
create a win-lose attitude on the part of labor and management by rulings
which fail to consider the fact that the parties have to live with each other.

Grievance procedures in labor agreements provide for a step-by-step
means of handling problems which arise out of administration of the
contract. Voluntary arbitration (agreed upon by the parties) is a last
step, affording a means of solution while continuing business operations
without strife. The process is only quasi-legal. It avoids the delay (possibly resulting in a worsening of relationships) which would occur if the
courts were used, and it is less expensive than litigation. The process is
well recognized by NLRB and the courts as a viable means of settling
labor disputes.

Agreements to arbitrate vary. Generally, however, they establish that if
disputes are not adjusted by the grievance procedure, either party, after
a brief period, may submit the issue to arbitration. Ordinarily, the contract
provides that an agency such as the American Arbitration Association, the

Federal Mediation and Conciliation Service, or a state mediation board be requested to supply a list of arbitrators. (FMCS is not an arbitration agency; it merely maintains listings of arbitrators from which names can be selected.)

The arbitrator should be carefully chosen. Generally, contracts provide for a process of mutual elimination of names from the lists submitted. Services are available which give the background, qualifications, and case-ruling histories of arbitrators.

Most arbitrators are ad hoc (for a particular grievance only), but many industries and unions have agreed on permanent arbitrators who serve the parties for a specific term and hear all arbitration cases. For the most part, a dispute is submitted to a single arbitrator, but there are also tripartite boards, made up of one representative from each party and a third member called the impartial chairman. The ruling by such a body usually finds either the union or the management member in concurrence with the impartial member so as to provide a majority decision.

NLRB will honor arbitration awards if certain standards are met. For example: Was there a valid agreement to arbitrate? Were the proceedings fair and regular? Did the arbitrator squarely face the issue?

Arbitration clauses in labor agreements can be enforced in a federal court under Sec. 301 of the Taft-Hartley Act. The Supreme Court, in the "steelworkers trilogy" (three landmark cases ruling for arbitration in 1960), set forth rather specific rules ordering arbitration of disputes brought to lower courts. The substance of these decisions was that (1) an order to arbitrate, even in the absence of an arbitration clause, should not be denied except where it is clearly established that the issue is not subject to arbitration by a reasonable interpretation of the contract; (2) no federal court should decide the merits of a dispute in order to require arbitration; and (3) no federal court shall consider the merits of an award in enforcing it. No-strike clauses which are breached do not disallow the use of an arbitration clause by a union that seeks, for example, to arbitrate strikers' discharges.

The arbitrator's purpose is to hear issues, testimony, and evidence and to make awards. Many times arbitrators are lawyers, as are the representatives of management and labor who present their respective cases. Some arbitrators conduct formal hearings; others allow informality to reign. Briefs can be submitted before and after hearings, dependent upon the arbitrator's preference and ruling. Transcripts of hearings can be made by stenographers, and orthodox rules of evidence may or may not apply.

Precedents stemming from a "common law of labor relations" are widely used. There are volumes of arbitration awards which rival judgments of courts. Awards are respected by both parties (as generally required by contract language), and few judicial enforcements are necessary.

STRIKES AND THE LAW

Strikes take several forms—the unfair labor practice strike (protected by law), the wildcat (a strike in contravention of an agreement not to strike), subtle forms of sitdown or slowdown by employees, and secondary strikes which extend beyond the primary dispute between union and employer.

The Wagner Act clearly established the right to strike, but not without regulation. Coercion of employers for secondary boycott or other objectives is an unfair labor practice, and strikes ensuing from this sort of activity are clearly illegal. They may be enjoined by NLRB. The Taft-Hartley Act, however, prohibits strikes by Federal Government employees, and many state and municipal workers similarly are barred from striking, although such laws have proved difficult to enforce.

Organizational strikes by primary unions do not constitute unfair labor practices when the union has filed a petition for certification and another union is not currently recognized. Informational picketing to apprise the public that an employer does not employ members of or have a contract with a labor organization is not, of itself, illegal. The use of a "reserved" gate on a company's property when secondary employees enter can prevent picketing by a contractor's employees from interfering with peaceful entry of primary-plant employees.

Jurisdictional strikes by a union which result from a dispute over which union shall perform specified work are considered by the Board to be illegal owing to the effect they have of forcing the employer to an action.

Not all strikes, however, are unfair labor practice strikes. Economic strikes, which occur as a result of nonagreement on contract terms, are perfectly legal provided proper notice has been given.

NLRB imposes a 60-day cooling-off period by means of notice-of-termination requirements. Taft-Hartley sets forth cooling-off requirements in industrywide strikes affecting national health or safety. The intent is to delay strike action in order to allow fact finding, board reports, Presidential involvement, and other mediating devices to take effect.

A boycott is a concerted refusal to deal with an employer, either by refusing to give services or declining to buy his products. Primary boycotts are directed against the employer involved in the dispute. Secondary boycotts are directed against those who deal with the primary employer. Strikes for boycott purposes are specifically forbidden.

Forms of Union Security

The forms of union security under law are the closed shop, the union shop, the agency shop, and the maintenance-of-membership clause.

The closed shop, requiring membership in the union as a condition of employment, is no longer permitted except that compulsory union membership is allowed under certain conditions in the building and construction industry.

The union shop requires that all employees must join the union as a condition of continued employment on or after 30 days of employment or 30 days from the date of a collective bargaining agreement.

The agency shop provides that employees who are not union members must pay the union an "administrative fee," usually an amount equal to union dues and assessments.

Maintenance of membership requires that an employee who has joined the union, or who joins the union in the future, must continue as a member in good standing for the term of the labor agreement. There is generally an "escape" period during which members may withdraw from membership.

In union-shop and maintenance-of-membership clauses, the employer contracts to discharge an employee at the union's request if he fails to maintain his membership in good standing. The law has specifically established that good standing refers only to the periodic payment of dues and initiation fees.

NLRB can be petitioned by employees for deauthorization of a union-shop agreement. An election similar to representation procedures is held; and, if a majority of employees vote against continuing the union shop, the pertinent clause will terminate immediately.

Finally, Section 14(b) of the Taft-Hartley Act provides that state law shall determine whether a union security clause is legal. A number of states now forbid any type of union-security agreement, but several allow agency-shop arrangements.

Alternative Forums

There are, as we have seen, four agencies involved in dispute settlement and hence in the creation of a body of labor law: the National Labor

Relations Board, the federal courts, arbitrators, and the state courts. All have had an active role in deciding the fate of the parties concerned.

The labor lawyer, of late, has had to consider what entitlements he is privileged to use in presenting his case. There are, of course, circumstances in which an arbitration award may be sought by a company which requests damages from the union for breach of contract and, at the same time, seeks in state court to have the strike enjoined. The union in this case might contend that the dispute is a matter for NLRB determination and enforcement in federal court.

Such dilemmas are more frequent as the complexity of labor strife involves several questions for decision. The management lawyer therefore needs to weigh the advantages and disadvantages of forum selection before he enters his case.

COALITION BARGAINING

NLRB, supported by the courts, has held to be unlawful the refusal, by management, to bargain with representatives of a locally established union from other locations or with representatives of other unions who act as advisers to the local union. This tactic, known as coalition or coordinated bargaining, is supported by the Board where unions ostensibly seek advice and counsel from other unions within a company and ask such unions to sit in on conferences with the employer. Companies generally argue that the union's aim in such cases is to achieve multiplant or national bargaining.

Much more will be heard in the future about the Board's developing position in this important area.

A Look Ahead

Labor legislation is much talked about, but new statutory enactments have been few and far between. The prospect for *major* law change seems remote. However, areas of particular interest at present include the right to work, antistrike legislation, and NLRB review.

Right to work. Of concern to labor is the repeal of Section 14(b) of the Taft-Hartley Act. This would allow unions the freedom to negotiate union-shop clauses in the states where compulsory union membership is now prohibited.

Antistrike legislation. The need for new antistrike provisions has been cited by many lawmakers, particularly during the years 1967 and 1968 when strike activity has been at its peak. Particular attention is being paid to strikes by public employees whose work stoppages have a profound effect upon the workings (or nonworkings) of a community.

A manufacturers' group has recommended that compulsory arbitration, as advanced by some lawmakers, be avoided in dealing with national emergency strikes.

NLRB review. Another management group urges labor law reform by limiting the authority of NLRB—especially as respects its power to determine what the law should be at the expense of employees' and employers' rights. Others recommend the creation of a special labor court to decide cases of both representation and unfair labor practices. This would abolish NLRB and ad hoc remedies.

The Protection
of Industrial Property
and Trade Secrets

Oliver P. Howes, Jr.

WHAT IS THE MOST FANTASTIC SPY STORY IN HISTORY? WELL, SECRET AGENT 007 fantasies notwithstanding, surely one of the front contenders would be a little known but truly bizarre tale of trade secret espionage, murder, and derring-do in the silk industry in the early 1700's.

For a century and a half, Italian engineers had possessed a monopoly over colossal silk-throwing machines capable of accommodating 100 operators who spun more silk thread per day than 5,000 hand spinners. This monopoly was destined to be broken by a brilliant young English weaver, John Lombe. By the age of 20, John Lombe had become an accomplished engineer, mathematician, and weaver and had learned to speak fluent Italian. He was fully aware that the Italians so prized their silk machines that the penalty for spying was death by hanging from a gibbet by one foot and the forfeiture of all property. He knew, too, that fabulous rewards

OLIVER P. HOWES, JR., is a partner of the New York law firm of Nims, Halliday, Whitman, Howes & Collison.

awaited the man who could bring the spinning machines to England and so establish a true factory system there.

Using forged documents, he voyaged to Italy and established himself as a maintenance engineer in a Piedmont silk mill. During a year filled with unbelievable tension and narrow escapes, he memorized and copied each part of each machine and smuggled the drawings back to England. Lombe bribed two fellow workers to leave with him and, after a sea chase worthy of Captain Horatio Hornblower, arrived safely in England. In 1718 he was granted a 14-year patent by George I. Subsequently, he and his backers erected a huge factory and waterwheel. The complex was considered one of the wonders of the age.

Not surprisingly, the enraged Italians cut off their shipments of raw silk to England. They were further infuriated when the enterprising English began importing silk of superior quality from China. Revenge was in order. The Italians sentenced Lombe to death in absentia and appointed a beautiful woman spy to execute the sentence. She went to England, ingratiated herself with Lombe, and was given employment at his plant. She also ingratiated herself with one of the Italians whom Lombe had brought with him back to England.

Over a period of 18 months, this charming counterspy and her cohort administered small doses of poison to Lombe. In the last painful stages of his affliction, Lombe discovered the woman's duplicity and had her arrested for attempted murder. She was able to charm an incredulous court, however, and was released on bail, promptly disappearing with her accomplice. A few days later, the now wealthy genius of the early English factory system died at the age of 29.

From Lombe's day to this, problems of protecting trade secrets and other forms of industrial property have ever been present. The following pages discuss some of the questions involved and point out salient legal issues likely to be of concern to corporate management today.

Characteristics of a Trade Secret

The value of a trade secret lies in the commercial advantage its possession gives one over one's competitors. To be protectable, it does not matter whether the subject matter qualifies as a traditional trade secret—which may consist of a formula for a chemical compound, a pattern for a machine, or a compilation of information, such as a list of customers or suppliers—or whether it is as nebulous as a scheme for promoting an uncopyrightable song. What is essential is that it be secret and provide a commercial advantage.

In a recent case, Monolith Portland Midwest Company chose not to categorize its claimed property as a trade secret, but referred instead to "valuable information" as the subject of its claim.[1]* This phrase was adopted by the court, and it is a good term of reference for corporate management to use in its consideration of the problems involved in receiving or exchanging information with potential customers or suppliers.

"Valuable information" need not have the novelty of a patentable invention to be protectable, nor need it be conceived by the "spark of genius."[2] Machinery designs and specifications developed through experimentation over a period of time or special knowledge developed through skill and ingenuity will qualify for protection as a trade secret. Courts have enforced rights in a unique combination of procedures which came about through the use of commonly known elements or steps that produced a superior product or a competitive advantage.[3] In such cases it is no defense that each of the separate steps has previously been mentioned independently in technical or scientific writings. However, matters in the public domain or methods involving only trivial advances will not be protected.[4]

Enforcement of rights in such industrial property is based on the social and economic benefit of protecting an investment in time and money against socially undesirable methods of obtaining valuable information which has been kept secret; that is, which is a private matter known only to a few and kept from others. The rules with respect to what is an actionable wrong involving this form of property recognize a distinction between preserving the integrity of confidential relationships and merely protecting the secrecy of industrial information as such.[5]

Disclosure of a secret by placing goods on the market, or by failing to use such security measures as will insure that goods which reveal a secret technique or method will not be examined by competitors or the public before going on the market, will destroy the basis for protection. However, even when a product is on the market and a competitor could determine essential information by reverse engineering, if such information is acquired by improper means (such as duplicating engineering drawings obtained by means of an explicit or implied confidential relationship), the "secret" will be protected. By failure to develop his own models or engineering drawings, a competitor reduces the development time necessary to get into

* Notes to the text are to be found at the end of the chapter.

competition. Thus a competitive advantage of a product already in the market is destroyed. In such a case, the courts will try to restore the parties to their rightful competitive positions by delaying the second comer's entrance into the field, but they will not deprive the public of the benefit of competition by preventing the second comer from eventually becoming a competitor.

Who Is Responsible in a Case of Misappropriation?

Relief in a case involving theft of secret intellectual property, to be effective, must be directly available against someone in addition to the person who takes the property, since the actual culprit is not usually a competitor. Even when armed with ill-gotten intellectual property, the actual culprit is not so financially situated that he alone can destroy the competitive advantage that secret intellectual property can give the owner. The victimized party must be able to proceed against the person benefitting most by the misappropriation—usually a competitor.

In order to obtain such relief it must be shown that the competitor had knowledge or implied notice of a confidential relationship between the owner of the secret and the culprit who unlawfully disclosed it. However, the competitor's knowledge or notice that the secret had been divulged in such a relationship may be inferred.

Employee's Responsibility

Employees have an obligation not to divulge confidential information and know-how which they acquire during their employment. The obligation not to disclose trade secrets is enforceable by injunction whether or not there is an express contract against disclosure of information communicated to the employee in confidence.[6] To prevent the disclosure or competitive use of such confidential information the employee is subject to injunctive relief so long as the information in question remains a trade secret.[7]

The restriction on disclosure of a trade secret by employees who acquire knowledge of it in the course of their employment extends to those cases where the trade secret is in fact developed by the employee in the course of his employment. However, the employee is not restricted from working for a competitor and using the skills he has learned and the knowledge he has acquired in the course of developing the secret information for his ex-employer. Thus an employee who, for a period of six years, was responsible for the direction of a 28-year project which resulted in a unique and highly experimental product was enjoined from disclosing the trade secrets of his ex-employer which he had learned during his employment. However, he was not enjoined from taking employment in a competitive business which was seeking to develop the same product or from using his knowledge and experience, aside from the ex-employer's trade secrets, for the benefit of his new employer.[8]

The public policy is to enforce an equitable morality upon mobile employees. This includes an obligation not to divulge confidential information and know-how developed during the term of employment. Although the obligation will be enforced whether or not there is an express contract, such a contract has the advantage of putting the employee on actual notice that he is likely to receive confidential information which he cannot use to the detriment of his employer. The express contract will not, however, be enforced if it is found that the restraint imposed on the employee is unreasonable. Factors in deciding this are as follows:

1. Whether it is injurious to the public—as, for example, where it is likely to reduce the supply of semiskilled labor or make the ex-employee a public charge.
2. Whether it is unduly harsh and oppressive on the employee— as where it prevents him from using certain skills acquired by training in the course of his employment.
3. Whether it is greater than necessary to protect a legitimate interest of the employer—as where it restricts the employee from taking employment outside the normal geographic radius of the employer's business.

Thus, where the same employment contract is used for all employees, there is a danger of not sufficiently restricting the sophisticated and highly educated engineers who direct research and development projects while, at the same time, imposing an unreasonable restraint on workers performing more mechanical functions. There is also the danger that by spelling out a particular area of sensitivity the contract will not cover collaterally valuable information developed during the course of employment. Since the courts use the same tests of reasonableness in enforcing an implied obligation not to disclose an ex-employer's trade secrets many concerns avoid the problem by not employing express contracts for personnel other than those in research and development.

In considering employment contracts, it must be kept in mind that they are viewed as a form of restraint of trade which is presumptively void and which is looked on with disfavor. The burden of proving the restraint reasonable is placed on the shoulders of the employer.

Actual notice. Clearly, deliberately inducing a competitor's employee to break his duty to his employer with knowledge of a confidential relationship will incur liability for injunctive relief, money damages, or both. The existence of such a relationship can be shown by a written employment contract or can be inferred from the position or title of an employee. The case of the competitor who advertised a job which could only have been filled by his competitor's supervisor of quality control is illustrative of such a situation.[9]

Implied notice. However, notice need not be affirmatively approved. Where an employer does not actually know that his new employee had a contract not to disclose information confided to him by his ex-employer, but should know that in accordance with fair business principles the precise character of the employee's former work was in all likelihood covered by an express or implied agreement not to divulge trade secrets, the same penalties will be imposed as if actual notice of the relationship had been proved.[10]

Thus, if there is actual knowledge or implied notice that a confidential relationship exists, anyone who uses another's trade secret is equally and individually liable with the person who knowingly breaches that relationship. Similarly, if a corporate officer acquires a trade secret from a third person who has acquired possession of the secret by other than lawful means, the corporation is liable as well as the individual corporate officer.[11]

RESPONSIBILITY OF NONEMPLOYEES

The courts recognize that secret information may have to be communicated to a person or persons not in the employ of the owner for limited purposes such as securing supplies or otherwise enjoying the benefits of the secret more fully. "It is not requisite that only the proprietor of the business know it."[12]

Once it is determined that a trade secret exists, any person to whom it is disclosed in a confidential relationship for a limited purpose will be enjoined from divulging it to others or from using it except for the benefit of its proprietor. Where valuable information which has been kept secret must be imparted to a supplier or subcontractor in order to enable him to fill a particular need, an express statement as to the confidential nature of the information and the particular purpose of disclosing it should be made. However, in the absence of an express contract, the obligation not to divulge a trade secret may be implied and will govern data imparted in confidence in the course of negotiating a contract, purchasing the business in which they have been used, establishing a relationship as licensor and licensee, or entering into a joint venture.[13] This implied obligation has also been found where an inventor employed a manufacturer to develop the inventor's idea.[14] In other words, the communication of secret information to a number of persons in a confidential relationship will not constitute publication of it and will not destroy the right to prevent its disclosure.

Each case naturally presents different facts, and the courts will judge each on its own particular circumstances. This is especially true where there is no relationship between the owner of the secret and the competitor who is charged with misappropriation of it. Where equipment is supplied by the owner of the secret to a common prospective purchaser, a series of steps by a competitor such as photographing the equipment and using drawings of it rather than preparing new engineering drawings or independently building a working model may be held actionable as unjustly enriching the competitor.[15]

In such a case the court's measure of damage provides a sound principle to follow where a prospective customer is in possession of a working model or engineering plans of a competitor's product. If the information disclosed is proved to be valuable, as by an established competitive advantage, the damages awarded the owner of the information may be the amount it would have cost the misappropriator to acquire the same information by its own experimental efforts. Damages have been awarded for the value of the time saved in solving a production problem by such a shortcut even where no trade secret was proved.[16]

A similar rule is applied where material (such as specifications) is stolen or otherwise misappropriated even though the material is not secret. This is illustrated by the case in which a group of employees founding a competing business chose to copy their former employer's blueprints despite the fact that they could have produced their own models without them. Their failure to do this resulted in their being enjoined from pursuing their competing business until they made their own drawings.[17]

In setting the measure of damages the courts have carefully distinguished cases of misappropriation and cases where a true trade secret is involved. In a 1966 decision one Trieman and other defendants were found to have taken and used some of National Rejectors, Inc.'s drawings, which were not trade secrets, in preparing their own drawings. The measure of damages applied by the court was for misappropriation.[18] Trieman and his associates were ordered to compensate National Rejectors for the loss from misuse. This was measured by Rejectors' lost profits by reason of Trieman's competition in the period of time gained by using the drawings instead of examining and measuring Rejectors' product, which was on the market, or experimenting independently. The opinion indicates that if a trade secret had been involved, Rejectors also would have been entitled to Trieman's profits during that period of time. In such a case, the time gained should be determined on the basis of the defendant's actual manpower and not on the basis of a larger staff such as the plaintiff might have employed.

Therefore, although material reveals nothing secret, if it is acquired under circumstances which expressly or impliedly create a confidential relationship, failure to expend time and money in producing similar material will be punished.

Types of Recovery After Theft

Court opinions continually point out that a trade secret is valuable because it gives its owner a competitive advantage in the marketplace. Maintenance of that dominant position is of prime importance in considering the question of remedies.

RELIEF BY INJUNCTION

One purpose of an injunction against the use of unlawfully acquired information is to prevent destruction of the comparative marketing positions of the parties. Speed in obtaining relief is therefore desirable. If a strong showing of secrecy, confidential disclosure, or theft and use of misappropriated property can be made, a preliminary injunction may be secured in advance of trial. However, the plaintiff's burden is great, as it should be, for if it is established upon trial that the plaintiff has no trade secret or the appropriation was not unlawful, the injunction will have given him an unwarranted advantage. The courst, recognizing that the evidence presented on a preliminary injunction motion is incomplete, invariably impose the obligation on the plaintiff to furnish a bond covering the defendant's damages if it should be shown that issuance of a preliminary injunction was wrong.

Swift and drastic relief is given to thwart outrageous misappropriation, as in the New York case where four ex-employees took not only customer lists, confidential price lists, and procedural and processing information but also a machine tool and then formed a corporation, called Tefco Electronics, Inc., to sell products in direct competition with their former employer, Sealectro Corporation.[19] Proof of misappropriation was established for the purpose of obtaining a preliminary injunction by a police raid on Tefco's premises. The court granted a preliminary injunction which not only enjoined Tefco from using the plaintiff's trade secrets but also prevented it from manufacturing and selling any products which Sealectro manufactured or sold or which were competitive with Sealectro's products. This was an extreme case of misappropriation, and the remedy also was extreme, for it prevented Tefco from continuing the business for which it had been organized.

Scope and duration of relief. If injunctive relief is granted, what should be its scope and duration? Here again the facts of a particular case are controlling. The duplicity of the defendant and the merit of the secret, among other factors, have led the same panel of judges on the U.S. Court of Appeals for the Second Circuit to deny injunctive relief in one case and to award a perpetual injunction in another.

In the first case, involving what might be termed merely a slight breach of faith, plaintiff Schreyer attempted to interest Casco Products Corporation in a license to manufacture a product for which a patent application had been filed. Negotiations broke off after the secret had been disclosed to Casco. Prior to issuance of the patent, Casco marketed its own product made by using Schreyer's secret. When the patent was issued, Schreyer sued for patent infringement, damages arising out of the use of its trade secret prior to issuance of the patent, or both. (It should be noted that issuance of a patent on what had been a trade secret destroys the trade secret.) If Casco had awaited issuance of the patent and chanced infringement, it would have lost an advantage over the rest of the trade. Giving Casco the benefit of the doubt, we can surmise it believed, from what Schreyer had disclosed, that the product was not patentable— a judgment borne out by the court, which held the patent was invalid. However, in jumping the gun Casco breached a confidential trust, and for that it had to pay. No injunction was granted, but, since Casco had made no profit, the court awarded damages to Schreyer in the amount of the sales which Casco gained by accelerating its production date.[20]

In the second case, a salesman called Wiltschek, by falsely stating his ability to represent a manufacturer named Franke, induced Franke to disclose production costs, plant capacity, sales records, and manufacturing process. Franke's product was already on the market. Shortly after the disclosures, Wiltschek began to manufacture and sell a similar product. It was determined that "any ordinary, moderately adept workman could have easily discovered . . . (Franke's) . . . process since a previously expired patent disclosed all the elements for making it." Despite this, it was held that Wiltschek's breach of confidence must result in a perpetual injunction, not only against making use of the information unfairly gained, but also against making and selling any product similar to Franke's.[21]

A perpetual injunction has also been granted where an officer of a rival corporation learned his competitor's secret process by posing as a laborer and gaining employment in the competitor's plant to observe its methods.[22]

It is clear, therefore, that an injunction can be used punitively as well as to restore to the plaintiff a previous competitive advantage. However, since it is difficult to calculate damages for permanent loss of a secret, a perpetual injunction is not always granted as a punitive measure but can be viewed as a means of compensating the deprived owner. Moreover, he who acquires knowledge of another's trade secret through a thief and then uses it is just as liable as the thief. When an industrial spy learns a competitor's trade secret by gaining access to the premises under false pretenses, a perpetual injunction should be issued against any use of the secret.

Mandatory injunction. Where the unlawful appropriation of a trade secret has been especially reprehensible, a mandatory injunction may be issued requiring destruction of tools and models. In a recent case defendant F. H. Frantz, an ex-employee of General Aniline Corporation, hired several of Aniline's employees and used knowledge and drawings which he had taken from Aniline, plus material obtained from an unfaithful employee who remained with Aniline, to produce within three months a product comparable to Aniline's—a task which ordinarily would have taken two to three years to complete. Frantz even went so far as to file a patent application, representing himself as the inventor. In addition to exemplary damages in the amount of $50,000 and an accounting of Frantz's profits, a mandatory injunction was issued requiring Frantz to deliver up for destruction such items, among others, as tools, dies, jigs, models, and machines and machine parts relating to or used in connection with any product employing or utilizing Aniline's trade secrets. Frantz was also permanently enjoined from manufacturing, selling, or distributing any product employing these trade secrets. Aniline, however, not having begun to sell its product, was not entitled to an award of actual damages.[23]

Relief from injunction. If an injunction becomes outdated through actual or potential knowledge of the supposed secret, application can be made to the court for modification of the injunction. This is a matter for the discretion of the court; and, while it has been held in some cases that because of past unfair conduct certain defendants will be enjoined from using information publicly known to all their competitors, here again, cases are decided on their own peculiar or particular facts.

In a leading case, the Allen-Qualley Company had made confidential disclosures to Shellmar Products regarding a machine for producing the plaintiff's wrapper for the purpose of having Shellmar supply such wrappers to A-Q. On the basis of the information disclosed, Shellmar was able to find a patent which had been issued on a very similar machine and which it then purchased. After a trial, Shellmar was ordered to assign the patent to A-Q and was permanently enjoined from ever using A-Q's secret.[24]

Obviously still smarting under this defeat, Shellmar sought to have the decree modified some eight years later on the ground that the issuance of the patent had destroyed Allen-Qualley's secret. This contention was dismissed. The court stated that "by defendant's inequitable conduct it had precluded itself from enjoying the rights of the general public to the patent disclosure and will not be permitted to place upon plaintiff the burden of suing for patent infringement when its proprietary rights in the process have already been adjudicated against defendant."[25]

Since such a decree extends protection to the plaintiff beyond the life of its patent, it is questionable whether this case would be decided the same way today in light of subsequent U.S. Supreme Court decisions setting aside state decisional law on unfair competition which conflicted with the federal patent law.[26] Partly as a result of those decisions, legislation has been proposed which provides that any person who engages in any act, trade practice, or course of conduct in commerce which may be regulated by Congress and which results or is likely to result in the wrongful disclosure or misappropriation of a trade secret or confidential information shall be liable in a civil action for unfair competition. Under such an enactment, the rights in a trade secret will clearly be protectable under federal law and will not be subject to the uncertainties of possible conflict between state action enforcing those rights and the federal patent law.

ACCOUNTING FOR PROFITS AND DAMAGES

The principal factors affecting a plaintiff's economic good health, the commercial advantage of possessing a trade secret, and the need for quick action to protect it are well illustrated by the case involving Rise shaving cream.[27] Sales of Rise made by a secret process, were $400,000 in the first year (1950), $800,000 in the second year, $1,800,000 in the third year, and $2,600,000 in the first six months of the fourth year (1953). After a competitor had "repeatedly failed in its attempts to produce a marketable pressurized shaving cream," it hired as a chemist one of the patentees of the product sold under the Rise mark. Within nine months, the competitive product became the market leader, and in 1954 it achieved sales of $5,000,000. Although the competitor's rapid achievement in increasing sales impressed the courts with the importance of the trade secret claimed by the makers of Rise, these sales also severely damaged the competitive advantage of Rise.

The court ordered an accounting of the competitor's profits on the use of the trade secret before issuance of the patent and, thereafter, for use of the infringing process. (To repeat: Once a patent has been issued on the subject matter that was previously a trade secret, damages are no longer attributable to its use.) Since a valid patent covered the trade secret at the time of trial, the duration of the injunction with respect to the trade secret was not discussed.

Typically, although it was awarded damages for loss of sales by reason of its competitor's misappropriation of its trade secret, the Rise management, because of the enormous difficulty of proving such damages, did not attempt to do so. In a case like this the plaintiff may prove an established royalty, or the court may determine one from the circumstances of the case, and the royalty will then be applied to the defendant's net sales. In fixing the royalty rate for the trade secret, the facts at the time of its first misappropriation are the facts to be considered.

It is interesting to note that in the Rise case the royalty allowed was 10 percent of the net sales of the first product produced by the use of the secret. Use of this secret was found to have contributed all the commercial value of the product. On a second product, in which a second secret was used, the royalty was 1 percent of net sales. This secret was found to have added to the commercial value of the product which first embodied it but was not deemed an essential element. In the accounting of profits the competitor was not allowed to deduct all its advertising expenses for the condemned products since it continued to sell similar products under the same trademark after the court enjoined its use of the trade secret, which was now embodied in a patent.[28] Thus there was recognition that, even without the trade secret, the competitor would continue to benefit by selling a shave cream bearing the same trademark which had been used and advertised on its commercially successful product.

Attorneys' fees, another means of compensating an injured competitor, are allowed in cases where conduct is unconscionable, fraudulent, or in bad faith. In the Rise case, fees were allowed in excess of $500,000.

In another case, where employees took their corporation's confidential information and diverted it to their own use through a dummy corporation which employed their wives at handsome salaries, the court took a realistic approach to the accounting of the employees' profits.[29] Recognizing that the expenses claimed by the dummy corporation were artificially high, the court ordered that the employees' profits be determined by what their employer's margin of profit would have been if the employer had retained the business diverted by the defendants. The case also involved a unique problem in that the employees had remained on the payroll while diverting their employer's business to their corporate alter ego. They were held to have forfeited all compensation subsequent to the overt act of unfaithfulness—that is, the formation of their corporation.

Recourse Under Penal Laws

Ordinarily, in the case of theft, it is normal to seek recourse under criminal law. Unfortunately, criminal law is based on traditional property concepts and does not provide effective relief in the case of a trade secret. The owner of property must be deprived of possession and use of the property before a crime can be established, and where formulas or blueprints are copied there is no actual taking and depriving of ownership and possession within the classical meaning of these terms under criminal law.

Attempts are being made to amend the state and federal criminal laws to cover the theft of scientific and technical information, as distinguished from the documents in which the information is set forth, and to eliminate the requirement that the owner of the information be deprived of its possession. Such legislation should be uniformly enacted in the near future.

Conclusion

In summary, one can set forth general principles but no hard and fast rules as to what is secret, what particular circumstances will establish a confidential relationship, and what penalty will be imposed in a case of misappropriation.

In applying equitable principles to cases between two private litigants, the court also seeks to protect the public interest, which may benefit from added competition in the form of better products and lower prices and from a better-trained labor force. This undoubtedly enters into the court's decision as to what employment may not be taken, what is a protectable trade secret, and how long its use will be enjoined. The court attempts to balance these various interests by enjoining certain conduct for specific periods of time, by requiring destruction of certain materials, and by awarding damages or profits. These measures seek to put the parties in the same relative competitive positions they occupied before the misappropriation took place.

The general principles discussed in this chapter will assist in deciding whether certain information has been supplied in confidence, whether it may be used, and, if so, to what extent and in what manner. In considering these questions it is well to remember that the court in the Rise case decided that the defendant knew or should have known, simply as a matter of fair business practice, that it had an obligation to do more than it did to ascertain the extent to which there was a restriction on what might be disclosed or used.

Notes to the Text

[1] *Monolith Portland Midwest Company* v. *Kaiser Aluminum & Chemical Corporation*, 152 USPQ 380 (D.C. Calif., 1966).

[2] *Atlantic Wool Combing Company* v. *Norfolk Mills, Inc.*, 357 F. 2d 866 (1966).

[3] *Head Ski Company* v. *Kam Ski Company*, 138 F. Supp. 919 (D. Md. 1958).

[4] *Nickelson* v. *General Motors Corporation*, 361 F. 2d 196 (C.A. 7, 1966).

[5] *Winston Research Corp.* v. *Minnesota Mining & Mfg. Co.*, 350 F. 2d 134 (C.A. 9, 1965).

[6] *Allen Mfg. Co.* v. *Loika*, 145 Conn. 509 (1958).

[7] *Kaumagraph Co.* v. *Stampgraph Co.*, 235 N.Y. 1 (1923).

[8] *B. F. Goodrich Co.* v. *Wohlgemuth*, 192 N.E. 2d 99, 137 USPQ 804 (Ohio, 1963).

[9] *Minnesota Mining & Mfg. Co.* v. *Technical Tape Co.*, 23 Misc. 2d 671 (N.Y. Sup. Ct. 1959).

[10] *Colgate-Palmolive Co.* v. *Carter Products*, 230 F. 2d 855 (C.A. 4, 1956).

[11] *Solo Cup Co.* v. *Paper Machinery Corp.*, 240 F. Supp. 126 (E.D. Wisc., 1965); aff'd 359 F. 2d 754 (C.A. 7, 1966).

[12] Restatement of Torts, Section 757 Comment (b).

[13] *Heyman* v. *Winarick*, 325 F. 2d 584 (C.A. 2, 1963); *Smith* v. *Dravo Corp.*, 203 F. 2d 369 (C.A. 7, 1953); *Sandlin* v. *Johnson*, 141 F. 2d 660 (C.C.A. 8, 1944); *Air Waukies, Inc.* v. *Pincus*, 86 USPQ 182 (N.Y. Sup. Ct. 1950).

[14] *Kamin* v. *Kuhnau*, 232 Or. 139, 374 P. 2d 912, (1962).

[15] *Servo* v. *General Electric Co.*, 337 F. 2d 716 (C.A. 4, 1964).

[16] *National Rejectors, Inc.* v. *Trieman*, 152 USPQ 120 (Sup. Ct. Mo. 1966).

[17] *Schulenberg* v. *Signatrol*, 50 Ill. App. 2d 402, 200 N.E. 2d 615, 142 USPQ 510 (1964); aff'd in part 33 Ill. 2d 379, 212 N.E. 2d 865, 147 USPQ 167 (1965).

[18] *National Rejectors, Inc.,* v. *Trieman, supra.*

[19] *Sealectro* v. *Tefco Electronics*, 32 Misc. 2d 11 (Sup. Ct. N.Y., 1961).

[20] *Schreyer* v. *Casco Products Corp.*, 97 F. Supp. 159 (D. Conn., 1951); aff'd 190 F. 2d 921 (C.A. 2, 1951).

[21] *Franke* v. *Wiltschek*, 209 F. 2d 493 (C.A. 2, 1953).

[22] *Eastern Extract Co.* v. *Greater New York Extracting*, 126 App. Div. 928 (1908).

[23] *General Aniline Corp.* v. *Frantz*, 50 Misc. 2d 994 (Sup. Ct. N.Y., 1966).

[24] *Shellmar Products* v. *Allen-Qualley Co.*, 36 F. 2d 623 (C.C.A. 7, 1929), aff'ing 31 F. 2d 293 (N.D. Ill. 1929).

[25] *Shellmar Products* v. *Allen-Qualley Co.*, 87 F. 2d 104 (C.C.A. 7, 1936).

[26] *Sears, Roebuck & Co.* v. *Stiffel Co.*, 376 U.S. 225 (1964); *Compco Corp.* v. *Day-Brite Lighting*, 376 US 234 (1964).

[27] *Colgate-Palmolive Co.* v. *Carter Products*, 230 F. 2d 855 (C.A. 4, 1956).

[28] *Colgate-Palmolive Co.* v. *Carter Products*, 214 F. Supp. 383 (D.C. Md., 1963).

[29] *Defler* v. *Kleeman*, 19 A.D. 2d 396 (1963).

Patents, Trademarks, and Copyrights

David Toren

I. Patents

THE PATENT SYSTEM IS AS OLD AS THE NATION ITSELF. AS EARLY AS 1790, IN enacting the first patent act, Congress heeded the constitutional directive "to promote the progress of science and useful arts, by securing for limited times to authors and inventors the exclusive right to their writings and discoveries."

From a struggling beginning, our patent system has risen to its unchallenged position as the primary tool and incentive for technical progress. It is one of the principal means by which the United States attained the dominant role it has today as the world's technologically most advanced nation. More than 3,375,000 U.S. patents have been granted. They constitute an essential currency of the industrial community, and a healthy economy without an effective patent system would be unthinkable.

DAVID TOREN is a partner in the New York law firm of McGlew & Toren.

What Is a Patent?

Essentially, a patent is a reward for inventiveness and provides an incentive for ingenuity. It is a two-way deal in the nature of an ordinary contract in which the inventor and the government are the parties, each contributing its share to the bargain. The inventor must disclose in detail a new and useful thing in a government prescribed form—the patent application. The government, in turn, after having satisfied itself through its patent office that the thing in question is in fact new and useful and that it contributes to technological knowledge and advance, grants the inventor the right to exclude others from making the thing for 17 years from the date of the grant. The right of the inventor ceases after the expiration of the 17 years; then the patented thing is deemed to be public property, and everyone may freely use it.

Why Must We Have Patents?

Detractors of the patent system contend that patents create monopolies that stifle progress. This argument ignores human nature and is belied by the tremendous technological advance that has taken place within the framework of the patent system of this and other countries. Even the socialized economies of the Eastern Bloc countries (including Russia) have recognized the importance of providing incentives to their inventors by granting patents or "inventors' certificates" to them as rewards for their contributions. But a patent is not only a reward; it fulfills many other important functions in a competitive and progressive society.

Patents encourage public disclosure of technological information. In the absence of patent protection, inventors would guard their discoveries as secrets and would prevent their disclosure as much as possible. This, in turn, would deprive the public of valuable information and would result in duplication of effort since others might attempt to solve a problem which has already successfully been dealt with. By disclosing their discoveries in the form of patents, inventors thus supply information which forms the starting point for and encourages further research, modification, and improvement.

Patents encourage capital investment and research. Private enterprises with research facilities would, of course, hesitate to spend their funds on research and development in the absence of the prospect of financial reward and exclusivity. Take the drug industry, for example, that invests tens of millions of dollars each year in developing new medicines, many of which prove ineffective after years of expensive experiments and testing. Once a new drug has been found effective and is market-ready, the manufacturer surely should be entitled to reap the benefit of its research by preventing others from copying the product unless they are willing to pay a reasonable royalty. Effective patent protection is thus a prerequisite for research expenditure by private enterprises. But the individual inventor also seeks and needs private risk capital for developing his products. Only the patent system affords the protection that is needed to encourage the expenditure of such capital.

Patents encourage exchange of products and information on an international scale. Without exception, patents are granted by all countries to foreign nationals as well as to their domestic inventors. Many thousands of patents are thus granted each year by the United States to nationals of European, South American, and Asian countries while U.S. inventions are patented in large numbers throughout the world. This, of course, stimulates international trade and promotes beneficial exchange of products and information across national boundaries. It is particularly important to technologically underdeveloped countries, which in this manner obtain the benefit of modern developments.

Patents are valuable assets. A patent is personal property that may be sold, bought, and licensed. To build up a strong patent position gives an enterprise a competitive edge that may prove invaluable. The success of many corporations is almost exclusively due to their dominant patent position. In case of doubt, it is a good rule of thumb to invest in the expense for obtaining a patent rather than dedicating the invention to the public by public disclosure without seeking patent protection or attempting to maintain the invention in secrecy. An invention that is of no commercial importance at the time may later turn out to be a valuable asset for the owner. In the ever changing picture of today's technology, it is often difficult to foresee the ultimate use and importance of an invention. If the owner is not able to exploit the patent himself, he may be able to sell it to a competitor and perhaps obtain in return a patent that he needs for his production.

BEWARE OF FOUR COMMON MISCONCEPTIONS

A patent gives no right to practice the patented invention. It is a common misconception that a patent gives the owner the right to manufacture and use the thing patented to the exclusion of all others. On the contrary, the patent grant is of a restrictive rather than permissive nature and merely empowers the patentee to *exclude others* from using the invention without, however, giving the positive right actually to exercise the invention. This distinction, which is the source of much confusion and disappointment, is of great practical importance as shown by the following example.

Assume that Smith invents the original chair and that the U.S. Patent Office allows him a claim reading:

> An article of furniture comprising a seat and at least three legs attached to said seat.

Brown subsequently improves on Smith's basic chair structure by inventing the armrest. He obtains a patent with the following claim:

> An article of furniture comprising a seat, at least three legs attached to said seat, and an arm-supporting means extending above said seat.

Assuming the "arm-supporting means" to be novel and useful, the Patent Office certainly is justified in granting a patent for the new combination. This, however, does not mean that Brown can lawfully build or sell his armrest chair without Smith's permission. As a matter of fact, he cannot since Brown's chair also has a seat and at least three legs. Thus, by making use of all the elements of Smith's claim, Brown would clearly infringe on the former's patent rights. On the other hand, Smith, who owns the dominating chair patent, can build and sell his chair, but he cannot incorporate Brown's armrest in it without obtaining permission from Brown. In other words, Brown's patent gives him the right to exclude others, including Smith, from using the armrest; but it does not permit him to sell his armrest chair since it is dependent on the structure protected by Smith's patent.

From a practical point of view, large numbers of patents are such dependent or improvement patents and can thus not be exploited in the absence of permission from the owner of the dominating or pioneer patent.

The claims, not the overall disclosure, tell what is protected. While the cigarette commercial may have taught us that "it's what's up front that counts," in patents It Is the end we have to look for since the "end" means the claims. The printed patent as published by the government upon conclusion of the examination on the day of grant consists essentially of a detailed description of the invention—usually referred to as the specification—and the claims. If the invention relates to mechanical or electrical subject matter, the printed patent also includes a drawing which is described in the specification. In process inventions, the drawing is replaced by specific working examples explaining the process. However, in interpreting the scope of a patent, it is only the claims, not the general disclosure of the specification, that count.

The claims measure the scope of the protected invention, and only in rare cases are they as broad as the general disclosure. Therefore, when it is said that "this machine is patented," the assertion has to be taken with a grain of salt. Although the patent may disclose the entire machine, the claims will in most instances be directed to a specific aspect of the machine that is considerably narrower than the overall disclosure. This explains the surprise often expressed by laymen that several patents have been issued to different inventors for essentially the same subject matter disclosed in the printed patents. A study of the claims of the several patents on such similar disclosures will demonstrate that the claims of each of these patents are directed to and thus cover different aspects of it. While the claims of the patent application as originally submitted to the Patent Office may have been broad, they more often than not are restricted during the examination to distinguish over the known subject matter.

There are no international patents. The protection afforded by a patent is restricted to the jurisdiction of the granting country. A U.S. patent thus gives no protection in Canada or Mexico. There are presently several pending proposals for international patents, such as a "Common Market patent," but nothing to this effect has materialized so far. This means that patents must be applied for in all those countries in which protection is deemed advisable. From a practical point of view, the following considerations should play an important role in decisions on foreign filings:

1. Does the invention have a potential use or market in the respective country?
2. Is it intended or feasible to manufacture or license the invention in the respective country?
3. Is there a major competitor in the respective country that could benefit from the invention if not patented?

Although there are no international patents, there is an International Convention of which most industrialized countries, including the Eastern

Bloc countries, are members. Essentially, the International Convention provides that an application for a patent which has been filed in a member country may be filed in any other member country within one year of the effective date of the first application. This means that a U.S. applicant has one year from his U.S. filing date to decide whether to file in other countries. If the decision is affirmative, the foreign application or applications can be filed without loss of priority within the one-year time limit. This one-year period is of considerable value as it provides time to investigate the advisability of foreign filing. A note of caution, however, is in order here. U.S. patent law provides for a one-year grace period before filing a patent application. The invention may be used, sold, or published in the United States during this year without affecting the validity of the patent subsequently granted. But several foreign countries, such as France, Italy, and Sweden, do not provide for grace periods; divulgation anywhere in the world prior to filing is a bar to a patent grant. A U.S. inventor who intends to file in foreign countries should consequently be careful to avoid public dissemination of the invention prior to his U.S. application.

The following example illustrates this point: Inventor Smith, employed by the Brown Corporation, invents a new duplicating machine. Smith assigns his rights in the invention to the Brown Corporation. Brown Corporation builds the machine and exhibits and uses it publicly in New York City on January 1, 1968. A U.S. patent application is filed by Smith on December 1, 1968. The prior public use is not detrimental to the grant of a U.S. patent. Brown Corporation has foreign subsidiaries and files applications in several European countries, including Italy and France, under the International Convention on November 30, 1969. Any patents granted in Italy and France under these facts will be invalid in view of the prior use in New York City. However, use after December 1, 1968, will have had no effect on the validity of the Italian and French patents in view of the filing of the U.S. application, which carries the effective filing date of the foreign applications back to December 1, 1968.

"Patent pending" is not the same as "patented." As soon as an application has been filed in the U.S. Patent Office, the object for which the patent is sought may be lawfully marked with the notation "patent pending." These words merely indicate the filing of a patent application, and no true patent rights attach to the marked object until the patent has been actually granted.

From a practical point of view, a "patent pending" marking may be a valuable advertising aid since it tends to impress the public. The notice, however, is without true legal significance as the patent may never be granted. To give an extreme example: There is nothing to prevent a smart businessman from applying for a patent on, say, an ordinary pencil and marketing the pencil with a "patent pending" notice to promote his sales until his patent application is rejected. Since, obviously, no patent will ever be granted on the pencil, the "patent pending" notice in this case is a sales gimmick. In more serious cases, a "patent pending" marking is at best a warning for the future. It puts a potential imitator on notice that a patent has been applied for and that the patent owner will enforce his rights once the patent has been granted.

A "patent pending" notice should be clearly distinguished from a true "patented" notice, which may be lawfully applied only after the patent has been granted. A "patented" marking, according to the statute, should read "patent" followed by the number of the patent. Such marking is not only desirable but required, lest the patentee lose important rights. Our law deprives a patent owner of the damages which otherwise might be awarded against an infringer if the "patent" marking has been omitted and the infringer had no actual knowledge of the existence of the patent.

WHAT IS PATENTABLE?

In the context of this brief summary it may suffice to state that—with a few exceptions which will be discussed—patents may be obtained on the results of human ingenuity of the most varied kind. Specifically, the statute classifies patentable subject matter as (1) process, (2) machine, (3) manufacture, and (4) composition.

Most inventions can be fitted within these broad classes. The exceptions are primarily those which involve mental steps or mere ideas not resulting in any perceptible effect. Because this is a free country, a person cannot be permitted to "exclude others" from thinking, and inventions involving thought processes are therefore not patentable.

A few representative examples may illustrate the exceptions. Traditionally, patents have been refused on merchandising methods, accounting systems, and methods of doing business and waging war as involving mental processes that do not obtain physical results. Discoveries of laws of nature have been held unpatentable on the theory that the discoverer merely uncovered an existing—although unknown—phenomenon without creating anything new. A borderline case, decided against the inventor in

1862, was Dr. William Morton's discovery of the use of ether for relieving pain during surgical operations.

The grant of patents in the atomic energy and space exploration fields has been severely restricted by Congress during recent years. Similarly, many foreign countries do not grant patents on chemical, food, and pharmaceutical substances. As a matter of public policy, adequate protection can, however, be obtained in these countries by patenting the processes for making the substances.

TYPES OF PATENTS

In addition to ordinary patents which are granted for the four classes of inventions enumerated earlier, patents may be obtained for asexually reproduced plants and ornamental designs. Plant patents were introduced in 1930 and have proven to be a most valuable protection to the nursery industry. Since it takes many years to develop a new flower to the marketing point, the importance of plant patents is obvious. Design patents are of lesser importance; in fact, the President's Commission on the Patent System recommended in 1966 that they be abolished. The purpose of design patents is to protect appearance rather than utility. The shape of an object and its surface ornamentation are thus proper subject matter for design protection.

From a practical point of view, design patents can be easily circumvented by changing the respective shape or ornamentation, thereby rendering this form of patent protection rather ineffective.

CRITERIA FOR PATENTABILITY

For an invention to be patentable, it is not sufficient for it to fall within one of the statutory classes for which patents may be granted. Three additional criteria have to be satisfied—novelty, utility, and nonobviousness.

Novelty. The concept of novelty or newness in patent law is not to be understood in a dictionary sense. Absolute originality is not always required for a thing to be considered "new" from a patent-law point of view. Since the guiding principle of the patent system is the constitutional mandate "to promote the progress of science and useful arts," newness is not affected by secret knowledge since such knowledge is of no benefit to the public.

Two examples illustrate this doctrine. If Smith invents a new shaver but keeps it to himself for an unreasonable time, the law deprives him of the benefit of his invention in favor of a subsequent inventor who invents the same shaver and applies for a patent, thereby making the invention ultimately available to the public. In the eyes of the law, the second inventor has contributed something new in spite of the fact that the shaver is not new in an absolute sense. Smith's concealment of his invention is considered abandonment. On the other hand, had Smith published or openly used his shaver, the publication or use would have destroyed the novelty of the shaver and the patent application of the second inventor would have been invalid even if Smith did not apply for a patent. The decisive factor is that the invention must be made available to the public in some form lest it become a nullity from a legal point of view.

This interpretation of novelty has important consequences. Assume that a domestic corporation has an active research department that produces many patentable inventions. For budgetary or other reasons, the corporation may decide that it does not want to file for patent protection on some of these inventions. If it withholds them from the public, the corporation runs the risk that a competitor may subsequently invent similar objects and obtain patents on them. The concealment by the corporation would then be considered abandonment of the inventions, and the corporation could conceivably be held liable for infringement, although it originated the respective inventions.

In order to avoid this risk, it is good practice to publish inventions for which no patents are sought, thereby rendering invalid any subsequent patents obtained by another. This protection is considerably facilitated by the fact that publications published anywhere in the world and in any language are considered "prior art"—material that may be used to invalidate a patent. By publishing inventions in some obscure foreign publication in a foreign language, the chance that a competitor may obtain knowledge thereof is greatly reduced, while the impact of the publication is the same as if the disclosure had taken place in *The New York Times.*

The second example of prior knowledge that does not affect novelty is use—as distinguished from publication—of an invention in a foreign country. Assume that the shaver referred to previously was originally invented and used in England, but that no publication has taken place anywhere in the world and no knowledge of the shaver has reached the United States. The subsequent invention of the shaver in the United States would then entitle the second inventor to a valid U.S. patent. Since the unavailable foreign invention did not enrich domestic U.S. knowledge, the useful arts were not promoted, and the second inventor thus created a new thing from a United States point of view.

Utility. In order to be patentable, the invention must be "useful," and the patent application must explain how to use it. Inventions which are obviously unworkable or impractical are not considered useful in the meaning of the statute, and patents on them are consequently denied. The U.S. Patent Office thus consistently rejects applications for perpetual-motion machines or other devices or procedures which violate established laws of nature. Inventions whose objects offend public policy or are immoral also are considered outside the utility requirements. Therefore, gambling devices or inventions injurious to public health do not possess the attribute of patentable utility.

The general attitude of the Patent Office in respect to the issue of utility was aptly summarized by Justice Story when he stated that a useful invention is one

> which may be applied to a beneficial use in society, in contradistinction to an invention injurious to the morals, health, or good order of society, or frivolous and insignificant.

In the field of mechanical and electrical inventions, the Patent Office rarely raises the question of utility or operativeness, although it has the right to ask for submission of proof in case of doubt. The utility requirements are, however, most stringent for chemical and particularly pharmaceutical inventions. For reasons of public policy, the Patent Office requires statistically significant clinical tests demonstrating the effect and safety of a new drug before a patent is granted. The policy of the Patent Office in respect to drug patents is succinctly stated in the 1957 decision of the District Court for the District of Columbia in *Isenstead* v. *Walron*, 157 F. Supp. 7, as follows.

> Great care and scrutiny should be particularly taken in connection with applications for medical patents. While the granting of a patent does not legally constitute a certificate that the medicine to which it relates is a good medicine and will cure the disease or successfully make the test which it was intended to do, nevertheless, the granting of such a patent gives a kind of official imprimatur to the medicine in question on which as a moral matter some members of the public are likely to rely. In view of these circumstances, it is right and proper that the Patent Office should be very careful and perhaps even reluctant to grant a patent on a new medical formula until it has been thoroughly tested and successfully tried by more than one physician.

Many recent court decisions have interpreted the statutory utility requirements for chemical and pharmaceutical patents. The U.S. Supreme Court thus held in a 1966 landmark case, *Brenner* v. *Manson*, 383 U.S. 519, that

> a patent is not a hunting license. It is not a reward for the search, but compensation for its successful conclusion

and that only patents for chemical inventions of proven utility should be granted. In this particular case, the court determined that a process for making a chemical product that had no proven use itself, but was a subject of serious scientific investigation and useful as an intermediary for preparing other useful products, did not constitute a patentable invention.

The *Manson* doctrine—enunciated by the nation's highest tribunal and thus the law of the land—has been severely criticized as having a detrimental impact on chemical research. Chemistry is a highly interrelated field, and a concrete, beneficial result is more often than not dependent on different, cumulative discoveries. Denying patent protection to a discovery that has no apparent independent use at the moment but may serve as a building block for further useful discoveries will make researchers hesitate to disseminate their knowledge until a use has been found and a patent may be applied for. This, in turn, runs counter to the very purpose of the patent system "to promote . . . science and useful arts. . . ."

Nonobviousness. To determine whether an invention is "obvious" in the light of the prior art has plagued the patent profession from its beginning and is likely to do so as long as we have patents. No all-encompassing standard for the interpretation of obviousness can possibly be set. What appears obvious to one person may seem nonobvious to another. The element of subjectiveness is seemingly impossible to eliminate from the evaluation of the merits of an invention in light of the prior art, and Congress, the courts, and the Patent Office have struggled for years to establish proper guidelines.

The Supreme Court, aware of the conflicting standards applied by the lower tribunals, finally determined to clarify the matter and in 1966 decided a series of patent litigations, each involving interpretation of the nonobviousness question. In a lengthy opinion in *Graham* v. *John Dere Co. of Kansas City,* 383 U.S. 1, the Court reiterated one of its earlier decisions, its holding in the leading *Hotchkiss* case—*Hotchkiss* v. *Greenwood,* II How. 248 (1850)—which concerned a patent involving a mere substitution of materials (porcelain or clay for wood or metal) in doorknobs. In the *Hotchkiss* case, the patent was held to be invalid and the following attempt to define an obvious invention was made:

> Unless more ingenuity and skill were required than were possessed by an ordinary mechanic acquainted with the business, there was an absence of that degree of skill and ingenuity which constitute essential elements of every invention. In other words, the improvement is the work of a skilled mechanic, not that of the inventor.

The court found that the definition in the *Hotchkiss* case is still applicable today and amplified the previous guideline by stating that the question of nonobviousness lends itself to several basic factual inquiries. Thus

> the scope and content of the prior art are to be determined; differences between the prior art and the claims at issue are to be ascertained; and the level of ordinary skill in the pertinent art resolved. Against this background, the obviousness or nonobviousness of the subject matter is determined. Such secondary considerations as commercial success, long felt but unsolved needs, failure of others, etc., might be utilized to give light to the circumstances surrounding the origin of the subject matter sought to be patented. As indicia of obviousness or nonobviousness, these inquiries may have relevancy.

The Court conceded the inherent difficulties in applying these tests by stating:

> This is not to say, however, that there will not be difficulties in applying the nonobviousness test. What is obvious is not a question upon which there is likely to be uniformity of thought in every given factual context.

INVENTORSHIP AND INTERFERENCE

One of the guiding principles of our patent system is that the patent should be granted to the first inventor. As we have seen in our discussion of novelty, however, the term "first inventor" is not interpreted in an absolute sense. The acts of a first inventor who abandons his invention by inaction are thus disregarded, while a foreign inventor starts to be in the running only after he has introduced his invention into the United States.

Let us again consider Inventor Smith, assuming that he invented his shaver on January 1 of 1968 and made a sketch of its construction at that time. He files a patent application on the shaver on August 15, 1968.

Brown independently invents the same shaver on March 10, 1968, and files his patent application on April 15, thus beating Smith to the application by four months. Who is the first inventor to be awarded the patent? The Patent Office now has two applications before it, both disclosing the same subject matter, the applicant of each claiming to be the first inventor. In most foreign countries, the answer would be simple since the first applicant is regarded as the first inventor; so Mr. Brown would get the patent. In the United States, however, the Patent Office declares an "interference," which is a litigative proceeding to determine priority of invention—that is, first inventorship.

Three principal factors determine the outcome of an interference— the "conception" date of the invention, "diligence," and "reduction to practice." In our example, Smith's conception date will be January 1, 1968—that is, the day he made his drawing—while the filing of the application on August 15 is considered constructive reduction to practice. The intervening months between January 1 and August 15 constitute the decisive period during which diligence comes into play. Since Brown conceived of the invention on March 10, Smith, in order to prevail, must prove that he was continuously diligent toward reducing the invention to practice from just prior to that date. Whether this period of more than five months will be considered sufficient diligence is dependent on the particular circumstances. The Patent Office may hold that Smith was too tardy, in which event he will forfeit his first-inventor status and Brown will be awarded the patent. It follows from this—which only briefly touches on the complex interference practice—that for an invention to be considered complete, it is not sufficient merely to conceive it and to make notes or sketches of it. The law requires that the invention be reduced to some practical form; the inventor must actually build the device or file a patent application on it.

Record keeping. In order to prove the evolution of an invention from its conception to its reduction to practice, it is thus of utmost importance that proper and detailed daily records be kept by all personnel engaged in research and development activities. Our tribunals are not satisfied with records as evidence unless they are corroborated. For this reason, all entries in notebooks, sketches, and so on should be signed and dated not only by the person making them but also by a witness who is sufficiently knowledgeable to understand the subject matter in question. Properly organized research establishments have elaborate procedures for this purpose that are often invaluable in case of conflict.

THE PATENT OFFICE

The U.S. Patent Office is located in Crystal City, Virginia, opposite the National Airport of Washington, D.C. It is a part of the U.S. Department of Commerce and is headed by a commissioner. Its operations are on an enormous scale and its functions manifold. The Patent Office prints all U.S. patents and supplies them to the public at 50 cents each; and, since some comprise hundreds of pages, the purchase may be a real bargain. Through the Patent Office, also, the United States exchanges patent copies with the major industrial countries of the world, including the Soviet Union.

The search facilities. All subject matter has been classified by the Patent Office into more than 300 classes, which in turn are divided into more than 50,000 subclasses. All patents are assigned to the class and subclass to which the respective invention belongs, and the class indication appears on the printed patent. Conveniently arranged indexes with ample cross referencing make it a relatively easy task to pinpoint the class and subclass which cover any specific subject.

The Patent Office maintains a search room in which copies of the patents are available in consecutively numbered order and also arranged according to subclass. Searchers may also consult with the examiners in their rooms, where foreign patents and relevant publications are available.

Although the public libraries of major cities throughout the country also offer patent copies on their shelves, effective patent searching is carried out most conveniently in the Patent Office search room. Patent searching has developed into a separate profession requiring much skill, know-how, and experience. Independent searchers in Washington serve both patent attorneys and industry, and large, patent-conscious corporations often maintain their own patent-searching staffs in Washington.

Great efforts are presently being made to improve search methods and to introduce computerized techniques. At present, internationalization of patent systems is rendered more difficult by the fact that different classification systems are used by the various countries.

"The Official Gazette." An important function of the U.S. Patent Office is the publishing of the weekly *Official Gazette*, which, in addition to containing announcements and decisions, lists and abstracts all newly granted patents and registered trademarks. It is probably the world's most kaleidoscopic and least expensive treasure trove of information. Leafing through its pages, which mirror the combined ingenuity and inquisitiveness

of the world's technological geniuses, is a fascinating and rewarding experience.

The patents are abstracted numerically according to class, which makes locating the new patents in a specific category a simple matter. The *Official Gazette* also includes an alphabetic index of the inventors and their assignees, so that competitors' patents are easily located. It should be a "must" for every enterprise, large or small, to assign a technically knowledgeable man to survey the *Official Gazette* each week for developments in the company's area of activity.

The Patent Office, however, offers a subscription service. Once your classes of interest have been determined, you can enter your subscription for them, whereupon the Patent Office promptly supplies copies of all newly granted patents in these particular areas.

The examination. By far the most important task of the Patent Office is, of course, its function as the primary judge of the patentability of inventions. Expertness and experience in passing on patents are the major attributes of the Patent Office, and, once a patent has been duly issued, it is presumed to be valid. This presumption may be rebutted, and the federal courts may and do frequently declare patents invalid, particularly on evidence that was not available to the Patent Office. In general, however, it can be fairly stated that considerable weight is attached to the rulings and decisions of the Patent Office.

The Patent Office maintains a large corps of technically trained examiners—many of them with legal schooling—who are presumed to be knowledgeable in their fields. The caliber and uniformity of the examination procedure have suffered for many years, however, because of the considerable turnover among examiners. Since industry and private patent law firms pay higher salaries than the Patent Office, numerous examiners use the Patent Office as a springboard for their careers and leave their jobs as soon as a better opportunity is offered by a private enterprise. The situation is aggravated by a provision in the law which automatically grants every examiner the status of a patent agent upon retirement after four years of Patent Office employment. The Patent Office is attempting to alleviate the situation by raising the salaries and increasing the promotion opportunities of examiners.

The examining corps is divided into four major examining groups—mechanical, chemical, electrical, and general; and each group, in turn, has a number of subgroups. A patent application, after filing, is assigned to an examiner in one of these groups and, depending on the backlog in its respective group, is acted upon within about 4 to 18 months. The examiner communicates his findings to the applicant or his attorney in the form of an "office action," to which a reply may be filed within three months. The reply—referred to as an "amendment"—must deal with all the objections raised by the examiner and may change the claims to overcome the objections raised and prior art cited by the examiner. No new subject matter can be submitted in an amendment. The amended application is finally either allowed or rejected. The examiners may also be interviewed in person or by telephone—a procedure which is highly recommended to settle disputed points and to expedite the process. More recently, however, the Patent Office has encouraged examiners to initiate telephone interviews. The examination procedure is presently governed by so-called "compact prosecution," a term introduced a few years ago to reduce backlogs and to eliminate protracted examination.

Rejected applications may be appealed to the Board of Appeals, which is part of the Patent Office and has been established to review adverse decisions of the examiners. If the applicant is dissatisfied with the decision of the Board of Appeals, he may seek review either in the Court of Customs and Patent Appeal or by way of civil action against the Commissioner of Patents in the District Court for the District of Columbia.

AVOIDING PREMATURE ISSUE

Once the Patent Office has determined that the invention is patentable and the patent application is in proper form, it advises the applicant or his attorney by a "notice of allowance." A final fee has to be paid within three months, after which the patent is granted and printed. The 17-year protection begins with the date of the grant. This is in contrast to the provisions of many foreign countries in which the term of the patent starts with the filing of the patent application.

Assume that the product is not market-ready at the time when the patent application is allowed. This happens very frequently, particularly if the respective product requires extensive premarketing testing. A grant of the patent now will more often than not be undesirable. Since the invention is not ready to be commercially utilized, a portion of the 17-year period is wasted. Further, competitors are put on advance notice when the patent is published on the day of the grant.

U.S. patent law fortunately provides for a procedure that avoids premature grant of the patent. The applicant may abandon his patent application after refiling its disclosure in the form of a new patent application that receives a new number and date. However, the applicant may rely on the filing date of the abandoned application, so that continuity is established. The second application—usually referred to as a "continuation"—is examined anew, and in this manner valuable time is gained since the period between filing and allowance may take several years. Moreover, the procedure may be repeated several times, thereby further delaying the grant of the patent.

This practice is not entirely without risk, however, since, as stated, the continuation application is subject to a new examination by the Patent Office. It is thus conceivable that the continuation application may be rejected on a point that had not been questioned by the Patent Office in the original application. Actually, this happens only in rare instances. Patent Office examiners, after all, are human beings; if one of them has allowed a patent application, another—out of sheer inertia—will be loath to re-examine and undo the work of his colleague. In addition, many continuation applications are examined by the same examiner who dealt with the parent case.

Make sure that the patent covers the commercial product. The foregoing procedure is of significant importance for the purpose of delaying the grant of patents not only on fully developed inventions but, perhaps more so, on inventions that are modified or improved after an initial patent application has been filed. The construction or appearance of the commercial product is only rarely identical with the product as it was originally conceived. In many instances, there is little resemblance between the product as it originally appeared on the drawing board and the final version that reaches the consumer. The patent application, however, is usually filed at a stage at which only the drawing-board model was available, and, if the patent were allowed to issue on that version of the invention, the patent owner might find himself with a patent that does not properly cover the commercial product.

The remedy for this dilemma is to be found in the continuation procedure. If it is found that the allowed patent application does not effectively cover the ultimate product, the application should be abandoned in favor of a second application which is amplified to include the changes and modifications. As in continuation applications, the second application—referred to as a "continuation-in-part"—carries back to the filing date of the original application. Here again, this procedure may be repeated several times if the invention is altered by further modifications that are not disclosed in the first continuation-in-part.

Since premature issue can have grave consequences, a prudent patent policy requires that careful consideration be given to the stage of development of an invention before a patent is issued. If an important feature of the commercial product is not covered by the patent, it may be too late to obtain additional patent protection since the particular feature may not possess sufficient inventive attributes as to be patentably distinct from the previously patented aspects of the invention.

MARKING WITH PATENT NOTICE

As has previously been stated, patented products should be marked with the word "patent" followed by the number of the patent. Such marking serves two distinct objectives: First, it notifies the public of the patent and warns potential infringers. Second, it is also a promotional tool, as the general purchasing public associates patent markings with originality and improved quality.

Proper marking presents considerable practical difficulties particularly if the patented product is small in size and patents have been granted in several countries that require different notices. In order to avoid substantial loss of rights, the marking question should be carefully considered before the patented product is sold and exported.

SHOP RIGHTS AND ASSIGNMENTS

A fundamental concept of U.S. law is that a person is entitled to the fruits of his endeavors. In the absence of any agreement to the contrary, an inventor retains the ownership of the patent granted on his invention. If the inventor is employed and develops the invention while using the assets of the employer, the latter obtains a "shop right."

"Shop right" was defined in the 1960 decision of the Supreme Court, in *Banner Metals* v. *Lockwood, et al.*, 289 U.S. 178, as follows:

> Where an employee (1) during his hours of employment, (2) working with his employer's materials and appliances, (3) conceives and (4) perfects an invention for which he obtains a patent, he must accord his employer a nonexclusive right to practice the invention.

The inventor thus remains the owner of the patent but cannot use it against the employer.

Companies engaged in research and development generally require that all employee-made inventions pertaining to company business be assigned to the company in a written agreement. This assignment is tantamount to a sale in which the inventor conveys his rights in the invention and patent to the assignee. Assignments should be recorded in the Patent Office to give notice of the change of ownership. If this is not done, the assignee has no recourse against a third party who, in good faith, subsequently buys the patent from the defrauding inventor who has sold it a second time.

PATENT LITIGATION

A patent, although it pertains to technical subject matter, is a legal document whose scope and validity have ultimately to be interpreted by a court of law, not by technical experts. This fact is often overlooked when drafting the patent application, which is traditionally couched in "patentese" —jargon not easily understood outside the patent profession.

The fact that many patents, and particularly their claims, are not easily translated into the ordinary idiom is a source of many difficulties since the overwhelming majority of the judges who decide patent suits have no technical or scientific training. Jurisdiction of patent litigations rests exclusively with the federal courts, and, with the exception of the Court of Customs and Patent Appeals, patent cases are not decided by technically knowledgeable courts. Therefore, an essential element in any patent litigation is the education of the court as to the technical subject matter involved, a task which may prove insurmountable if the invention involved is complex. To aid the court in technical problems, the parties may call expert technical witnesses, who are usually reputable scientists or engineers in their fields. This, of course, contributes to the expense of the litigation, and patent suits tend to be exceptionally costly and protracted. For this reason, litigation is (and should be) avoided if at all possible. Many patent conflicts are thus settled out of court. Because of the high costs of patent litigation, "nuisance" suits for patent infringement are sometimes initiated (particularly by small inventors against large corporations) in the hope that the corporation will decide to pay a money settlement rather than invest in a costly defense.

Before embarking on patent litigation, the prospective litigants are well advised first to weigh the economics of the conflict. Except for minor costs, even a successful litigant does not often recover his litigation expense—as for preparatory work and counsel and expert witness fees—and since this expense can be considerable, it may exceed any damages awarded. Accused infringers often do better to take a license and pay royalties, while a victory for the patent owner may turn out to be of a Pyrrhic nature.

If litigation cannot be avoided, thorough preliminary steps should be taken. The validity of the patent involved should be exhaustively investigated, all relevant records should be collected and evaluated, prospective witnesses should be interviewed, and the most favorable jurisdiction in which to bring the action should be chosen.

In addition to infringement suits in which the patent owner charges unauthorized use of the patented invention, the law provides for a species of suit—a declaratory judgment action—in which a party threatened by the patent owner requests the court to declare the patent invalid. This type of action can be brought only if an actual controversy exists between the parties—for example, if the patent owner has notified a competitor that the competitor's product infringes the patent.

Because of the complexity of patent litigation, it is handled by a relatively small group of experienced patent counsel, and even large corporations with patent departments usually retain outside counsel to prosecute their litigation problems.

Inventions Submitted by Outsiders

Larger corporations receive numerous suggestions from outsiders for new products or improvements of the corporation's existing products. The proper handling of such suggestions presents considerable legal and public relations difficulties. They may have merit and therefore should be examined. On the other hand, the corporation may be engaged in research along the suggested lines and may even have solved the same problem before the suggestion was received.

Many concerns refuse to consider outside suggestions unless the submitter signs an agreement that no confidential relation is created between the parties and that the rights of the parties are to be governed by the patent laws. This practice, of course, does not work when the submitter sends in the details of his suggestion with his initial letter. To avoid lawsuits, such unsolicited suggestions should either be returned immediately or be kept in a confidential file under the care of a nontechnical person until the submitter has signed an agreement of the indicated nature.

Be sure your company has professional patent advice and liaison. The trite cliché "Ignorance of the law is no excuse" is applicable to the patent problems that constantly arise in any business. Many infringement situations could have been avoided, and patent rights maintained or strengthened, had corporate management not neglected professional advice on patent matters. It is simply prudent company policy to seek professional advice as soon as a patent problem arises. As the result of the staggering growth of the patent field—involving not only the procurement of patents here and abroad but also their defense and licensing and the surveillance of competitors' patent positions—patent awareness has steadily increased. Larger corporations maintain their own patent departments, employing patent practitioners and other trained personnel. Smaller enterprises seek advice from outside patent counsel. A good patent policy should consider the necessity for at least the following:

1. An adequate record-keeping system for research and development in which daily records are properly signed and corroborated.
2. Constant liaison between management and research and development.
3. A team of managers and professionals who appraise inventions and make decisions on the filing of patent applications domestically and abroad.
4. Adequate professional staff or retention of outside patent counsel for speedily filing patent applications.
5. A searching and surveillance service, including library facilities.
6. Established policy as to the right of the company to inventions made by employees.
7. Established policy as to unsolicited suggestions submitted by outsiders.

In the absence of patent protection, an imitator may produce "Chinese" copies of an object with impunity. This is true even though the object has particular functional or decorative features that identify the copy with a particular manufacturer, so that the copy is likely to be regarded as a product of the originator. The impact of this doctrine was forcefully brought home in 1964 by the famous *Stiffel* case—*Sears, Roebuck & Co.* v. *Stiffel Company*, 376 U.S. 225. Stiffel was the originator of the pole lamp, a vertical tube with lamp fixtures along the outside, the tube standing upright between floor and ceiling. Pole lamps proved a decided commercial success. So, knowing that patents had been held invalid for lack of invention, Sears, Roebuck marketed substantially identical lamps. Justice Black, speaking for the Supreme Court, said:

What Sears did was to copy Stiffel's design and to sell lamps almost identical to those sold by Stiffel. This it had every right to do under the federal patent laws. That Stiffel originated the pole lamp and made it popular is immaterial. "Sharing in the goodwill of an article unprotected by patent or trademark is the exercise of a right possessed by all—and in the free exercise of which the consuming public is deeply interested."

PROPOSED DEVELOPMENTS

The foregoing pages have presented a brief overview of the significance of inventions and the patent system for the benefit of corporate executives directing company operations where patents are, or should be, involved. It must be observed, however, that both the reader and the writer may have largely wasted their time and that this chapter may turn out to have been an exercise in futility. This is due to the likelihood that the basic concepts discussed may be overturned and replaced by radically different ones in the very near future.

Technical and scientific information is being generated in ever-increasing amounts, creating an enormously complex technology during the past few decades. Emerging agrarian nations, unequipped to cope with the technological revolution, are rapidly being industrialized. Internationalization of trade has reached fantastic proportions. During this dramatic transformation of the world scene, the patent systems of the world have tended to remain largely static. Now, however, they are in a state of upheaval unmatched by any of the other branches of the law. They have reached a point at which they can no longer function properly or meet the demands made on them. As a result, many fundamental changes are being proposed and effected throughout the world with a view to streamlining the various systems, to simplifying procedures, and to creating a functional patent system that will adequately serve the ever-increasing demand.

The United States occupies a special position in the picture. Although its patent system is perhaps the most advanced and developed, it differs from most, if not all, the systems of the other industrialized nations in both concept and procedure. This is a serious obstacle to international coopera- tion in the technological field. The Patent Reform Act of 1967, pending before Congress as this is written, is intended to remedy the situation by moving the U.S. system closer to the foreign systems and to lighten the burden of the Patent Office without sacrificing the basic purpose of patent protection. The Patent Reform Act proposes a multitude of drastic changes, two of which stand out.

First, as already noted, a fundamental doctrine of present U.S. patent law is that the patent is to be granted to the first inventor, who is not necessarily the first to apply for the patent. In case of conflict, the burdensome and time-consuming interference procedure is necessary to determine the true inventor. The patent systems of most other countries, by contrast, are based on the principle that the first to file for a patent is entitled to it. The Patent Reform Act proposes to discontinue the first-inventor principle in favor of the first-to-file doctrine, so that interference procedures would be unnecessary.

The proposal is opposed, however, by a large segment of the patent profession as contrary to the essence of our patent system, and several counterproposals have been made.

The second dramatic change is concerned with examination and publication. At the present time the patent systems of the world may be classified into examination systems and registration systems. The United States has an examination system; that is, patent applications are substantively examined before the patent is granted. Other examination system countries are Japan, Great Britain, the Scandinavian countries, and, until recently, Germany. According to the registration system, by contrast, patents are granted without substantive examination, and a third party who feels aggrieved by the patent must find recourse in the courts. The dominant registration countries are France and Italy. Owing to the ever-increasing amount of prior art, which at this stage is essentially unmanageable by conventional means, reliable examination of patent applications is rendered more and more difficult and time consuming. For this reason, the tendency of the examination-system countries is to adopt a hybrid registration-examination system. This system, which was first adopted by The Netherlands and then, recently, by Germany, has been proposed in the Patent Reform Act in somewhat modified form. According to this proposal, all patent applications will be published within a certain period—that is, between 18 and 24 months after filing—regardless of the status of the application. In this manner, the public obtains the immediate benefit of the invention. The examination of the application will be deferred until a request for examination is filed by the applicant or by a third person, who may be a competitor. The examination request must be accompanied by a prescribed fee. The application will be considered abandoned if no examination request is filed within five years of the filing date.

The rationale underlying this system is that, in many instances, the value or importance of an invention either is not known or cannot be foreseen at the time of the filing, while within the subsequent five years the applicant should be able to make up his mind whether the invention merits patenting. It can be reasonably assumed that, in the case of many inventions for which applications are initially filed, no examination will be requested and the examining burden of the Patent Office will thus be lightened. A competitor who feels threatened by a pending application is not affected by deferred examination since he has the right to request examination at any time during the five-year period. Thus the new system is designed to reduce wasteful examinations of applications that are ultimately abandoned. Since the applicant has the option to request examination immediately upon filing, no delay in the issuance of the patent need occur.

The Patent Reform Act would provide for many other important changes. It proposes that an application may be filed by the assignee of the inventor—for example, the corporation employing the inventor—and that the term of the patent be 20 years from the date of filing instead of the present 17 years from the date of grant.

Of late, the first series attempts have been made to interest the various countries in a unified world patent system with central search facilities. According to the most recent proposal, embodied in a suggested Patent-Cooperation Treaty, an applicant would file a patent application in an international office located in Switzerland. The international office, in cooperation with the search facilities of the major patent offices, would supply a search report. On the basis of the results of the search, the applicant could then decide to proceed with applications in selected countries whose patent offices would utilize the search report.

These proposals, which are viewed sympathetically by the U.S. authorities and sponsored by international patent organizations, have a long way to go before ripening into concrete treaties. There is no doubt, however, that the time will come when the patent systems of the world will be unified to provide for a world patent.

II. Trademarks

In a competitive, brand-conscious society like the United States, a business needs conspicuous identification to distinguish its products from those of competitors. The public becomes familiar with the identification, recognizes it in the marketplace, and associates it with the particular product. Trademarks are the principal means used by businesses for this purpose.

WHAT IS A TRADEMARK?

A trademark is a word, symbol, device, or combination thereof adopted and used by a manufacturer or merchant to identify his goods and distinguish them from those manufactured or sold by others. The antithesis of a trademark is the common descriptive name; for example, "Coca-Cola" versus "soft drink." The Shakespearean "What's in a name? That which we call a rose by any other name would smell as sweet" is antagonistic to trademark thinking. While the common descriptive or generic name of the goods may be freely used by anyone and has no distinguishing function, the trademark sets the goods of one source apart from those of another.

Marks assure consistent quality. A mark not only indicates origin but also guarantees to the purchaser that the quality of the goods bearing the mark will remain consistent. The housewife who prefers a particular brand of detergent expects to get a product of the same quality when she returns to buy another box of it. Consistency of quality is, however, not a prerequisite for preserving trademark rights. The owner of the mark has, of course, the right to change his merchandise. A 1969 "Dodge" automobile may thus be superior to the 1968 model without affecting the trademark situation.

Marks are valuable promotional tools. The third function of a mark lies in its advertising and promotional value; its ability to generate and maintain a demand for the trademarked product. A catchy trademark is an important selling asset, as every marketing executive knows. The promotional function of a trademark often overshadows that of indicating origin. Thus the source of goods in our era of mass distribution may remain unknown to the public, the chief purpose of the mark being promotional and stimulative. Few women will be able to identify the manufacturer of "Lux" soap, but the word "Lux" is nevertheless an American synonym for good soap.

Trade name distinguished from trademark. It is not uncommon to use the term "trade name" when reference to a trademark is actually intended, but a clear distinction exists between the two. While a trademark identifies a product, a trade name is descriptive of the manufacturer or merchant and applies to a business, vocation, or occupation. "Coca-Cola" is the trademark for a soft drink made by an enterprise whose trade name is The Coca-Cola Company. It is clear from this example that a certain overlapping of the two concepts does frequently occur if all or the significant part of a trade name also serves as a trademark. From a practical point of view, such overlapping does not result in any serious problems because, in case of conflict, a court will protect the trade name in the same manner as the trademark even if the former does not technically serve a trademark function.

TYPES OF MARKS

Service marks. With the rise of service industries, identification of services as well as products became desirable. This resulted in the development of service marks. Just as a trademark serves the function of indicating origin of goods, service marks are intended to connote the origin of services. Specific services in such fields as advertising, insurance, communication, and education may thus be properly identified by service marks. The names of television and radio programs are proper subject matter for service marks.

Collective marks. Collective marks are trademarks or service marks used by members of an association, union, or other collective group or organization to indicate membership. Such marks should be used, not by the owner-association, but only by its members.

Certification marks. Typical examples of certification marks are "Roquefort" for cheese and "Harris Tweed" for woven fabrics. Such marks certify regional origin or a set standard of quality which is met by several manufacturers.

It should now be apparent that the true purpose of marks is to protect not only the owner but also the public interest. Use of an established mark by an infringer on inferior or different goods damages the owner and misleads the public, because a customer may purchase the infringer's product in the mistaken belief that he is acquiring the product of the trademark owner. This dual purpose of trademarks is not stated in patent law since, in patent litigation, the patent owner merely seeks to protect his own rights.

STATUTORY PROTECTION

In contrast to patent rights, which come into existence only by statutory grants, rights in marks are acquired by use, not by grant. An inventor forfeits the exclusivity in his invention by failing to obtain a patent. A trademark owner, by contrast, must merely adopt and use his mark in commerce to acquire common-law rights that are superior to those of a latecomer who adopts the same or a confusingly similar mark. This does not mean, however, that statutory protection is not available or should not be applied for. On the contrary, registration of a trademark has many substantive and procedural advantages. A trademark registration is thus official recognition of the common-law rights of the owner.

Federal registration. Federal registration of marks is handled by the Trademark Operation of the Patent Office and is governed by the Lanham Act of 1946. Distinctive marks may be registered on the "principal register," while the "supplemental register" is intended for nondistinctive marks. A principal register registration is prima facie evidence of the registrant's ownership of the mark and exclusive right to use it in interstate commerce; and thus it is an important weapon in case of conflict. The existence of a registration permits the trademark owner to bring suit in federal court even in the absence of diversity of citizenship. Once the registration has been in force for five years, the right of the owner to use the mark in commerce may become incontestable under certain conditions. An important right resulting from a registration is that the importation of goods bearing an infringing mark can be stopped at customs.

State registration. The several states have their own trademark registration system. The effect of state registrations does not extend beyond the boundaries of the registering state and thus is exclusively directed to intrastate activities that are outside the jurisdiction of Congress.

CHOOSING A MARK

Since the common descriptive name of a product cannot serve as a trademark, the strongest marks are those which are fanciful and meaningless. Coined words and arbitrary symbols are marks entitled to the broadest protection because the particular word or symbol is unique and the creation of the owner. A good example of this type of mark is "Kodak." The principal problem with this kind of mark lies chiefly in marketing, since it may prove more difficult to make it familiar enough to establish the desired association between mark and product.

A trademark may, however, be an ordinary, arbitrary word as long as it is not descriptive of the goods. "Arrow" (shirts) is a proper trademark.

Many manufacturers have a tendency to prefer marks that are suggestive of the properties, effect, or use of the goods. Such marks supply information about the product in a subtle and indirect manner—for example, "Coppertone," for a suntan lotion. Suggestive marks are more difficult to defend and are therefore considered weaker marks.

Secondary meaning. A word or symbol that originally has no trademark significance may, as the result of prolonged use and promotion, acquire a new or secondary meaning in a particular trade which differs from the dictionary definition of the word or symbol. Once this stage of development has been reached, the word or symbol is a good trademark regardless of the initial shortcoming of the mark. This doctrine of secondary meaning is of significant interest in respect to words that are not inherently considered proper trademarks. In addition to prohibiting the assertion of trademark rights in descriptive words, the right to exclusivity in geographical terms, surnames, and laudatory expressions is severely restricted. But by being able to demonstrate that the original meaning of the word in question has been supplanted in relation to the particular goods, the owner may validly claim and maintain the desired exclusivity. While Johnson is a common surname and thus not originally capable of serving as a trademark, no one can seriously deny today that "Johnson" is a distinctive trademark for baby powder.

Although a descriptive word may thus eventually acquire a secondary meaning that indicates the source rather than the nature of the product, it is obviously not good practice to adopt such a word in the hope that it may some day become an effective trademark. In no event should a mark be adopted that is deceptively misdescriptive of the product since the courts are loath to acknowledge any rights in it even though a secondary meaning may be established.

In choosing a trademark, it is also important to check on any unpleasant implications or connotation the mark may have in any other language, especially if the manufacturer contemplates using the mark in foreign markets. The word "gift," for example, could be a trademark for toothpaste in English-speaking countries, but it means "poison" in German.

The generic mark. Strange as it may seem, one of the greatest dangers to a trademark is that it may become too popular. When a trademark becomes a household word and when it begins to function as a noun to identify the product rather than the source, it is in danger of becoming part of the public domain and thus no longer the property of the originator and no longer capable of distinguishing his goods.

The history of trademarks is full of sad examples of lost trademark rights because of degeneration of the mark into the common descriptive term for the product. "Aspirin," "cellophane," and "thermos" were once good trademarks but have lost their trade distinctiveness and no longer identify the products of particular manufacturers. A mark may become generic because of the lack of a suitable or simple common term for the product. The public cannot be expected to ask for acetylsalicylic acid when it gets the same thing by requesting aspirin.

The manufacturer should therefore make certain that a simple descriptive term is available to encompass his and competitors' goods. The tendency of a mark to become generic can also effectively be countered by proper and distinctive use of the mark both on the product and on promotional material. Thus the mark should always be capitalized or set off in quotation marks or italics. In promotional material, it should preferably appear in distinct and boldface type. If the mark is registered, it should be followed by the symbol ®. Nonregistered trademarks can be identified by the symbol "TM" or the word "Trademark."

USE OF ANOTHER'S TRADEMARK

A patent grant conveys the absolute right to exclude others from making, using, or selling the patented invention. Trademark rights, by contrast, are more limited. A competitor may legitimately use another's trademark as long as the use is truthful.

The landmark decision on this point was rendered by the United States Supreme Court in 1924 in *Prestonettes, Inc.* v. *Coty*, 264 U.S. 359. The defendant bought genuine "Coty" perfume in bulk, rebottled it, and marketed it under a label that read: "Prestonettes, Inc., not connected with Coty, states that the contents are Coty's . . . (name) . . . perfume." Coty brought suit for trademark infringement and asked for injunctive relief. Justice Holmes in his opinion stated:

> The trademark does not confer a right to prohibit the use of the word or words. It is not a copyright. A trademark only gives a right to prohibit the use of it so far as to protect the owner's good will against the sale of another's product as his. When the mark is used in any way that does not deceive the public we see no such sanctity in the word as to prevent it being used to tell the truth. It is not taboo.

The holding in the *Prestonettes* case has been severely criticized. Thus, for example, in *Bourjois, Inc.* v. *Helmida Laboratories, Inc.*, 106 F. 2d 174, the court stated:

In that case (Prestonettes) Mr. Justice Holmes lent the prestige of his great name to a doctrine that does not appeal very greatly to the sense of fairness of the ordinary man.

Notwithstanding the criticism, however, the doctrine of the *Prestonettes* case is still controlling.

In 1961 the Christian Dior enterprises, owners of the "Dior" trademark,, failed in their attempt to stop a New York City department store from advertising and selling unauthorized copies of "Dior" originals as "Dior copies" or "reproductions of Dior originals." The truth was deemed to be an absolute defense in this case of *Société Comptoir de l'Industrie Couturière, Établissement Boussac et al.,* v. *Alexander's Department Stores, Inc.,* 109 F. Supp. 594.

The use of another's trademark is, however, prohibited if it tends to be injurious to the reputation and goodwill of the business of the trademark owner. A typical case in point is *Polaroid Corp.* v. *Permarite,* 186 F. Supp. 755. The defendant had purchased genuine but surplus "Polaroid" goggle lenses from the U.S. Government. The lenses had been manufactured during World War II and were of large size for use by pilots. The defendant cut the lenses to fit ordinary sunglasses, whereby distortion resulted. Further, the Polaroid Corporation had in the meantime considerably improved its new sunglass lenses. The defendant advertised the product as follows: "Sunglasses with genuine Polaroid lenses. U.S. Government surplus, Polaroid lenses $2.49, frame by Permarite." The word "Polaroid" appeared in larger letters than the remainder of the text.

The court held that

> . . . buyers may reasonably be expected to conclude that Plaintiff made or was responsible for having made the lenses as a whole as lenses of sunglasses, contrary to the fact.

The defendant was therefore enjoined.

The use of a competitor's trademark for comparative advertising purposes has increased widely during the past few years, particularly in the automobile industry. Ford thus asserts that its cars are quieter than the Rolls Royce. Renault claims a lower rate of gas consumption than the Volkswagen has. This use of another's trademark is considered objectionable by many trademark purists. It should be distinguished from "teasing" advertising—as, for example, is represented by the Hertz-Avis battle—or from implied use of another's trademark as symbolized by the slogan "Look is bigger than life."

TRADEMARK LICENSING

Licensing of trademarks is of considerable practical importance in an expanding economy. A manufacturer in the East may not be able to satisfy the demand for a popular product in the West, and manufacture of the product by a licensee in the West reduces distribution problems. Licensing is, however, fraught with pitfalls, and stringent safeguards have to be taken lest the owner's rights in the mark be diluted or lost.

It will be remembered that an important function of a mark is to protect the public, not only the owner. In granting another the right to use his mark, the owner must make sure that the public will continue to associate the mark with a particular product or standard of quality. Otherwise confusion or deception may result. The public interest is deemed to be satisfied if the owner sets the quality standards for the product and maintains and actually exercises control over the nature of the goods which are manufactured by the licensee under the mark. A quality control and inspection clause is thus necessary in every trademark-license agreement. If the owner fails adequately to control the goods of the licensee or knowingly acquiesces in the licensee's failure to live up to the set standards, the rights of the owner in the mark may be considered abandoned.

The theory underlying trademark licensing is that the goodwill created by the licensee's use of the mark actually benefits the owner and that the owner and the licensee are related companies as far as their activities involving the mark are concerned. If the trademarked product is also patented, a combined patent-and-trademark-license agreement is often of advantage to the owner. Since a patent has a limited life, while a trademark may last forever and, in fact, increases in value upon prolonged use, the license may survive the term of the patent.

III. Copyrights

In the present context, copyrights are perhaps best discussed in comparison with patents. Although both patent and copyright protection in the United States spring from the same constitutional clause—recited in the opening paragraph of this chapter—these two types of property rights are essentially different in respect to subject matter, scope, standards, procedure, and duration. A patent is directed to innovation and progress in the technical and scientific fields, while a copyright protects authors of literary, dramatic, musical, artistic, and other intellectual works.

The right conferred by a patent is absolute; it permits the owner to exclude all others from using, making, and selling the patented thing. By contrast, the copyright owner has a remedy only against one who has actually copied his work. If another, without having had access to the copyrighted work, independently produces a similar creation, he may reap the benefit of it in spite of the copyright. Copyright, as the inverse of the word implies, is essentially the right to copy, to the exclusion of others.

Vastly different standards apply to the requirements for patent and copyright protection, respectively. The criteria for patents are novelty, utility, and nonobviousness. The sole standard for copyright protection is originality. An author is accordingly entitled to copyright protection as long as his work is original and is not copied from another's.

Procedural requirements also highlight the differences in standards. The inventor must persuade the Patent Office of the patentability of his invention by explaining it in detail and in a prescribed form, which requires a high degree of technical skill. A copyright is, however, secured by merely publishing the work with a prescribed copyright notice. Subsequent registration of the copyrighted work with the Copyright Office is merely a formality. The Copyright Office does not examine or grant copyrights; it merely registers them.

Another important difference between the two types of protection lies in the duration of the protection. The term of a patent is 17 years, and it cannot be extended. Copyrights last for 28 years and are renewable for a further 28-year term.

What Can Be Copyrighted?

The Copyright Law lists 13 broad classes of works in which copyright may be claimed. These classes may be briefly summarized as follows: books; newspapers and periodicals; lectures and scripts prepared for oral delivery; dramatic works; musical compositions; maps; works of art; reproductions of works of art; drawings or sculptural works of scientific or technical nature; photographs; commercial prints or labels; motion picture photoplays; and motion pictures other than photoplays.

The Copyright Notice

The copyright notice is the most important requirement for obtaining copyright on a work that is to be published. Once a work has been published without proper copyright notice, copyright protection is permanently lost; the work is in the public domain and can be freely copied. A proper copyright notice includes the following elements:

1. The word "Copyright," the abbreviation "Copr." or the symbol ©. The use of the symbol is to be preferred since it can be used in securing copyright in foreign countries under the provision of the Universal Copyright Convention.
2. The name of the copyright owner.
3. The year of publication.

An adequate notice may thus read: © American Management Association 1969.

Common-law copyright versus statutory copyright in unpublished works. An unpublished work may be eligible for one of two kinds of copyright— common law or statutory.

Common law recognizes that an artist or writer has a personal property interest in his work. This property interest arises as soon as the artistic idea has been expressed in some tangible form—for example, in writing. Under common law, the author has an absolute right to his unpublished works without time limit. The common-law right ends, however, on publication, dedication to the public, or deliberate registration to obtain statutory protection.

Statutory copyright for unpublished works is available for only certain types of works. Musical compositions, works of art, dramas, motion pictures, and drawings and sculptural works of scientific character may be statutorily protected by complying with certain requirements. Unpublished books or periodicals, however, are not subject to statutory copyrights.

Statutory copyright for published works. Three steps are necessary to obtain statutory copyright protection:

1. Copies of the work bearing the copyright notice have to be produced.
2. Publication of the work, with the copyright notice, must take place.
3. The claim to the copyright must be promptly registered in the Copyright Office in a prescribed form, accompanied by the required fee.

Suits against infringers can be brought only after the three steps have been complied with.

Major revisions of the Copyright Law are contemplated and proposals to this effect are before Congress at this time.

The protection of industrial and intellectual property rights—of which patents, trademarks, and copyrights are the prime examples—is the key to the progress and success of many companies. The problems they entail are manifold and cut across the broad spectrum of business activity from research and development to marketing and advertising. To stimulate awareness of these problems has been the sole purpose of this chapter.

Taxation of Income from International Business Transactions

Paul D. Seghers

EVEN A BRIEF SUMMARY OF SIGNIFICANT LEGAL PRINCIPLES WHICH A BUSI-
nessman should be aware of in connection with international business
transactions would far exceed the scope of this volume. This chapter deals
almost exclusively with legal principles relating to U.S. taxation of income
from international business transactions. Every executive concerned with
foreign trade needs to have a general understanding of these principles
in order to minimize tax burdens, to avoid unnecessary penalties, and to
obtain available tax and related benefits. Such an overall grasp is essential
from the moment of embarking on the stormy sea of foreign trade,
through the years of business operations in the international field, until
the sale or liquidation of the business.

U.S. foreign fund controls initiated by President Johnson's January 1,
1968, Executive Order 11387 and the U.S. Department of Commerce
"Foreign Direct Investment Regulations" also are of significance to all

PAUL D. SEGHERS is an attorney with his own firm in New York City. He is a
Certified Public Accountant in New York and Illinois.

U.S. businesses having funds or property abroad or deriving income from abroad.

Now that taxes—both foreign and domestic—normally swallow up more than half the profits of business, it is vital for the business executive to have a working knowledge of tax dangers and possibilities, even though he eventually must turn to specialists within this field for guidance in making final decisions and in executing them.

Compared with the complexities of tax statutes, the common law is an admirable model of common sense. Principles of law (that is, of common law) change very slowly—tax statutes can be and frequently are changed radically overnight, often retroactively.

Many well-established principles of U.S. income tax law, unchanged over the years despite a constant output of tax statutes and statutory amendments, were swept aside in 1962 at the Treasury's demand, and efforts in that direction continue. Hence any statement of *principles* of U.S. income taxation is today far more difficult to make than it was before 1962, and it is of lesser value as a guide in obtaining an overall understanding of U.S. taxation of income from international business transactions. Nevertheless, it is possible to obtain a general idea of the tax consequences of overseas business activity.

Making a choice of forms and methods for doing business abroad. Two basic tax questions must first be asked: (1) what corporate forms (domestic or foreign) and (2) what methods of operation are available and desirable? In order even to consider what choices are available, it is necessary to have some understanding of how the United States taxes income of various kinds that is earned abroad by domestic (U.S.) corporations and by foreign corporations owned by U.S. stockholders.

U.S. tax advantages may be in the form of a smaller tax "bite" out of every dollar of income earned or of a postponement of the time of payment of the tax. *The ultimate objective is a maximum U.S. dollar return after all taxes.* In evaluating the advantages of the different forms and methods of earning income abroad, the ultimate payoff should be kept constantly in mind—how many U.S. dollars earned net on the investment will be left after all tax bites and recovery of the capital invested. All that follows is written in the light of that objective.

THE BASIC APPROACH

Determination of what is taxable income from foreign sources, when it is taxable, how it is taxable, and at what rates depends on the classification of the taxpayer and of the person (corporate or individual) that earns the income, as well as the nature of the income itself. The ultimate answers to these questions must be found in the provisions of the Internal Revenue Code of 1954, as modified by a great number of amendments constantly being enacted by Congress and as interpreted in the U.S. Treasury Regulations and by courts.

Unless otherwise indicated, all that is stated in this chapter relates to U.S. taxes on income derived by corporations from normal business activities abroad. Prior to the 1962 act, it could be stated positively that a U.S. taxpayer was taxable on income from business activities only if the activities were those of the taxpayer and if the income was earned or received by the taxpayer; that a foreign corporation was subject to U.S. tax only on its income from U.S. sources; and that there was no U.S. penalty imposed on stockholders for failure to cause a foreign corporation to pay dividends out of its business income from non-U.S. sources. Today no such sweeping statements can be made.

The "source" of income. Income from the sale of goods purchased by the seller is deemed, for U.S. income tax purposes, to have its source in this country if title to the resold goods (and the risks and benefits of ownership) passes from the seller to the buyer in the United States; otherwise the source is deemed to be outside the United States. Where the goods are produced by the seller in one country and sold (that is, title is passed) in another country to the buyer, the source of the income is apportioned between the two countries. The source (country of realization) of income from other activities is determined, for U.S. income tax purposes, in accordance with more or less specific rules. For example, the source of rental income is the country where the rented property is situated; the source of patent royalty income is the country that granted the patent. The source of income from rendering services is the country where they are rendered. Rules for determining the source of other kinds of income are more technical and complicated.

How U.S. Corporations Are Taxed on Foreign Income

A company that is incorporated in the United States and derives most of its income from sources in this country is subject to U.S. tax on its entire income. However, if any portion of its income is also subject to tax in the country where it is earned, the U.S. tax on this portion may be reduced or eliminated by a "foreign tax credit" allowed against the U.S. tax on such income.

Western Hemisphere trade corporations. A U.S. corporation which conducts its business entirely in the Western Hemisphere and derives not less than 95 percent of its income from sources outside the United States and not less than 90 percent from the active conduct of business is allowed a special "Western Hemisphere trade corporation" deduction equal to 14/48ths of its otherwise taxable income. This has the effect of reducing the tax to about 15.5 percent on the first $35,300 of actual income and to 34 percent on all income in excess of that amount. Such a U.S. corporation is allowed credit against its U.S. tax on income from any foreign country for the amount of foreign tax paid on this income. (It should be noted that the U.S. tax rates cited here and elsewhere in this chapter are those in effect prior to January 1, 1968, and do not give effect to the 10 percent surcharge tax, with its 10 percent reduction in the amount of the foreign tax credit.)

U.S. possession corporations. A U.S. corporation that derives most of its income from business activities in a U.S. possession (other than the Virgin Islands) may be exempt from U.S. tax on all its income from sources outside the United States.

The use of the words "may be" in such general statements in this chapter indicates that they are subject to many conditions and exceptions, but that the stated result can be achieved if the proper steps are taken. To give an example: Income earned in Puerto Rico, which otherwise would be exempt from U.S. tax under the provisions just summarized, loses its exemption and immediately becomes subject to U.S. tax if the income is received directly by the exempt corporation in the United States. Yet that same income would be exempt if first deposited in a bank in Puerto Rico, even if the funds were immediately withdrawn and remitted to the corporation's own bank account in the United States.

This example emphasizes that general statements regarding U.S. taxes on foreign income, while useful in pointing out possible tax consequences of using various corporate forms and methods of doing business abroad, are not to be taken as comprehensive statements of the law.

Before leaving the subject of activities in Puerto Rico, it should be mentioned that income earned there may be subject to tax under the laws of that possession (at rates lower than the U.S. tax). However, there are possibilities of obtaining exemption from Puerto Rican tax on income from certain activities. Such income earned by a U.S. corporation may be entirely tax-free. It is even possible for such a corporation to be liquidated, tax-free, if it is a subsidiary of another U.S. corporation. Thus the capital produced by its business activities in Puerto Rico may remain undiminished by taxes and be available for use in producing more income, as long as these funds are not distributed to individual shareholders.

U.S. tax on corporations improperly accumulating surplus. This tax is applicable only to U.S. source income and is not applicable to a foreign corporation having less than $100,000 of accumulated surplus.

U.S. TAXATION OF FOREIGN CORPORATIONS

Except for income "effectively connected" with U.S. activities, a corporation organized under the laws of any country other than the United States is subject to U.S. tax only on income from sources within the United States. Prior to 1962 this meant that such a corporation could accumulate income earned abroad and use it to earn further income, without its first being depleted by the immediate payment of U.S. tax. Subject to the exception mentioned earlier, this still is literally true; but, for the reasons given later, since 1962 this is no longer true in substance in many cases.

U.S. TAXATION OF U.S. SHAREHOLDERS OF FOREIGN CORPORATIONS

Under the 1962 amendments of the Internal Revenue Code a U.S. corporate shareholder of a "controlled" foreign corporation may be subject currently to U.S. tax on its undistributed income, even though the taxpayer may never actually or constructively receive any of this income.

"Subpart F" and foreign funds controls. The Code provisions that embody the novel device of taxing as dividend income that which is *not* income of the taxpayer is commonly spoken of as "Subpart F." Strangely enough, the constitutionality of this tax provision has not yet been tested in any court proceeding. Now, on the authority of the President's January 1, 1968, Executive Order 11387, U.S. shareholders are required to cause foreign corporations in which they own interests of 10 percent or more to pay out certain specified portions of their income within the taxable year in which the income is earned. This is not a tax measure but an administrative order which in many cases will result in the immediate realization of income and the immediate payment of U.S. tax on income that otherwise would be retained abroad, used to earn more income, and ultimately brought home to benefit U.S. shareholders.

How Subpart F taxes the U.S. shareholder. Subpart F requires certain U.S. owners of stock in certain foreign corporations to include in their income, subject to tax as dividends, their distributable share of certain kinds of undistributed corporate income. For this purpose a "U.S. person" (citizen, resident, or corporation) is deemed to be a U.S. shareholder only if he (including certain family members and associates) is deemed to own, directly or indirectly, 10 percent or more of the voting power in a foreign corporation.

A foreign corporation is held to be controlled and its U.S. shareholders are subject to these tax provisions if more than 50 percent of its voting power is owned by such shareholders. U.S. shareholders so taxed on imaginary dividends which they have not received are allowed the same foreign tax credit (if any) to which they would be entitled if they had actually received such an amount as a dividend. (No duplicate credit is allowed when an amount, previously taxed as an imaginary dividend, is thereafter received, tax-free, as an actual dividend.)

The law which imposes the tax on imaginary dividends is extremely technical and impossible to explain in simple terms. One of its objectives may have been to drive U.S. corporations to abandon the use of foreign corporations as a means of operating abroad. Another objective may have been to require so much planning and effort to minimize the tax burden under the complicated provisions of Subpart F that attention would be diverted from the weight of the burden on overseas business and the doubtful constitutionality of this form of tax. Be that as it may, any business executive faced with the necessity of making decisions regarding forms and methods of doing business abroad must have at least a general understanding of this taxing device.

Income taxable as an imaginary dividend. A U.S. shareholder is taxable under Subpart F on his (or its) distributive share of the sum of three amounts:

1. The Subpart F income of the controlled foreign corporation, earned in its taxable year, which ends in or with that of the U.S. shareholder.
2. The Subpart F income of such a corporation which was not so taxed in a prior year because it was deferred as foreign trade corporation income under Subpart G, but which becomes taxable in the current year because of a decrease in certain assets of the corporation.
3. Income of the controlled foreign corporations not otherwise taxable or not previously taxed under Subpart F equal to any increase during its taxable year in the amount of certain property owned by it in the United States.

Income otherwise classified as Subpart F income may, however, be excluded from such classification pursuant to the "30 : 70" rule or the minimum distribution exemption discussed later.

Gain on the disposition of shares of a controlled foreign corporation. Gain on the sale or exchange of stock in a controlled foreign corporation may be taxable as ordinary income (rather than as capital gain) to the extent of the corporation's undistributed and previously untaxed profits accumulated after December 31, 1962.

An exchange includes the receipt of a sum of money in the event of partial or complete liquidation of a corporation. The rules for determining the circumstances in which gain is so taxed are too technical to be given here. One exception is noteworthy—where the foreign corporation is an LDCC (Less Developed Country Corporation) and the shareholder is deemed to have held its stock for more than ten years, no part of the gain may be taxed as a dividend.

What Is Subpart F Income?

Subpart F income consists of the following:

1. Certain income derived from insuring U.S. risks.
2. Foreign base company income of the following classes:

   + Certain foreign personal holding company income (in the form of income from passive ownership of stocks, bonds, patents, rental property, and so on).
   + Foreign base company sales income.
   + Foreign base company service income.

No income of the foreign corporation is deemed to be Subpart F income unless it comes within one of these classifications. Hence, as will be seen, many types of income—such as from the sale by the foreign corporation of goods it manufactures abroad—are not currently taxable to its U.S. shareholders as Subpart F income. A foreign corporation is, however, itself subject to U.S. tax on income it derives from sources in this country—for example, from its sale of goods *in the United States*—or on foreign income "effectively connected" with activities here.

Under the 30:70 rule, if less than 30 percent of the *gross* income of the foreign corporation would be classified as Subpart F income, it is deemed to have no such income; if it has more than 70 percent, *all* its income for that year is deemed to be Subpart F income.

Foreign base company sales income. This classification imposes a U.S. income tax penalty on income from the sale abroad of goods manufactured here or in another country by a related company. However, this tax can be avoided if the foreign corporation manufactures abroad the goods it sells or incorporates a separate enterprise in each foreign country in which purchased goods are sold for use or consumption.

The penalty—in the form of immediate U.S. tax on income *not* received by the U.S. taxpayer—applies where the foreign corporation sells goods for use, consumption, or disposition outside the country in which it is incorporated and where such goods are purchased from or for the account of a related person or corporation or are sold to or for a related person or corporation. Furthermore, in some circumstances goods manufactured by a foreign corporation in one country and sold by a branch it maintains in another country may be held to be taxable as Subpart F income. This falls under the "branch rule," which treats such a branch as if it were a separate corporation that purchases from the factory the goods it sells.

Where the foreign corporation buys from a U.S. parent company goods which it further processes before sale, the question arises: Are the goods sold by the controlled foreign corporation purchased from the U.S. company? If so, the income from the resale of such goods may be Subpart F income and may immediately be subject to U.S. tax. If the goods sold are deemed to be *produced* by the foreign corporation which sells them, they are not deemed to be purchased by it. Thus it is essential in such a case to determine whether the activities of the foreign corporation constitute *production* of the goods sold. To aid in making this determination, there is a "percentage of added cost" test: a "common understanding" rule; and the rule that mere labeling, repackaging, or assembly does not constitute production. The term "assembly" is the one most likely to cause dispute.

These Subpart F provisions of the 1962 law penalize what had once been an ideal method of entering a foreign market—through the use of a foreign subsidiary that purchases goods from its parent manufacturing company and resells them in many countries through distributors, branches, and selling sub-subsidiaries. Today, all such income of the first subsidiary (except that derived from sales in its country of incorporation) may be, and usually is, immediately subject to U.S. tax—despite uncertainty as to the ultimate realization or receipt of such income by any U.S. taxpayer.

It still is possible, however, for a controlled foreign corporation to make sales in foreign countries without becoming liable for U.S. or foreign tax until the resulting income is brought home and is subject to U.S. tax in the hands of individual U.S. shareholders.

When the Subpart F penalty does not apply to sales abroad. One way to avoid the Subpart F penalty, as mentioned previously, is for a U.S. corporation to own a U.S. corporation which manufactures products in Puerto Rico and thus is exempt from both U.S. and Puerto Rican taxes on its income. In such a situation, there may be no tax even on the gain realized by the parent company upon receipt of the assets of the subsidiary when it is eventually liquidated.

Another way to avoid the Subpart F penalty is for the U.S. parent company to own the stock of a foreign corporation that manufactures goods in Ireland for sale in other countries, with no U.S. tax on its income and no Irish tax on such income for ten years or more. However, the parent company would be taxable on any gain realized on the receipt of the assets of such a corporation upon its ultimate liquidation. Furthermore, to the extent of the foreign corporation's previously undistributed income accumulated after 1962, such a gain on liquidation might be taxable as if it were received by the parent company as a dividend. If the foreign subsidiary had paid any foreign income tax on the income thus taxed to the U.S. parent company, the parent would be allowed credit for the foreign tax against the U.S. tax on the amount taxed as a dividend. This may result in *less* tax than there would be at the capital gain rate.

Foreign base company service income. Income received by a controlled foreign corporation for services it renders outside the country in which it is incorporated, to or for the benefit of a related person or company, constitutes Subpart F income. Services rendered directly to an unrelated person may fall within this classification if they are connected with sales made to such person by a corporation or person related to the foreign corporation.

Subpart F foreign personal holding company income. Foreign personal holding company income, as defined in Subpart F, consists principally of so-called passive income—dividends, interest, rents, gains on sales of securities, and the like. However, there are many exceptions. For example, if a controlled foreign corporation (CFC) receives dividends or interest from another CFC which is a less developed country corporation (LDCC), such income does not constitute Subpart F income to the extent that the recipient CFC *increases* in the same year the aggregate amount of its investments in certain less developed countries or LDCC securities or debt obligations. If the aggregate amount of such investments of the CFC *decreases* in any subsequent year, the amount of the decrease then becomes Subpart F income (limited to the amount previously excluded from Subpart F income and not previously taxable to the U.S. shareholder because of an increase in such investments.)

CAPTIVE FOREIGN INSURANCE COMPANIES

Income of a foreign corporation that is derived from the insurance of non-U.S. risks is not Subpart F income and hence is not taxable to its U.S. shareholders until it is distributed to them as a dividend. This means that, prior to Executive Order 11387, it was possible to accumulate all such income abroad, free of all income tax. The funds representing such accumulated profits could be used in many ways to produce further tax-free (actually, tax-deferred) income.

Certain investment income which otherwise would be classified as Subpart F income is not so treated if it is received by a foreign company in connection with its insurance business.

Because of these and other tax and nontax advantages, many multi-national U.S. corporations have organized so-called captive insurance companies. These are used to provide insurance protection of all kinds for foreign property and casualty risks, directly or indirectly, through reinsurance. The gross income of such a CFC can afford a substantial umbrella, under the 30:70 rule, for income which otherwise would be taxable to its U.S. parent company as Subpart F income.

LESS DEVELOPED COUNTRY CORPORATIONS

Briefly stated, a less developed country corporation is a controlled foreign corporation, actively engaged in the conduct of business, 80 percent of whose income is from sources in less developed countries and 80 percent of whose assets during the entire year consist of property of certain kinds in less developed countries.

Less developed countries comprise all the countries outside the Iron Curtain, with the exceptions prescribed in the statute (Sec. 955) and by Presidential Executive Order. Among these excluded countries are the industrial countries of Europe, the United Kingdom, Canada, Japan, non-Communist China, and a few small nations such as Monaco. Ireland, however, enjoys the advantage—for U.S. income tax purposes—of being classed as a less developed country.

The U.S. tax consequences of a foreign corporation's being classed as an LDCC are widely misunderstood. Certain tax advantages do flow from that classification, but a U.S. shareholder does not escape taxation on the undistributed Subpart F income of a controlled foreign corporation by reason of its being an LDCC.

One of the U.S. tax advantages of an LDCC is that dividends paid by it to another foreign corporation may escape classification as Subpart F income in the circumstances described earlier under *Subpart F foreign personal holding company income.*

Another advantage of LDCC classification is that dividends received (or imaginary dividends deemed to be received) by a U.S. shareholder corporation from an LDCC are *not* subject to "gross-up" in the computation of the foreign tax credit.

A third possible advantage is that a U.S. shareholder who has held the stock of an LDCC for more than ten years may obtain capital gain rather than dividend income treatment on the sale or other disposition of such stock.

THE "MINIMUM DISTRIBUTION" EXEMPTION

A U.S. corporate shareholder of a controlled foreign corporation may elect not to be taxed on any of the latter's Subpart F income for any year in which the amount of profits distributed to and received by the shareholder meets a percentage test prescribed in the Code.* This test is designed to insure that the aggregate of foreign and U.S. taxes payable on the income of the foreign corporation and on the distribution received by the U.S. shareholder equal about 90 percent of the U.S. tax on an equal amount of income. For example, if the U.S. tax rate is 48 percent and the effective foreign tax rate is not higher than 43 percent, the enterprise is allowed to retain, in the aggregate, about 57 percent of its before-tax income without any further U.S. tax on the balance of the income for that year until it is distributed to a U.S. stockholder. (Where the foreign tax is levied at a higher effective rate than 43 percent, no U.S. tax is payable under Subpart F.)

This provision affords acceptable relief to well-established U.S. multi-

---

* Subpart F, Section 951 *et seq.* of the Internal Revenue Code of 1954, as amended.

national organizations which already have expanded foreign operations to the point where the receipt of the required amount of dividends from its foreign subsidiaries presents no problem and does not result in serious interference with its desired rate of growth abroad.

Thus the minimum distribution provisions not only provide an escape from much of the miseries of Subpart F, but also may offer some unexpected benefits.

An Individual's Option to Be Taxed as a Corporation

An individual is given the option to be taxed on his share of undistributed Subpart F income as if it were received by a U.S. corporation. Should this be elected, the individual thereafter is taxable on the amount of any actual distributed income received by him as if it were received by a U.S. corporation. In certain circumstances, election of this method may afford tax benefits. One advantage is the allowance of the "deemed paid" foreign tax credit, which is permitted only against U.S. tax on a U.S. *corporation* taxable on the actual or imaginary receipt of a dividend from a foreign subsidiary. By obtaining this credit, an individual may eliminate any immediate U.S. tax payment on Subpart F income for which he would otherwise be taxable.

Foreign Tax Credit

A U.S. citizen, resident, or corporation that pays or is deemed to have paid a foreign income tax is allowed to *deduct* the full amount of this tax in computing income subject to U.S. tax or, as an alternative, to *credit* a portion or all of this amount against (that is, treat it as a reduction in) the U.S. tax on the foreign-source taxable income. This credit is limited to the amount of U.S. tax on the foreign income.

No *deduction* is allowable for *any* foreign income tax if credit is claimed for any such tax. However, the taxpayer may elect either method in any year and may change that election at any time prior to the running of the statute of limitations on assessment of additional tax for that year.

Generally, it is more advantageous to claim credit for foreign taxes than to take them as deductions. Credit is allowable for taxes levied by foreign governments on net income or in lieu of net income taxes. Credit is not allowable for taxes of any other kind, such as on sales or gross income.

Any excess of foreign tax over the U.S. tax on foreign-source income (computed on either the per-country or overall basis) may be carried back two years and forward five years. There are various restrictions and penalties on any change in the method of computing this limitation on the allowable foreign tax credit.

A failure to comply with the provisions of IRC, Sec. 6038 (*b*), which calls for the filing of information regarding foreign corporations in which a U.S. taxpayer owns an interest, may result in a reduction in the amount of foreign tax credit otherwise allowable.

Caveat. A study of the tax effect of any new step or change in the form or method of doing business abroad should include a careful consideration of the related foreign tax credit effects. The complexity of these provisions results in both the dangers of unnecessary losses and penalties and the possibilities of substantial tax benefits.

EARNINGS, PROFITS, AND TAXABLE INCOME

Earnings and profits generally may be taken to mean the amount of actual income minus the sum of all costs, expenses, and losses. For this purpose foreign income taxes are treated as expenses. Accumulated earnings and profits as of any date usually means the amount remaining after all distributions to stockholders have also been deducted. However, the Code and Regulations at times give different meanings to these terms. Let us consider some of the problems commonly encountered in determining taxable income from exports and overseas activities and in determining earnings and profits of foreign corporations.

Sec. 482 adjustments of intercompany sales. Internal Revenue Code Sec. 482 authorizes the Internal Revenue Service to "distribute, apportion, or allocate gross income, deductions, credits, or allowances between or among" related businesses if IRS finds this "necessary in order . . . clearly to reflect the income" of any such business.

It is the position of IRS that this provision of the Code gives it authority to increase the taxable income of any U.S. taxpayer if, in the opinion of IRS, any sale of goods between related corporations or other related "persons" is made at a price other than an arm's length price.

The attempts by IRS to apply this rule to sales between U.S. corporations and their Western Hemisphere trade corporation (WHTC) and foreign corporation subsidiaries constitute one of the most serious and harassing problems with which U.S. manufacturers are confronted in selling their products abroad.

The courts have held, in effect, that an arm's length price is the price at which a willing seller, under no pressure to sell, would sell to a willing and able buyer who is under no pressure to buy. Such a price, therefore, never can be proved as a *fact*; it can only be an opinion or informed guess as to what an imaginary person would do in imaginary circumstances. The value of such an opinion must depend on the qualifications of the person expressing it.

In the usual case, which involves the sale of many different items in a large number of transactions during the taxable year, the problem in reality boils down to what is a fair amount of profit to the seller—not the arm's length price of each item sold.

In order to bar revenue agents from using their own judgment in proposing or making adjustments of income resulting from intercompany sales, in August 1966 the U.S. Treasury for the first time proposed regulations instructing revenue agents how to adjust intercompany sales so as to reflect arm's length prices.

The regulations are not addressed to taxpayers and, in most cases, cannot possibly be applied in the prescribed manner by U.S. manufacturers in day-to-day pricing of goods they sell to their subsidiaries. Nevertheless, it is essential that all U.S. manufacturers making sales to related buyers be familiar with these instructions to revenue agents. Any adjustments actually made by the Internal Revenue Service to the prices of sales to WHTC and foreign subsidiaries by a U.S. parent company are likely to prove costly and embarrassing, despite the relief measures which are discussed here.

These proposed Treasury intercompany pricing regulations require that, in determining arm's length prices, the revenue agent take the following steps, in the order given, and in accordance with strictly prescribed procedures.

+ First, he is to adjust such prices, if possible, to comparable uncontrolled prices, on the basis of comparable sales to unrelated persons.

+ Next, if the first method cannot be applied because of the absence of sufficiently comparable sales, the resale price method must, if possible, be used to determine the arm's length prices to be employed in adjusting the U.S. taxpayer's income.

✦ Then, if the first two methods cannot be used for lack of the requisite information, the cost-plus method *may* be used; however, if the revenue agent deems it inapplicable, he may apply the resale price method—even though he may have to use statistics that are not clearly appropriate.

The comparable uncontrolled price method is largely self-explanatory. The resale price method determines the theoretical arm's length price by working back from the price at which the goods purchased from the U.S. parent company (or other related person) are resold by the related buyer to unrelated buyers. This is done by deducting from the ultimate resale price a normal markup percentage, determined on the basis of comparable sales made by a comparable reseller to unrelated persons.

Finally, there is the prescribed cost-plus method of determining the theoretical arm's length price at which the goods in question should have been sold to the related buyer. This requires a determination of the normal percentage of profit on the cost of similar goods sold to unrelated buyers.

The comparable uncontrolled price and resale price methods are relatively simple in theory, but difficult or impossible to apply in day-to-day pricing of goods sold to related buyers. The difficulty lies in determining what are comparable sales prices and normal percentages of markup on comparable sales to unrelated buyers.

The basic principles reflected in one or more of these three methods necessarily enter into a competent sales manager's determination of selling prices, whether to related or unrelated buyers. The difficulty lies in justifying the markup or cost-plus percentages to be used: How can the percentage be proved to be fair and reasonable? Where values are to be established in a court proceeding, testimony of a qualified expert, supported by evidence of relevant facts, normally takes precedence over any theoretical computations made by a person who cannot qualify as competent to express an opinion about such values.

Only future court decisions will determine whether intercompany pricing adjustments made by revenue agents on the basis of the regulations are conclusive or whether they may be overcome by competent evidence which establishes, by any other method of analyzing and evaluating the facts, what are fair and reasonable arm's length prices (or seller's profits) with respect to the goods sold.

Much of the rigidity of the originally proposed intercompany pricing regulations, however, has been taken out of these three prescribed methods by the following statement, which is included in the introductory portion of Section 482 of the pricing regulations as finally published in the *Federal Register* on April 16, 1968:

> Where none of the three methods of pricing described . . . can reasonably be applied under the facts and circumstances as they exist in a particular case, some appropriate method of pricing other than those described . . . or *variations* on such methods, can be used (emphasis added).

This amplification of methods largely restores to revenue agents the authority to determine arm's length pricing on the basis of all relevant factors. It is hoped that results of these intercompany pricing regulations now will prove to be more satisfactory than they threatened to be under the regulations as originally proposed.

Sec. 482 adjustments of other intercompany transactions. The authority granted by Sec. 482 to allocate gross income, deductions, credits, or allowances among related businesses clearly is not limited to the adjustment of prices charged in sales of goods between related persons. IRS adjusts income and deductions arising out of other types of intercompany transactions, in accordance with Treasury regulations that deal with interest on intercompany loans and advances, rental of tangible property, use of intangible property, services rendered to related parties, and other intercompany transactions.

Adjustments in this field, as well as pricing adjustments, may in some cases affect a U.S. parent company not only directly (by increasing its taxable income), but also indirectly, by reducing the amount of the allowable foreign tax credit and in other ways.

Gains and losses resulting from fluctuations in value of foreign currencies. For U.S. income tax purposes, foreign currencies in whatever form are property but not money. Only U.S. currency is considered to be money.

Under the rules generally applicable to the ownership of property, a fluctuation in the value of foreign currencies cannot be taken into account until realized by sale or exchange—except if the taxpayer conducts a foreign business which uses the foreign currency in normal operations. In computing taxable income in such a case, all current assets and liabilities must be translated, at appropriate exchange rates, into U.S. dollars at the beginning and end of the year. (In some cases special rules are applicable in valuing inventories for this purpose.) Thus net income or loss will automatically reflect the net gain or loss resulting from fluctuations in value (in U.S. dollars) of the foreign currency during the year. The same rules are applicable in determining the earnings and profits of a foreign corporation.

As an example of these principles, a U.S. corporation that owns a foreign corporation operating in the United Kingdom cannot deduct for U.S. income tax purposes the shrinkage (owing to sterling devaluation in 1967) in value of its stock in that subsidiary. At the same time, if prior to the 1967 devaluation the U.S. company had sold sterling for future delivery, gain on that transaction would not be taxable until realized by delivery of the sterling or sale of the contract. However, if the contract held by the U.S. taxpayer requires a bank (the other party to the contract) to pay an agreed price for the pounds sterling when tendered by the taxpayer at a future date, that contract itself is property in the hands of the taxpayer. Hence the *sale* of the contract to a third party would give rise, not to ordinary income, but to capital gain. Because of the relationship of the source of income to the statutory limitation on the amount of the foreign tax credit, it might be preferable, in such a case, to effect transfer of title and all risks and benefits of ownership of the contract from the taxpayer to the buyer in some selected foreign country.

The tax significance of "blocked currency." The basic principle is well established that only income realized (actually or constructively) in U.S. dollars or in other property having a determinable value in U.S. dollars is taxable. (As has been said, the taxation of imaginary dividends under 1962 legislation is a departure, of questionable constitutionality, from this principle.)

One application of this basic principle is in the case of income received or receivable in foreign currency or its equivalent which, by reason of restrictions imposed by a foreign jurisdiction, cannot be exchanged for or converted into U.S. currency or its equivalent. The rule that such unrealized income is not taxable is well established by court decisions, although it is not embodied in the Internal Revenue Code *except* with respect to the computation of earnings and profits of a foreign corporation for the purpose of Subpart F.

For determining taxable income and for all other purposes where blocked currency is involved, it is the Treasury's position that, in order to apply the principle of nonrecognition of income or gain tied up in blocked currency, the U.S. taxpayer must file a tax return on such blocked income (showing no tax thereon) in the manner prescribed in Internal

Revenue Service "Mimeo. 6475." Although it is doubtful that what is not "income" would be taxable because of failure to comply with Mimeo. 6475, there seems to be no case of this ruling having been questioned in the courts.

Income in the form of blocked currency becomes taxable when the currency is unblocked. This may throw a large amount of income into a single year.

Expenses related to excluded (nontaxable) income in blocked currency are not allowable as *deductions* until the currency is unblocked and such income then becomes taxable.

Gain on transfers of property to a foreign corporation. In certain circumstances, property may be transferred to or received from a corporation in an exchange without recognition of gain or loss. These provisions of the Internal Revenue Code, generally spoken of as the reorganization provisions, include Sections 332, 351, 354, 355, 356, and 361. IRC Sec. 367, however, denies the benefit of those provisions, when one or more of the parties to the transaction are foreign corporations, unless the Commissioner of Internal Revenue has determined in advance of the transaction that the avoidance of U.S. income taxes is not one of the principal purposes of the exchange. Such clearance under Sec. 367 is generally difficult and often impossible to obtain from the Internal Revenue Service. In many cases the clearance is obtainable only at the price of agreeing to pay a tax which would not be imposed if all corporations involved were organized in any of the United States or in the District of Columbia.

For example, gain on the liquidation of a subsidiary, which would be tax-free if the subsidiary were a domestic corporation, is taxable if it is a foreign corporation, unless Sec. 367 clearance is obtained before any step is taken in the actual liquidation. If taxable, the U.S. parent company may be confronted with a tax proposed by a revenue agent based on a very high alleged value of goodwill or other intangible assets of the liquidated subsidiary.

Another example is to be found in instances where the U.S. corporation transfers to a wholly owned subsidiary tangible or intangible property having a value in excess of its cost. If the subsidiary is a domestic corporation no gain is recognized (taxable), whether the exchange is for shares of stock of the subsidiary or as a "contribution of capital" to it, unless shares of stock or other consideration is received from the subsidiary. If the subsidiary is a foreign corporation, however, and it issues shares of its stock for the property, the gain realized by the U.S. parent company is taxable if Sec. 367 clearance was not previously obtained. The amount of the gain is the excess (if any) of the value of the shares received from the subsidiary over the cost—or adjusted basis—of the property transferred to it by the U.S. parent corporation. It is the Treasury's position that the result is the same if the transfer is made by the parent company without the receipt of shares of stock or any other property from the subsidiary. This seems contrary to the principles applied in other situations involving gratuitous contributions to capital.

Gain on sale of patents and similar intangible property to a controlled foreign corporation. Prior to the 1962 U.S. tax legislation, it was possible for a U.S. corporation to realize a capital gain on the sale of patents and similar intangible property to a foreign subsidiary. Today, however, gain on any sale or exchange of such property to a foreign corporation which is or is deemed to be 50 percent or more owned by a U.S. person is taxable as ordinary income (IRC Sec. 1249). Thus such gain is subject to U.S. tax at the same rate as royalty income.

Transfers of stock or securities to a foreign corporation as a contribution to its capital. At one time it seemed to be recognized that a transfer of property without the receipt of any consideration did not result in income. In order to block what it believed to be a loophole in this regard, the Congress imposed an excise tax of 27.5 percent on the excess of the value of stock or securities transferred as a contribution to capital of a foreign corporation over the cost (or other statutory adjusted basis) of such property in the hands of the transferer (IRC Sec. 1491). Here, also, the tax may be avoided if clearance is obtained from the Internal Revenue Service. Unlike Sec. 367, however, this provision gives the Internal Revenue Service authority to grant such clearance after the event as well as before it.

REDUCTION OF EXPORT TRADE CORPORATION INCOME—AND RECAPTURE

What is generally referred to as Subpart G of the Internal Revenue Code (Secs. 970–972) provides for a reduction in the amount of income of an export trade corporation which otherwise would be classified as Subpart F income, subject to immediate U.S. taxation to its U.S. shareholders. An export trade corporation is a controlled foreign corporation which derives more than 90 percent of its gross income from sources outside the United States and more than 75 percent from export trade income which consists primarily of income derived from sale or lease abroad of property produced in the United States.

There are various percentage limitations upon the amount of this income which can be excluded from Subpart F treatment. In addition, there is an overall limitation on the exclusion equal to the increase in the foreign corporation's export trade assets in the year in which the income is earned.

The provisions of Subpart G are considered unsatisfactory by most of those it was intended to benefit, and it has been availed of by very few U.S. taxpayers.

There is a recapture provision whereby the amount of income of the export trade corporation taxable to its U.S. shareholders is increased in any subsequent year to the extent of any decrease in its export trade assets in that year. (Such recapture is limited to the amount which has been allowed as a reduction in Subpart F income for prior years.)

The overall effect is that the U.S. tax on certain undistributed Subpart F income is postponed only so long as there is no distribution thereof and no decrease in the export trade assets of the export trade corporation. The deferment ends at the time and to the extent that there is a decrease in such assets in any year.

Income from Sea and Air Transportation

All "income derived from, or in connection with, the use (or hiring or leasing for use) of any aircraft or vessel in foreign commerce, or the performance of services directly related to the use of any such aircraft or vessel" is excluded from classification as Subpart F income. The provision for this favorable treatment was incorporated in Subpart F for reasons of national defense. This exemption is so broad and sweeping that no further clarification is required.

Owing to the structure of Subpart F, a corporation entitled to this exemption may use this provision to eliminate from Subpart F treatment income otherwise taxable as such, provided that the income of the latter kind does not exceed 30 percent of the total gross income of the corporation. In other words, each $.70 of shipping or aircraft gross income can furnish an umbrella of U.S. tax postponement for $.30 of corporate income which otherwise would be immediately taxable as Subpart F income to its U.S. shareholders. Thus the time for paying U.S. tax on such foreign income may be postponed until its actual receipt. This postponement has been found to be of great value by some U.S. taxpayers, as it permits the use of funds resulting from such deferment to produce further income abroad.

INCOME OF FOREIGN FINANCIAL INSTITUTIONS

Passive income such as dividends, interest, and so on, which normally would constitute foreign personal holding company income of a controlled foreign corporation, is excluded from Subpart F treatment where it is received by banks and other financial institutions and, subject to certain limitations, by certain insurance companies. There are other related provisions for exclusion of income of this kind from Subpart F classification where it is earned within the country of incorporation of the controlled foreign corporation.

Aside from those multinational U.S. organizations having captive foreign insurance or finance companies, these provisions are of concern only to the companies engaged primarily in financial and insurance activities.

FOREIGN PERSONAL HOLDING COMPANIES

Broadly speaking, a foreign corporation is classified as a foreign personal holding company if it is more than 50 percent owned by five or fewer "individuals" (including as one individual certain family members, and so on) who are U.S. citizens or residents and if more than 60 percent (or in some instances 50 percent) of the corporation's gross income is passive income—such as, but not limited to, dividends, interests, rents, and gains on sales or exchanges of stock or securities.

A few significant features of these provisions require consideration in tax planning for operations abroad. Ownership of stock is defined to include indirect ownership. For example, if five United States individuals (within the meaning of the law) own more than 50 percent of the stock of a U.S. corporation, which in turn owns all the stock of a foreign corporation, and if the income of the latter meets the test as to the amount of its passive income, it may be deemed to be a foreign personal holding company. This is the case even though the U.S. corporation derives most of its income from the active conduct of business in the United States and has a large number of other U.S. shareholders.

The U.S. shareholders of a foreign corporation which is classed as a foreign personal holding company are taxable currently (each year) on its undistributed income. Shareholders of such a corporation who are so taxable are not subject to tax on its income under Subpart F.

There are numerous special rules for determining whether a foreign corporation is a foreign personal holding company, but the foregoing are the principal points to be kept in mind in tax planning for business operations.

OTHER FORMS OF U.S. TAXES AND CONTROLS AFFECTING FOREIGN PROFITS

In addition to foreign taxes of many varieties and foreign government controls and regulations, a U.S. or foreign corporation owned or controlled by U.S. persons may be affected by other U.S. taxes and controls in addition to those already discussed.

Foreign Investors Tax Act of 1966. The so-called Foreign Investors Tax Act of 1966 introduced another radically new principle into the U.S. tax system. Prior to the Act, no corporation organized outside the United States was subject to U.S. tax on income it derived from foreign sources. This new Act, in addition to provisions that encourage foreign investments in the United States, also levies U.S. income tax on certain income derived by foreign corporations from foreign sources, if this income is "effectively connected" in certain ways with activities in the United States.

Without going into technical details, it may be said that income arising out of exporting or selling U.S.-produced goods outside the United States is very unlikely to be subjected to tax under this Act; that foreign corporations shipping goods to buyers in the United States may, in certain not-unusual circumstances, become liable to tax under this Act; and that foreign corporations deriving income from financial transactions in the United States may also become liable to tax.

Interest equalization tax. The provisions levying the interest equalization tax have frequently been changed since it was first added to the growing number of U.S. taxes designed to penalize income from foreign sources. However, this tax very rarely is of concern to U.S. taxpayers in connection with the active conduct of business inside or outside the United States either directly or through subsidiaries because it does not affect transactions involving stock or securities of a foreign corporation in which a U.S. person owns 10 percent or more of the stock.

EXECUTIVE ORDER 11387 AND FDI REGULATIONS

Executive Order 11387 was filed in the *Federal Register* on January 1, 1968, along with Commerce Department foreign direct investment regulations issued under its authorization.

The Order forbids almost every transaction involving foreign property, including foreign exchange and foreign funds, but gives the Commerce Department power to authorize transactions by regulations.

In brief, the Commerce Department regulations permit all transactions which are not specifically forbidden therein and make provision for special authorizations for transactions otherwise prohibited under the regulations. These regulations have already undergone numerous changes.

The regulations require the filing of an initial base period report (Form FDI-101) containing information regarding certain operations and transactions for the base period years 1964–1966, some figures for 1967, and quarterly reports (FDI-102) for calendar quarters beginning January 1, 1968. They require certain repatriations (transfers to a U.S. bank in dollars) of foreign funds and prohibit certain transfers of capital and retention of earnings of foreign corporations, which may be considered under three headings:

1. Requirements that a certain percentage of current earnings of related foreign corporations be remitted in U.S. dollars to their U.S. shareholders within the year earned (or perhaps within 60 days thereafter).
2. Restrictions on transfers of funds to foreign corporations (and others) and, in effect, restrictions upon the amount of earnings which may be retained undistributed by certain foreign corporations.
3. A requirement that certain foreign funds and other liquid assets owned abroad by U.S. persons are to be repatriated by June 30, 1968, and additional funds thereafter accumulated in excess of a certain amount are to be repatriated each month.

The countries of the world are divided into three groups:

Schedule A—For the most part, the less developed countries.
Schedule B—The United Kingdom, Ireland, certain oil-producing countries of the Near East, and a few other countries.
Schedule C—All other countries (except the United States and Canada).

The percentage of earnings which must be distributed currently depends upon the schedule in which the foreign corporation is deemed to be located. For this purpose the same foreign corporation, having branches in different countries, may be included in Schedules A, B, and C, and each branch of a U.S. or foreign corporation may be treated as if it were a corporation located in one of the countries in Schedule A, B, or C.

In general, the reports may be required to be made by any U.S. corporation or other person in this country having an interest of 10 percent or more in the voting power, earnings, or right to receive assets of any "foreign national." A foreign national includes a foreign branch as well as a foreign corporation.

Severe penalties may be imposed for failure to file the required initial report on Form FDI-101 or the required quarterly reports on Form FDI-102.

After several months, the regulations, forms, instructions, rulings, special authorizations, and other materials constitute a large volume and are available in a commercial service published by one of the large service publishers.

It is not only impossible but unnecessary and perhaps misleading to give further details regarding this Executive Order and its regulations. The important point is that every corporation or individual having a substantial interest in any foreign corporation or foreign funds, property, or income should determine whether Forms 101 and 102 are required and, if so, what further requirements and prohibitions are applicable and what steps should be taken.

U.S. tax treaties with other countries. The United States has entered into tax conventions (usually referred to as tax treaties) with many countries. These include Canada, most of the industrialized nations of Europe, and a few other countries, among them Pakistan. There are as yet no tax treaties with any of the Latin American countries, as the tax treaty with Honduras was terminated by that country on December 31, 1966, and has not since been resumed. The tax treaty with Brazil has not yet been ratified.

Those treaties are intended to avoid double taxation and also to assist the U.S. Treasury and the treasury departments of all the pertinent countries in enforcing their tax laws through the exchange of information.

In general, wherever there is a conflict between the Internal Revenue Code and a tax treaty, the latter prevails. IRC Sec. 894(a) provides that income is exempt to the extent provided in any such treaty. However, the 1962 Revenue Act contains a provision (not incorporated in the International Revenue Code) that IRC Sec. 7852(d) "should not apply in respect of any amendment made by this Act." The latter section provides that none of the income tax provisions of the Code applies in any case where it is contrary to treaty obligations of the United States.

The provisions of each tax treaty are applicable only to citizens, corporations, and residents of the two countries involved. For example, provisions of the tax treaty with France are not applicable to transactions of a French corporation owned by a Bermuda corporation which is a subsidiary of a U.S. corporation.

In many cases the advantages of a tax treaty to the U.S. corporation with subsidiaries organized in treaty countries are of doubtful value. For instance, a reduction in the rate of withholding tax on dividends paid to a U.S. parent company by a subsidiary organized in a treaty country will depend on the effect it has on the amount of the foreign tax credit currently available to the parent company. The benefit of the reduction may be completely wiped out or it may be of value in a particular case, depending on the limitation on such credit.

It is essential in all tax planning to take into consideration the applicable provisions of any existing U.S. tax treaties with any countries in which operations are to be conducted or a foreign subsidiary is to be organized.

Tax treaty provisions also are of great importance when the question arises as to whether a foreign corporation is taxable on income derived from sources or activities in the United States. There are numerous tax treaties and commercial treaties between various countries which also must be considered wherever applicable.

Reports Required of U.S. Stockholders in Foreign Corporations

Foreign personal holding companies. On the 15th day of the first month after the close of the taxable year of a foreign corporation which, with respect to that taxable year, is a foreign personal holding company, each U.S. citizen or resident who is an officer or a director of the corporation is required to file an information return with respect thereto, as is each U.S. shareholder who owns or is deemed to own 50 percent or more of the value of the stock of such a corporation on that date. (For this purpose, certain members of a family and other persons are considered to own the stock owned by any one of the group.)

A U.S. citizen or resident who is an officer or director of such a corporation on the 60th day after the close of its taxable year also must file on that date a return containing information as to its income for the taxable year.

Each U.S. shareholder of such a corporation is required to include in his income tax return his share of the undistributed foreign personal holding company income of such corporation for its taxable year ending with or within his own taxable year and to include details regarding the income, deductions and credits, taxable income, foreign personal holding company income, and undistributed foreign personal holding company income of such corporation.

Controlled (Subpart F) foreign corporations. Every U.S. shareholder who owns or is deemed to own 10 percent or more of the stock of a controlled foreign corporation which is not a foreign personal holding company is required to file with his U.S. income tax return a report on Form 3646 for each such corporation in which he was a U.S. shareholder at the close of his taxable year.

In addition, each U.S. person who has or is deemed to have controlled a foreign corporation for a period of 30 or more consecutive days during the corporation's annual accounting period ending within his taxable year is required to file, with his U.S. income tax return, a Form 2952, in duplicate, with respect to each such corporation.

Form 3646 is not too difficult to prepare for a foreign subsidiary included by a U.S. parent company in an election under the minimum distribution provisions of Subpart F or in the case of a foreign subsidiary having no Subpart F income. However, where the foreign subsidiary *has* Subpart F income and is *not* included in a minimum distribution election, the preparation of such a return may involve a tremendous amount of detailed accounting analyses and numerous tax accounting problems in order to complete the schedule of this return.

Form 2952 appears relatively simple but requires analyses which make it difficult. A balance sheet, a profit and loss statement, and a surplus analysis also are required as a part of this return.

Help in solving the problems involved in the preparation of Forms 3646 and 2952 may be obtained from the material published in ¶24,032 of *Tax Ideas—Transactions Tax Guide,* published by Prentice-Hall. It is especially important in connection with these returns to keep in mind the provisions of the Internal Revenue Code which impose penalties for failure to furnish the required information.

Every U.S. citizen or resident who is an officer or director of a foreign corporation is required to file an information return on Form 959 with respect to every U.S. person who, during the time when he is such an officer or director, acquires a stock interest of 5 percent or more in the corporation. Instructions on Form 959 give details regarding the contents and filing of this return. It is always necessary to file Form 959 when United States persons organize a foreign corporation or any change in ownership of shares occurs.

TAXATION OF U.S. CITIZENS EMPLOYED ABROAD

Earned income (compensation) for services rendered abroad by a U.S. citizen (but *not* an alien resident in the United States) may be exempt from U.S. tax—subject to a limitation of $20,000 or $25,000 of such income per annum—under either of two sets of definitions and limitations. The exemption does *not* apply to income other than earned income or to compensation paid by the United States or any instrumentality of the United States.

The exemption at the $20,000 rate is allowed where the U.S. citizen earning the income spends 510 full days out of a period of 18 consecutive months (about 548 days) in one or more countries outside the United States. For this purpose, the Treasury rules that less than full 24-hour days actually within a foreign country or countries are not counted, and a trip by air or water over international waters lasting more than 24 hours may result in the loss of one or more days. This ruling has trapped many U.S. employees abroad.

The other exemption, at $20,000 per annum for the first 36 months of foreign residence and $25,000 per annum thereafter, is allowed where the U.S. citizen earns the income while a resident in a foreign country or countries during a period including at least one entire taxable year. (For the purpose of either type of exemption, a U.S. possession or territory is not considered to be a foreign country.)

"Residence" and "domicile" are quite different in meaning. However, as stated by a learned judge, they "are slippery words," frequently confused as well as misunderstood. An individual can have only one domicile at any time, but he can and frequently does have two or more residences at the same time or a residence that is different from his domicile. For U.S. tax purposes residence requires an intention to reside or live in some one locality for an indefinite time, with no intention of leaving at any definite time in the future.

A U.S. citizen who lives outside the United States during a period which includes an entire taxable year and claims exemption at the $20,000 or $25,000 per annum rate may have the problem of proving that he was in fact a "resident" of one or more foreign countries during the period. Furthermore, the statute denies the exemption on the basis of residence in a foreign country where the U.S. citizen has successfully asserted, for foreign tax purposes, that he is *not* a resident of such country.

A U.S. citizen actually resident abroad does not lose that status or the benefit of the exemption on the basis of residence by reason of temporary visits to the United States for pleasure or business. Any portion of the compensation of such citizen attributable to his stay in the United States is, of course, *not* exempt, because it is not earned abroad.

The exemption, under either the 510-day provision or residence abroad, is determined on what might be called an "accrual" basis—that is, the time when the income is earned rather than when it is received determines its status (but *not* the time of its taxability). However, this is subject to a further restriction: Income, otherwise exempt, that is received *after* the end of the taxable year following the year in which it is earned, is *not* exempt. This provision is especially harsh in cases of deferred compensation and pension income.

No deductions are allowable for expenses in connection with income which is exempt under either of these provisions.

A U.S. citizen claiming exemption under either provision must complete Form 2555 and attach it to his income tax return for the year in which the exempt income otherwise would be taxable.

The regulations provide special relief provisions regarding filing U.S. tax returns and payment of taxes by U.S. citizens who earn income abroad.

Despite all the limitations on these earned income exemptions, many U.S. citizens employed abroad find them a real incentive to foreign service. For example, a U.S. citizen who is employed in Ireland by a U.S.-owned Bermuda corporation operating a manufacturing plant in the Irish Republic can obtain the benefit of the exemption from U.S. tax on up to $20,000 or $25,000 of his annual compensation. He also could obtain exemption from Irish tax on so much of his compensation as he did not receive in Ireland but caused to be deposited or paid out for his account outside that country. This is permitted by law also in the United Kingdom. There are other countries, however, where any attempt to avoid local taxes by this means could result in severe criminal penalties.

Problems of Executive Estate Planning

George S. Wolbert, Jr.

AN ESTATE PLAN IS A PROGRAM FOR THE ACCUMULATION, MANAGEMENT, AND disposition of assets in order to achieve, within the limits of your capabilities, the objectives that you have set for yourself and the others for whom you wish to provide.

This concept utilizes the same approach that you use in your business. Within such a plan, the proper role of tax minimization is simply a *means*, albeit a very important one, to achieving the desired end. Here is an extreme example: One sure way to avoid estate taxes entirely is to will all your property to a qualifying charity. But what does this do for your family?

Why an Estate Plan?

Implicit in our definition of the term "estate plan" is the recognition that all but the extremely wealthy must assess priorities. The unfortunate, but undeniable, fact is that we must do our best with what we have. However, "tradeoff" analysis should be second nature to an executive.

GEORGE S. WOLBERT, JR., is a member of the New York bar.

DANGERS OF DEFAULT

It has been said that failure to evolve an affirmative estate plan itself constitutes the adoption of an estate plan. This may follow as an exercise in semantics, but do you really want the results of such a "default plan"? What are some of its consequences?

Unaccomplished accumulation. One of the earliest benefits of an estate plan is the setting of targets for accumulation. A sound review of one's estate usually reveals how inadequate are the provisions one has made for one's survivors. Try a simple test: Capitalize the value of your net assets and project an income from it at, say, 4.5 percent. Could your family live in an acceptable manner on such an income (after income taxes are deducted) even if you take into account social security and any other source of income available to them? Unless you have realistically assessed your own situation and designed a course of action, it is unlikely that you will succeed in accumulating an estate which will come even close to assuring the continued comfort of your beneficiaries.

Misdirected distribution. The laws of the several states provide a statutory scheme for the distribution of the property of persons (known as "intestates") who die without leaving a will. The applicable law to personal property is that of the state in which the intestate was domiciled at the time of his death; real estate distribution is governed by the laws of the state in which the intestate's real property was located. While such distributory schemes are designed to be as equitable as possible, they are necessarily uniform in their application and, therefore, seldom really meet the individual needs of the deceased. Among the principal difficulties are these: The wife's share is too small; the marital deduction which could have been allowed under federal estate tax is not realized because insufficient qualified property goes to the wife; property vests outright in minors; statutory distributees receive property without regard to their competency; worthy beneficiaries are omitted because they don't fit into the prescribed statutory scheme; and there is no flexibility to meet changing circumstances.

Perhaps a simple example may bring the point home. Consider the case of Mr. L. Gone, who dies in Massachusetts leaving his dearly beloved wife and a wastrel second cousin, Rowdy, whom the couple hasn't seen since he disgraced them by getting abnoxiously drunk at their wedding 25 years ago. The disposition of the estate is $25,000 outright plus one half of the remaining estate to the widow and the rest to cousin Rowdy!

The heavy hand of the tax collector. Federal estate tax rates begin at 3 percent of taxable estates under $5,000 and rise rapidly to 77 percent in the top bracket. Thus the federal estate tax on a $500,000 taxable estate is $133,300, assuming the applicable state death tax at least equals the allowed maximum credit. To this must be added the state tax. Obviously, the most careful attention must be given to minimizing the impact of taxes on the passage of assets to one's beneficiary.

COORDINATION OF EFFORT

There are many different ways by which we may transfer wealth to our beneficiaries. Insurance may pass by designation; jointly held property may vest by operation of law; annuities may flow under a survivorship option; company benefits may be paid directly pursuant to a direction or because the recipient falls within a favored class; existing trusts may provide for income and principal payments to beneficiaries; and the provisions of our wills may channel funds to them. Only by developing an overall estate plan can we coordinate these various transfers so as to accomplish all our dispositive desires, make the most efficient use of tax-reducing mechanisms, and achieve the flexibility required for the plan to adapt itself to ever-changing circumstances.

An Overview of the Program

In determining our estate plan objectives, we must first decide whom we are planning for and what we want for them. We must evaluate, with the utmost candor, the abilities and disabilities of our beneficiaries and inventory our assets to determine the possibility of achieving the desired objectives. Then we must examine the various methods of transferring our property to these beneficiaries in such a manner as to minimize taxes, provide the necessary liquidity, fulfill our capital requirements, and, where applicable, preserve the family business.

A LOOK AT THE BENEFICIARIES

Yourself. Strangely enough, the person who is most frequently overlooked is you; yet this is where you should start. Today's odds are reasonably favorable that you will live to be 65, but the chances that you will avoid disablement are not as favorable. You should analyze the income that would be available to you in the event that you were unfortunate enough to become disabled. Sources of such income, in addition to interest and dividends on accumulated invested savings, might be workmen's compensation, state compulsory disability insurance, federal social security disability benefits, certain veteran's disability benefits, or company benefits. In other words, take a good, hard look at your situation and determine its shortcomings. Perhaps supplementary disability insurance can be obtained commercially at a reasonable cost by integrating it with company benefits. For example, your company plan might provide for salary continuation up to one year, which could be used as an exclusionary period under the commercial plan. This would mean marked decrease in premium as compared to that of a plan with no waiting period or even a short one. Remember, obtain this protection when you are in good health; don't wait until you need it.

You must also plan for retirement, which, unlike disability, is almost inevitable. Company retirement is mandatory in most instances. Will the company's pension plan provide sufficient income? What are your own plans for retirement? Have you accumulated, or do your plans provide for, enough supplementary income, even taking social security into account? There is also a nonfinancial problem that often is overlooked. Are you psychologically prepared for retirement? Have you developed fulfilling avocations? If not, do you have a substitute vocation lined up, and are you sure that it does not involve a conflict of interest with your present employer or in some way jeopardize your retirement benefits?

Your wife. The next object of your attention is your wife. What kind of person is she? If she is stout as a horse, financially acute, modest in her living standards, devoted to the children, wouldn't dream of remarrying and holds a master's degree in taxation, you can probably leave her your entire estate, knowing that she will put it to good use and so arrange her affairs as to provide for herself and the children, preserve the capital in sensible degree, and transfer to the children the remainder of the estate at the least possible tax cost. But how many of these paragons exist? To the extent that her characteristics depart from this level of perfection, you must modify your desire to give her maximum flexibility. In the event that she has, or may receive, property of her own, you will probably be impelled to adopt certain devices which reduce taxes on successive estates. These will be discussed in subsequent sections.

Children. Much the same personal characteristics should be examined with respect to your children. You will also have to make an important basic decision: Shall they all be treated the same? This question can cause substantial soul searching. Remember that your judgment is human. You may be wrong, and subsequent events may make a correct judgment incorrect. Equal treatment is the norm; but there are certain cases where differences are justified. Incompetency is one of them, health is another, an extremely fortunate marriage is yet a third. Each case should be decided on its own merits.

The guardianship of your minor children's person and property must also be thought through carefully.

Grandchildren. The usual question that arises in the case of grandchildren is whether they should be treated equally *per capita* or whether the distribution should be by representation *per stirpes*. To illustrate the difference, assume you had four children; one died leaving one grandchild, another died leaving two grandchildren, a third is still living, and the fourth died leaving four grandchildren. If you distributed among your descendants *per capita*, each would receive one-eighth of the property; *per stirpes* distribution would give the living child one-quarter, the sole grandchild surviving the first child would get another quarter, each of the two grandchildren produced by the second child would get an eighth, and the grandchildren born to the fourth child would each receive one-sixteenth of a share. Inequity can be claimed in either case; you wouldn't think of giving the last group of grandchildren birthday gifts worth only a quarter as much as the first grandchild's or half as valuable as your presents to the second set of grandchildren. By the same token, however, it doesn't seem right to give each of the four grandchildren begotten by the fourth child the same share that your own living child receives. Often a Solomon-like decision is made to distribute *per stirpes* so long as any children survive you but *per capita* among the grandchildren if all the children have predeceased you.

Parents. It may be that you have a parent who is dependent in whole or in part on you. It would not seem prudent to make an outright disposition to him. However, provision can be made to take care of the parent's needs through a trust.

Other relatives, servants, friends. If your immediate family is nonexistent, or otherwise well provided for, you might consider bequests to more distant relatives, a faithful servant, or even friends. Except in unusual cases of disability, outright dispositions usually are made, probably because there is no need to protect other beneficiaries.

Charity. Because of the special tax consequences arising from charitable dispositions, this subject will be discussed in a separate section.

Your Objectives

In reviewing our beneficiaries, we mentioned objectives, especially in the section on *yourself*. Objectives necessarily are extremely personal, and they must be arrived at with the characteristics of your beneficiaries firmly in mind. Some of the possible objectives that might occur to you in respect to your wife are:

1. To provide her with an adequate income for life or until she remarries.
2. To entrust her with complete control over your children's portion of your estate or to give her control only over such a portion of your estate as will forestall election against the will or over that portion which will produce the maximum marital deduction under the estate tax.
3. To assure that she receives professional financial management or to let her run her own show.
4. To minimize the estate tax on her estate by passing at least the nonmarital deduction portion directly or in trust for the children or to disregard the potential estate tax on her estate in order to be sure that she is protected financially.

The same exercise should be conducted for each beneficiary. However, you may have to modify the goals to achieve the appropriate compromise when the objectives of two or more beneficiaries conflict.

Inventory of Assets

At this point, we must remind ourselves that estate planning is concerned not only with the property of which we are the sole, outright owner but also with a wide variety of other property rights. An illustrative, but nonexhaustive, list follows.

- Real property, including dower and courtesy or a statutory substitute.
- Stocks and bonds in one's own name and those in the broker's street name.
- Mortgages, notes, certificates of deposit, and savings certificates.
- Contracts to sell land.

+ Cash on hand, checking accounts, and savings accounts.
+ Insurance on your life and insurance, owned by you, on the life of another.
+ Annuities and death benefits.
+ Pension, profit-sharing, stock-option, and deferred-compensation payments.
+ Property held jointly, property held by tenants in common or tenants "by the entirety," or community property.
+ Business interests held either as sole proprietor or as a partner, or a closely held, incorporated business.
+ Livestock, automobiles, boats, and airplanes.
+ Claims, rights, causes of action, and judgments.
+ Household goods and personal effects.
+ Social security and veteran's benefits.
+ Reversions or remainder interests in self-created trusts.
+ Benefits, including powers of appointment, under trusts created by other people and benefits which might accrue in the future by reason of the death of another.
+ Income sources owned by beneficiary.

Of course, a similar compilation of debts, liabilities, and estimated expenses must be undertaken.

Estate-Tax Obstacles

We have mentioned the federal estate tax rates, but we should also be aware of the extremely broad base upon which that tax is levied. The general rule of inclusion (known to tax lawyers as Section 2033) provides that the gross estate includes all property of every type (including foreign real estate) to the extent that the decedent owned a beneficial interest in it at the time of his death. Moreover, by virtue of several "loophole closing" sections of the Internal Revenue Code, gross estate may also include property which the decedent did *not* own at his death but which he had previously transferred, by trust or otherwise, for less than an adequate and full consideration in money or its equivalent. For instance:

1. Property which the decedent disposed of within the past three years "in contemplation of his death."
2. Property in respect to which the decedent reserved possession,

the right to income, or the right to designate who should have such rights.

    a. For the grantor's life. Example: "To *T* in trust, to pay all net income to me for life [remainder to *A*]."

    b. For any period not ascertainable without reference to the grantor's death. Example: "To *T* in trust, to pay all net income to me in quarter-annual installments, provided, however, that no part of such income received by the trust between the date of the last quarterly payment and the date of my death shall go to me or my estate [remainder to *A*]."

    c. For any period which does in fact not end before the grantor's death. Example: "To *T* in trust, to pay all net income to *A* for life; upon *A*'s death to pay all net income to me for life [remainder to *B*]." In fact *A* dies before I do.

3. Property which a beneficiary could possess or enjoy only by surviving the grantor *and* in which the grantor has a reversionary interest (not just the income) which exceeds 5 percent of the property's value. Example: "To *T* in trust, to pay all net income to my wife, Winifred, for her life; at her death to distribute all of the then existing principal to me if I am then living; if not, all said principal to be distributed in equal shares to my daughter, Sharon, and my son, George."

4. Property whose enjoyment was subject, at the decedent's death, to any change through the exercise of a power by the decedent to alter, amend, revoke, or terminate such enjoyment or where any such power is relinquished in contemplation of the decedent's death.

5. An annuity or other payment receivable by any beneficiary by reason of surviving the decedent under certain agreements or plans, to the extent that the value of the annuity or other payment is attributable to contributions made by the decedent or his employer. The tax section (IRC Section 2039) is made inapplicable by its terms to life insurance. An exemption is, however, created in favor of distributions from a "qualified" trust [under IRC Section 401(a)] forming part of a pension, stock bonus, or profit-sharing plan, and retirement annuities purchased by an employer pursuant to a plan [IRC Section 403(a)], to the extent that the amounts payable are attributable to the employer rather than the employee.

6. All property held jointly at the time of death by the decedent and another person, with right of survivorship, is included in the gross estate:

   a. To the extent of the decedent's fractional interest where the property was acquired by the joint owners through gift, devise, bequest, or inheritance.

   b. In all other cases, in its entire value, except for any portion which the survivor can prove that he or she never received from the decedent for less than an adequate and full consideration in money or money's worth. This negative fact is extremely difficult to prove.

7. Property in respect to which the decedent possessed, exercised, or released certain powers of appointment.

8. Proceeds of insurance on the decedent's life receivably by or for the benefit of the estate, and receivable by beneficiaries other than the decedent's estate if he possessed, at the date of his death, any of the "incidents of ownership" in the policy. This term refers to the right to enjoy the economic benefits of the policy, and it includes such terms as the power to designate or change the beneficiary, to surrender or cancel the policy, to assign or revoke assignments of it, to pledge the policy to secure a loan, or to obtain from the insurance carrier a loan against the surrender value. It also includes a reversionary interest in the policy or its proceeds, whether such interest arises from the terms of the policy or from the operation of the law, so long as the value of the reversionary interest immediately before the death of the decedent exceeded 5 percent of the value of the policy.

In this discussion, we necessarily have oversimplified many concepts and passed lightly over certain terms which are surrounded by technical tax lore. There are many fine questions of terminology, retroactivity of application (especially in the case of the loophole-closing sections), and overlaps between the general section and the special sections and among the special sections themselves, which become extremely important where the included value depends upon which section is applicable.

In general, the primary objective of the federal estate tax is to tax all transfers of interest in property at death. Therefore, in order to preserve the integrity of the tax, its scope has been broadened to include all other types of arrangements which are deemed to be substantially equivalent to such transfers. Because of this broad sweep, practically all the assets inventoried here will be included in your gross estate, except for any pension or profit-sharing distribution from a "qualified" plan (to the extent attributable to employer contributions) made payable to persons other than your estate; social security or veteran's benefits; and the assets which your beneficiaries have held entirely apart from you.

Our discussion has been limited to the federal estate tax; however, note must be taken of the various state estate and inheritance taxes. It would be impractical here to attempt a dissertation on them, and their impact usually is insubstantial compared to the federal tax. Frequently, the same steps that serve to minimize or avoid federal estate taxes will result in a corresponding reduction or avoidance of state death taxes.

OTHER ESTATE PROBLEMS

We must examine income taxes as they bear upon the problem of creating an estate, achieving liquidity of estate, or—as a factor in the consideration of alternatives—planning a program of lifetime giving. (The gift tax also will be considered in our review of lifetime giving.)

Capital management. At every stage of estate planning, we face the problem of providing sufficient capital to generate the income required to obtain our objectives, both short and long term. We first encounter this in the early phase of accumulating the estate; later it acts as a limiting factor in planning our lifetime giving.

In these first two stages, the dimension of the problem which concerns us is *how* to manage, rather than *who* is to manage, our capital. Generally we carry the basic responsibility ourselves. However, when the matter of postmortem management of capital comes up for review, we must resolve the question of who is going to do the managing. Most relevant to this issue is the homework we have done on objectives and the capabilities or disabilities of our beneficiaries. But we cannot safely assume that the persons or institutions we select to manage our estate will be willing or able to carry on this crucial task. We must assure ourselves of their availability in actual discussions with them.

Liquidity. There will be substantial expenditures involved in settling your estate: expenses of the last illness, funeral expenses, satisfaction of debts, taxes, costs of probate, counsel and executor's fees, trustee's commissions, and the like. Not to be overlooked are the cash needs of your beneficiaries while they await final distribution. Because these needs must be satisfied from *cash*, not just assets, you should mentally divide your assets into cash, those items that can be converted into cash without undue diminution or loss of control, and those items that must be retained intact.

Probate. There has been considerable criticism of the costs, delays, unwanted publicity, and loss of flexibility involved in probate. For example, without a contrary provision in the will, the general rule is that legatees may not be paid until after the time has expired for the filing of claims. This period can run up to six months after the grant of letters testamentary or of administration. Certain states require an order from the probate court before any distribution is made, and in some instances the nature of the property (for example, real estate and stock) requires an order before the distributee has clear title to it. In this connection, considerable and sometimes excessive costs can be involved in giving notices that are statutory but impractical. Often, the state law will zealously protect its transfer tax by restricting distribution until the tax is paid.

Nevertheless, it is possible to avoid most of the disadvantages of probate and still get the benefit of the protection it gives executor and distributees by the judicious channeling of certain clearly taxable assets through probate. This is particularly apt where the decedent desires to control death taxes by means of a specific provision in his will directing his executor to pay all such taxes (plus interest and penalties) without the right of reimbursement from recipients of testamentary and nontestamentary property.

Facing the Facts

One practical way to size up your situation is to conduct a simulation exercise or "dry run" with the aid of the Federal Estate Tax Return (Form 706). Schedules A through N, summarized on Schedule O, will serve as a checklist in making an inventory of your assets and assessing your liabilities. By completing Part I on page 1 a good estimate can be made of the amount by which the federal estate tax will reduce the capital available to your beneficiaries under your present estate plan. The listing of debts, claims, and estimated expenses will give you a feel for your liquidity requirements. A valuable byproduct will be a better understanding of the nature of your assets—those that are the ready equivalent of cash, those that presently would cause monetary loss or loss of control if they had to be converted into cash, and those that should be retained in their present form until the very end.

After the 706 simulation, you should apply the results against a profile of your objectives. Take the amount of assets that you have theoretically passed through your estate into the hands of your beneficiaries. Add to the income from these assets any additional income available to your beneficiaries from other sources, such as pension-plan benefits under a survivor option, social security, death benefits, or income generated by their own property. How closely did you come to meeting the objectives you have set for them?

This analysis will indicate what needs to be done—whether it is accumulation of assets, reduction of estate tax, rearrangement of the nature of ownership of one's assets, or combinations of these.

Corrective Action

We often assume, erroneously, that estate planning should be deferred until we have achieved a degree of success that will make such planning worthwhile. We tend to disregard our present activity on the false premise that it has little bearing upon our ultimate planning. Nothing could be further from the truth. Our present patterns can well determine our future capabilities.

STARTING AT THE BEGINNING

Take the matter of housing. If we locate ourselves too ambitiously, we never will be able to set aside the amounts necessary to build up our estate in the first instance. An expensive home in an exclusive neighborhood involves more than the heavy tax, mortgage, and interest payments. It structures a standard of living that may well leave nothing to purchase insurance or to fund our children's college education. Moreover, it can create a tremendous psychological problem if ever we should be unfortunate enough to have our income cut back.

Have you considered that *where* you live can affect your family-protection plan? Those working for companies frequently have no choice in the matter: If your office is in Houston, you must live in Texas. But suppose the head office is in New York City. You probably could live in New Jersey, New York, or Connecticut. New Jersey and Connecticut do not have income taxes; New York does. But New York taxes residents of New Jersey and Connecticut who work in New York to the extent that their salaries are attributable to a New York source. However, it does not tax the capital gains that are realized by the residents of the other two states, whereas it will tax the income of a New York resident regardless of the nature of his gain or its source. So—what is your "income mix"?

Again, how about local estate or inheritance taxes? New York imposes an estate tax at rates ranging from 2 percent on taxable estates under $50,000 to 21 percent on estates in excess of $10,100,000, but permits a full 50 percent marital deduction. New Jersey imposes an inheritance tax on the value of the bequests received by each beneficiary. The rates depend upon the relationship of the beneficiary to the decedent. A wife is taxed at 1 percent on bequests up to $15,000, and the rate progresses up to 16 percent where the value of the property exceeds $3,200,000. Although New Jersey allows a $5,000 exemption, it does not have a marital deduction. Connecticut has an inheritance tax which follows a pattern similar to New Jersey's except that in the case of property passing to a wife, the rates range from 3 percent on the first $150,000 to 8 percent on property in excess of $1,000,000. A $50,000 exemption is allowed, but there is a 30 percent surcharge on top of the basic tax. It likewise does not permit a marital deduction.

Obviously, these factors indicate different choices for different people. A man with substantial nonsalary income who travels almost continually in his job, whose wife has died, and who has no intention of remarrying will resolve the issue differently than a man whose salary forms the principal part of his income, who is required by his work to stay rather close to the office, and who has married a lady several years his junior.

One problem is common to both these executives—the old "double domicile" issue. Rationally, you can only have one domicile at a time, that being the state where your physical presence and your intent to reside have coalesced. However, if you have residences in more than one state, you subject yourself to the possibility that the courts of each state will make a judicial determination that you were last domiciled in that state. This means multiple taxation and administration.

LIFE INSURANCE—AN INSTANT, LIQUID ESTATE

In these days of high income-tax rates and galloping inflation, few of us are able to earn enough to build up sufficient capital to meet the objectives set for our beneficiaries in the event of our early death. It takes time to accumulate capital, and the only way to indemnify the risk during the building period is to purchase life insurance. How much and what kind?

Here, such widely used rules of thumb as four to five times your annual income are misleading.

Having just profiled your objectives, you are in the best position to appraise your need and determine your capability. However, there are certain tax attributes which merit consideration as you make this determination.

1. Proceeds paid upon the death of the insured are free of income tax in the usual case.
2. Where an installment-payment option (either fixed period or fixed amount) is elected by a surviving spouse, up to $1,000 per year of the interest element will be income tax free.
3. The buildup of cash value under a permanent insurance policy is income tax sheltered, and the insured will not be taxed on it unless he ultimately surrenders the policy and thereby receives more than he paid in premiums.

In addition to the indemnity or "instant estate" feature, life insurance has a liquidity role. Familiar applications of this role are:

1. Buy-out arrangements in small businesses.
2. Estates where the stock of a family corporation represents at least 35 percent of the value of the gross estate or 50 percent of the taxable estate and the owner wishes to provide the company with funds to redeem stock from the estate to pay estate taxes and administrative expenses.
3. Estates otherwise consisting of nonliquid assets which would suffer severe loss if they had to be sold on a crash basis to provide the cash required for settlement.

There is a further advantage in the case of nonterm life insurance—it is a fund builder. Even though the primary reason for its acquisition may be to buy time under the indemnity provisions, the buildup of cash value serves as an increasing protection against the exigencies of life. Here is a guaranteed source of loans at a fixed rate of interest and a fund of money available if you wish to cash in your policy.

In the past, and to a lesser degree today, the interaction of the cash buildup feature and the deduction against taxable income allowed by the Internal Revenue Code for the payment of interest created a substantial advantage for a person in the 50 percent or higher income tax bracket. By borrowing from the insurance carrier ("minimum deposit" plan) or from a bank ("bank loan" financing), essentially against the cash value of the policy, the interest payments in effect are used to purchase the pure-risk, or death-insurance, part of the premium. For a person in the 50 percent bracket, they do so at half-cost; alternatively, substantially more insurance can be obtained for the allotted money. Those in lower tax brackets will not find this plan to their advantage as they will end up paying more, rather than less, for their insurance.

The Revenue Act of 1964 restricted to the following cases deductions for interest paid on loans used to purchase insurance under a plan which contemplates systematic borrowing:

1. Policies purchased on or before August 6, 1963.
2. Policies on which the interest paid or accrued during the year is $100 or less.
3. Policies purchased on or after August 7, 1963, if any four of the first seven annual premiums have not been borrowed.
4. Loans made for a trade or business.
5. Loans incurred because of an unforeseen substantial loss of income or an increase in financial obligation.

Another way in which life insurance has been used to provide assets for beneficiaries at the least tax cost has been for an employer to purchase a group life insurance policy on the lives of its employees. Since it is truly life insurance, it qualifies for exclusion from the beneficiary's gross income for income-tax purposes; and by making the policy payable to preferentially ordered beneficiary classes (spouses, then surviving children, then parents, and so on) the proceeds are kept out of the employee's estate because he has no incidents of ownership. Caution must be taken to place such insurance in a state which does not have a statute giving the employee-insureds of such policies certain rights (such as conversion to ordinary insurance) that the Internal Revenue Service could seize upon as being "incidents of ownership."

A SHORT-TERM EXPEDIENT—THE CLIFFORD TRUST

A short-term (also called a reversionary or "Clifford") trust may be of value to the executive who has not yet amassed a sizable estate but who can foresee in the reasonably near future that one of his beneficiaries will require a substantial amount of capital. For example, suppose you have a seven-year-old son for whom you have college plans. Projecting today's tuition and living costs to allow for inflation, you can expect that $12,000 will be required. If you funded this amount with after-tax dollars, assuming a 5 percent rate of return (compounded quarterly) and a 50 percent income-tax bracket, you would need capital amounting to $30,000; whereas if you were in a position to use a ten-year trust, the job could be done with $15,000.

This device may also be used to good advantage to provide a dowry for a daughter, support an aged relative, maintain a home for your children and their families, provide life insurance for your children or set them up in a career, and so on. The basic advantage of the plan is that it skims the top-bracket income from you, the grantor, and guides it through the lower tax-bracket rates of the trust or the beneficiaries.

Before elaborating on the characteristics of the short-term trust, it should be said that it will *not* be useful to someone who has completed the accumulation of his estate. Such a person will be more concerned with permanently reducing his estate in order to minimize his estate tax, and he can accomplish his goals with an irrevocable trust which, if properly designed, will remove the capital in it from his gross estate.

In order to achieve the desired income-tax savings, the term of the trust must be for at least ten years and one day from the date when the property is transferred to the trust. However, you may limit it to the lifetime of the income beneficiary or to your own life if your life expectancy is ten years or longer. This requirement covers only the tax side; your attorney will have to pass on whether your state's rule against perpetuities requires a "measuring life." But perhaps you can combine tax and legal requirements, in a clause such as this: "Upon the expiration of ten years and one day or upon my death or upon the death of the income beneficiary, whichever is earliest." This will probably be desirable in most single-purpose cases anyway, since you will want to have your assets back as soon as the need ceases—otherwise your death will create a greater need elsewhere.

You must not have any power to revoke or to amend the trust, except to extend its duration. There are certain controls over the property which you can retain by naming as trustees yourself, your wife, or yourself and your wife and, say, a professional adviser. Note, however, that if you wish the trustee to be able to distribute the trust income among more than one beneficiary (a so-called spraying trust), you as grantor cannot be a sole trustee. You can, however, vote stock, sell stock, and reinvest the proceeds; exercise conversion rights and exchange bonds for regular securities; and substitute property of equal value owned by you individually for assets of the trust. You may borrow from the trust but such borrowing must be at an adequate rate of interest and adequate security must be given.

The question arises as to whether you should accumulate the income in the trust or have it distributed currently. Some states do not permit accumulation trusts for adults; thus, although you would have a choice in the college-education trust situation, you would not in the aged-relative situation. Assuming you have a choice, what is the purpose of the trust? If it is to build a fund, you probably are considering accumulation. However, you could accomplish the same object by distributing to a bank account for the beneficiary, although he would have an unfettered legal right to withdraw money from the bank at any time. In the aged-relative case, there is probably a need for the money currently; so you would want to distribute at least some of the income, even in a state where you could accumulate. Perhaps you might wish to decide each year whether to accumulate or to distribute and in what proportions. This is known as a sprinkling trust. Under such an arrangement, you can tailor the distribution so as to minimize the tax. Thus, in our college-fund example, you could arrange to make the first $1,100 trust income tax free—$100 dividend exclusion, $100 exemption to the trust, $600 personal exemption, and $300 minimum standard deduction.

In regard to gift-tax implications, accumulation in the case of an adult beneficiary will definitely lead you to use your $30,000 lifetime exemption, because transfer to such a trust is not considered a gift of a "present interest"; therefore, it does not qualify for the annual $3,000 exclusion ($6,000 if your wife joins). In the case of a minor beneficiary, as in the college-education trust fund, the better view is that if the accumulated income must be paid over to the minor or his estate before he reaches 21, a special section of the Internal Revenue Code [Section 2503(c)] treats such gifts as ones of a present interest and, hence, the annual exclusion will be available.

One note of caution: The income-tax shield will be penetrated, and you will become taxable, to the extent that any of the trust income is actually used for the maintenance of a beneficiary whom you are legally obligated to support. An interesting question arises as to whether a person is legally obligated to send his children to college. In the situation we have presupposed, even assuming that you have such a duty, you and your attorney still should be able to work your way around this problem. One way might be to have the trustee pay the income annually into a savings account in your son's name or in your wife's name as agent for the child.

When he is ready for college, he can withdraw his own funds for his own needs. You should avoid any express or implied contract with the college in respect to his bills and remain liable only as a guarantor.

ANOTHER ESTATE BUILDER—THE ACCUMULATION CORPORATION

Another device to shield your current income from high-bracket taxes is formation of a corporation to hold certain of your income properties. This can be accomplished tax-free provided you receive only the stock or securities of the corporation in exchange for the properties you put in it and that, immediately after the exchange, you are in "control" of the corporation; you receive 80 percent or more of all stock. You can guard against the possibility of needing money in the future by using a long-term debt instrument as part of the capitalization structure. Your attorney will advise you concerning the ratio of debt to stock imposed by the so-called thin incorporation doctrine and the proper mix of income to the corporation that must be set up to avoid a personal-holding-company status. You should discuss the matter of unreasonable accumulations of income and allow at least a three-year period from incorporation to liquidation because of the problem of collapsible corporations.

What is to be gained by all this? The saving arises from the fact that the corporation is entitled to an 85 percent deduction before tax on all dividends received from another domestic corporation. Hence, assume a dividend stream of $30,000. If you received the income personally and were in the 60-percent bracket, you would realize only $12,000 after taxes (disregarding state income tax). If the same income stream were received by the corporation and it avoided the problems just mentioned, it would pay tax on only $4,500, and at a rate of 22 percent, or $990, leaving $29,010 to be reinvested. To complete the comparison, upon liquidation of the corporation (ignoring the compounding effect of reinvestment) you would have to pay a long-term capital gain tax of 25 percent on the $29,010, leaving you with a net of $21,757.50, almost twice what you would have realized by holding the property directly.

OTHER POSSIBILITIES

There are a number of other methods used to avoid the steeply progressive income-tax rates. Basically, they fall into two categories: (1) income splitting through the creation of additional tax-paying entities, or the diversion of a portion of the income stream to another family member, and (2) taking full advantage of certain deductions or credits made available by the Internal Revenue Code. In the first category are the two devices which we have just discussed. Another example is the family partnership, especially valuable in the case of a family business. Examples from the second category are investments in oil and gas or timber properties which permit deduction of business expenses against your high-tax-bracket income from other sources and, when production is achieved, bring tax advantages in the form of a depletion allowance while you continue to hold the properties and capital gains rates when you sell. Still another example is cattle ranching, where operating expenses are deducted from ordinary income and sales of animals from the breeding herd are taxed as capital gain.

Lifetime Giving

Although we shall discuss several devices designed to reduce the overall tax take, significant savings are realized by the use of two methods: (1) lifetime transfers which remove property from your taxable estate and (2) the avoidance of successive estate taxes.

Proper planning for the minimization of transfer taxes must adopt a total approach to the problem. It is not enough to develop an artful design for disposition at the time of our death; we must also take into account the possibilities afforded by lifetime giving. Consider the matter of exemptions. In addition to the familiar estate-tax marital deduction and the $60,000 estate-tax exemption, there is a gift-tax lifetime aggregate exemption of $30,000 (which can be increased to $60,000 with the consent of your spouse), an unlimited gift-tax marital deduction of half the value of any property interest transferred by gift to the donor's spouse, and annual exclusions of $3,000 ($6,000 if joined in by your spouse) per donee. It is important to note that these gift-tax benefits can be lost by nonuse. Each year that goes by means another opportunity lost, and the $30,000-to-$60,000-maximum lifetime exemption will not carry over to your estate. It should also be noted that three recent studies—The American Law Institute Federal Estate and Gift Tax Project, The Brookings Institution study published in May 1966, and The Carter Commission Report in Canada—all recommend reduction of the annual exclusions. This suggests prompt action.

In addition to the complete avoidance of tax through judicious use of these exclusions, exemptions, and deductions, the fact that the gift-tax rates are only three-fourths of the estate-tax rates offers an additional opportunity for savings. Indeed, the possibility of savings is even greater because the amount of the estate tax is included in the base for computing the tax, whereas the amount of the gift tax is excluded in calculating the gift tax. Moreover, that which is given during a lifetime comes off the top of the estate and will usually fall into a much lower gift-tax bracket. You should be careful that your tax planning does not rest on generalities, but is reduced to the most exact figures you and your estate planners can estimate.

Another principle, of more limited application, is that of avoiding a great imbalance between your net worth and that of your wife. An example frequently cited in this regard is this: Suppose you died, leaving a net worth of $240,000 while your wife has nothing. Disregarding deductions for expenses and fees, but assuming a marital deduction and the $60,000 personal exemption, estate tax would apply on $60,000. However, if you had given your wife $120,000 at least three years prior to your death, there would be no estate tax (and no gift tax if the gift were timed properly).

Consider, also, the effect of inflation. If you give property today worth $500,000, any gift tax will be computed on $500,000; whereas, if you retained this property, the estate tax would be imposed on its value at the date of your death—say, $1,000,000. Moreover, another factor enters into the picture when you are giving to someone other than your wife. This is the possibility of income-tax savings.

There are certain pitfalls which must be considered when designing a program of lifetime giving. If you quickly review what we have said on the estate tax, you will note several instances in which lifetime transfers, even though outright in form, will not avoid the estate tax. This is an area where the most delicate touch is required; it is no place for "do it yourself" tactics. Be sure that you have the assistance of competent counsel who are familiar with this area of the law.

GUIDELINES FOR GIVING

Having glimpsed the potential tax savings, it is easy to go off the deep end. Once again, we have a choice; this time it is dollars versus intangibles. Take the example where you started out with $240,000 net worth, then gave $120,000 to your wife. You avoided estate tax on $60,000, but what good will that do you if your wife takes off with the $120,000?

This suggests a cardinal rule of lifetime giving. Don't give to the point of endangering your personal welfare. There are mutations of this rule: For example, don't give to the children unless you and your wife will, after the gift, have adequate funds, and don't hypothecate your present standard of living to save future estate taxes. This suggests another rule: Don't give so much to certain people that the death of a beneficiary (principally your wife) before you will completely upset your estate plan.

Don't let your lifetime gifts compromise the tradeoffs among beneficiary objectives that you have determined for your overall plan. If, say, you have assigned priority to your children's safety as against a higher standard of living for your wife, you should not violate this decision by making substantial lifetime gifts to her.

These, then, are the "don'ts." You yourself will have to fill in the "do's." They will be determined by you and your advisers, bearing in mind the size of your estate, the abilities and disabilities of your beneficiaries (including yourself), and the objectives you have set for them.

What Property Should Be Given

Once you have made an agonizing appraisal of how much you can afford to give, and whom you want to give it to, you may examine the questions of what and how.

Life insurance. Insurance is an especially attractive lifetime gift. Any gift tax that is imposed will be on the replacement value (which the gift-tax regulations equate with the interpolated terminal reserve) at the date of the gift, whereas the amount which is removed from the estate tax is the face value. Many of us have added policies from time to time to our estate; hence the replacement value of each individual policy could well be less than the $6,000 that can be transferred tax-free to wife or children each year. Even if the replacement value exceeded $6,000, it might be worthwhile to exchange the policy for several smaller policies, which subsequently could be given away one by one.

In order to keep the policy transferred out of your estate, you must completely divest yourself of any incident of ownership. One immediately asks: If I have to give up all incidents of ownership, won't I lose the ability to surrender the policy or borrow against it in case of emergency? Fortunately, the gift will be made to someone in the family who can normally be expected to cooperate and see that these needs are met.

One word of caution about paying premiums on insurance policies that you have given away. The Internal Revenue Service has promulgated a ruling that a premium payment by someone other than the owner is not just a gift of money but a gift of insurance. Under this rationale, the portion of the death proceeds which is attributable to premiums paid by the insured within three years of death is includable in his gross estate. Can this ruling be circumvented, and can litigation thus be avoided? It will not be safe to make indirect payments by simply giving your wife the cash to make the premium payments. However, if you give her other property which produces income which she uses to pay the premiums, you probably will be successful—judging from cases decided when the law used to make premium payment a ground for inclusion. How about killing two birds with one stone and letting her "minimum deposit" or "bank loan" the premiums? She will be paying the premiums from her own assets; that is, borrowings against "her" cash surrender value, and the interest payments will be deductible on your joint income-tax return, assuming the 1964 Act requirements for deduction are met.

Household furnishings and furniture. Frequently, the things a wife treasures most after her own personal jewelry and effects are her household furnishings and furniture. She probably was the one who shopped for them, selected them, and ordered them from the store, and she is the one who takes care of them. They are frequently bought piece by piece, or by suite, and thus can readily be transferred without gift tax.

Home. Many husbands and wives own their houses as tenants by the entirety. This form of ownership not only fails to remove the value of the home from the husband's estate when he dies, but it can also put him to the stiff task of proving that all the money originally came from him if his wife predeceases him. Why not give it to her by lifetime transfer? This will remove it from your estate and preserve the marital deduction for property that you must keep in your estate. A wife will have a real feeling of security if she knows that the home and its contents are hers. Avoid any agreement, express or implied, giving you a right as a matter of law to continue to use and enjoy the property for your lifetime. Courts have been unwilling to infer such an agreement merely because you continue to live there.

Jointly owned property. As previously mentioned, jointly held property will be included in the estate of the first of the joint owners to die, unless the survivor can prove the extent to which he or she contributed to such ownership. If you are embarking upon a program of lifetime giving, it may be well to consider unscrambling any joint tenancies so as to avoid a problem at estate time.

Miscellaneous considerations. If possible, don't give away property that has substantially appreciated in value. The donee must assume your low tax basis (cost adjusted by tax depreciation, depletion, and so on), plus any gift tax paid, and hence is taking over a large income-tax liability. If, however, the property is included in your taxable estate, the beneficiary will get as his income-tax basis the higher estate valuation. Conversely, if you have property which has lost in value and is to be sold to persons outside the family circle, you yourself should sell the property, take advantage of the income-tax loss, and give the proceeds to your donee. If, instead, you give the property to him, he cannot take advantage of the loss, because in such cases his basis for measuring loss is the *lower* of your basis or the fair market value at the time of the gift.

The question of whether to dispose of hard-to-value property can be argued either way. The problem will have to be faced either at the time of the gift or at the time the estate is settled. It may be preferable to face IRS now, while you are around to give valuable assistance. In the case of closely held stock, you can give or even sell a few shares to establish a valuation. Although the commissioner still can argue that "control" stock is much more valuable than a small block, you may be able to set the ballpark figure against which the bargaining will take place.

How Should the Transfer Be Made?

Outright gift. The very simplest transfer is by an outright gift. Be sure a complete transfer is effected and that you are completely divested of any incidents of ownership. Document the fact that you are not making the gift in contemplation of death. Note, too, that you must file a gift-tax return (Form 709) if you have made gifts of present interests to any one donee of more than $3,000 in value or gifts of any future interests to anyone. This is so despite the fact that, because your wife consented to gifts to a third person, neither you nor she will be considered to have made a gift in excess of $3,000. Each of you should file a return, and each should evidence his or her consent to the gift by signing the other's return. (A return is required even where, because of exemptions or deductions, no tax is due.)

Custodial gifts. A simple, outright gift to a minor raises a host of practical problems, including difficulties in registration and transfer of stock in a minor's name. There is the possibility of the natural guardianship of a parent, but this highlights the question of whether such a gift is one of a "future interest," ineligible for the annual gift-tax exclusion. Courts have found future interests where it considered the parents' obligation to make the property or income immediately available to the minor was less than absolute. A gift to your own children, with your wife as natural guardian, might be subject to attack under the circumstances.

Legal guardianship is cumbersome and expensive—usually there must be a court appointment or perhaps the posting of a bond. Annual accounting and investments must be made within the restrictive framework of statutorily enumerated "legal" investments.

Fortunately, most states have enacted a version of the Uniform Gifts to Minors Act or the Model Gifts of Securities to Minors Act. Under these acts, you can make an irrevocable gift of securities to a minor simply by having the securities registered in the name of a custodian (who can be you or your wife) for the child. The custodian is not subject to guardianship restrictions but can manage the securities, invest them, and reinvest them without further authorization or approval by a court. The Internal Revenue Service has ruled that gifts of registered securities, according to a special section of the Code, qualify for the annual exclusion. However, any income that is actually applied to the minor's support will be taxed to you; and when the child reaches 21, the property must be turned over to him.

It would appear prudent to name your wife instead of yourself as custodian because if you should die before the child reaches 21, the property would be included in your estate.

Sale of property within family in exchange for a private annuity. A frequently overlooked device which can produce both income- and estate-tax benefits is the transfer of property to someone in the family in exchange for his promise to make you periodic payments of money for the balance of your life. Provided you do not retain the property as security for the annuity payments, place restrictions on alienation of the property, or in some way tie the annuity payments to the income from the property transferred, you will remove its value from your estate. If the fair market value of the annuity, as determined by the present-value methods set forth in the regulations (which use a 3.5 percent factor) equals that of the property, there will be no gift tax.

With respect to the income-tax effects, the fact that you are receiving the mere promise of an individual (rather than an insurance company) in exchange for your property precludes an immediately taxable capital gain. There is no capital-gain tax until the total of that portion of each annuity payment which is attributable to the cost of the annuity to you exceeds the cost of the property. Of course, that portion of each payment which represents the interest element is taxable to you as received. To illustrate:

Suppose you are 58 years old and transfer a capital asset with a basis of $50,000 and a fair market value of $100,000 to your son in exchange for his promise to pay you $7,000 per year for life. The expected return, using the multipliers from the annuity tables in the regulations, will be $137,200 (19.6 times $7,000). The cost of the annuity—or investment in the contract, as it is known—is $100,000, the value of the property you exchanged for it. Your exclusion ratio (return of investment divided by total expected return) is 72.89 percent. Thus, of each $7,000 payment, $5,102 will be considered as return of your annuity cost, and the balance of $1,898 will be treated as ordinary interest income when received. Only when the total of the excluded portions reaches $50,000—that is, in 9.8 years—will you begin to be taxed on the exchange gain as such. Then, for the balance of the time—9.8 years—the $5,102 will be capital gain (at long-term rates if you held your asset for more than six months prior to the exchange). An interesting question arises if you live beyond your 19.6-year expectancy. If deemed a cash purchase of an annuity, you will exclude the $5,102 and treat the $1,898 as ordinary income. However, if the transaction is viewed as an "open" exchange of capital assets, all additional payments will be capital gain.

Controlled gift. You may not be in a position to give away control of an asset. And, as we have seen, you cannot give away property subject to your lifetime control and still remove it from your estate. We have discussed placing property in a corporation to shelter the income from your high income-tax rates. Should you now consider giving away a noncontrolling interest in it? By so doing, you continue to retain control, even though indirectly through the corporate structure, and at the same time you decrease your estate to the extent of the value of the stock which you give away.

Living (intervivos) trusts. Trusts are generally classified as testamentary (those which are created by will and become effective at death) and living or intervivos (those which are created by agreement and take effect during your lifetime but which frequently continue after death). Intervivos trusts may be subdivided into two types: (1) revocable—those which the grantor may revoke, alter, or amend at any time—and (2) irrevocable, those which cannot be revoked or terminated.

A revocable intervivos trust has no immediate tax advantages to you as grantor. Income from the trust is taxed to you because of your control over and the economic benefit you enjoy from the trust. Likewise, the power to revoke will keep the property of the trust in your estate for estate-tax purposes. There is no gift tax because a completed transfer has not been made. Why, then, should we be interested in such a device? Because there are a number of basic estate-planning needs that can be fulfilled by a revocable intervivos trust. If you should die with the trust unrevoked, the property will pass outside the probate estate, thus avoiding publicity and expense. You will have the benefit of professional management of the property, relieving you of the burden during your lifetime if the trust is funded, and your beneficiaries will have the benefit after you die; thereby you can achieve such objectives as protecting family members against their lack of experience in money matters and insuring income for your widow while, at the same time, preserving the property for your children. You can build into it all the flexibility you desire, making sprinkling or spraying provisions to vary the distribution pattern as the need arises. You can form multiple trusts for income-tax savings. You will have the benefit of previewing, while you still can make changes, how the trustee is likely to carry out your wishes after death. You can put in all the marital deduction and generation-skipping devices you wish. If you are satisfied with the operation, you can later make the trust irrevocable or cause your testamentary estate (that which is disposed of under your will) to be placed or "poured over" into the trust. Thus, if you're not ready to commit yourself now, this trust is frequently a good exploratory device. If it is formed to receive life insurance proceeds and company benefits which mature at death, there usually will be, at most, a nominal charge until the assets are received.

One of the most interesting features of an intervivos trust, which is applicable to either a revocable or an irrevocable one, is the ability to receive distributions from a qualified employee's trust. This makes possible qualification for exclusion from your gross estate of amounts attributable to contributions made by your employer, makes room for otherwise taxable property to qualify for marital deduction, and provides all the flexibility in distribution that a trust can offer.

When you have brought your estate to the point where you are ready to consider an irrevocable intervivos trust, you will find that you must trade off control in order to obtain the income-tax and estate-tax advantages made available by this device. To oversimplify the facts—you may avoid taxation on the trust income if

1. You receive none of the income yourself.
2. It is not used to support a beneficiary whom you are legally obligated to support.

3. You cannot determine who is entitled to receive the money or how much.
4. You cannot deal with, borrow from, or exercise control over the property in the trust except in a narrowly prescribed manner.
5. The income cannot be used to discharge your legal obligations or to purchase life insurance on your life.

On the estate-tax side, to summarize again at the expense of detail, you will be able to remove the property in the trust from your estate if

1. You avoid the "contemplation of death" trap.
2. You do not have any right to trust income.
3. You lack the power to revoke, alter, or amend the trust or to control the enjoyment or possession of the property.

You can be a trustee, but you must limit your acts to those of a fiduciary administering the trust in a standard way. You will incur a gift tax on the transfer or transfers unless you can qualify for one of the exclusions or exemptions we have discussed.

The singular advantage, in addition to flexibility, that the irrevocable trust has over an outright gift is the ability to avoid successive estate taxes. Giving property outright to your children will remove it from *your* estate, but it will be includable in your children's estate and be taxed upon its transfer to your grandchildren. By use of the trust, you can also keep it out of your children's estates by providing for income to your children for life, even permitting certain carefully prescribed provisions for invasion of principal, with the remainder going to your grandchildren. Thus it never goes through your children's estates—it skips a generation, as the saying goes. It is even possible to skip the grandchild generation by using successive life estates so long as living grandchildren are used as "measuring lives" to determine the duration of the trust.

Disposition at Death

Earlier in this chapter, we discussed the principal disadvantages of dying without a will. At this point, we should also mention that the absence of a will involves additional expense in administration, lack of flexibility in the administrator, and a court appointment of the administrator as opposed to one selected by you.

Your will is the final wrap-up of your estate plan; without it, your careful planning will lack its full force and effect. For example, take the need for professional management of your estate. By making a will, you can insure the selection of the manager you want for the testamentary trusts you create; or, if you have already selected a trustee of an intervivos trust, you can provide that the remaining property in your estate will pour over into that trust.

Your Wife's Will

It is very important to wives that their personal effects, jewelry, furs, and objects of sentimental value go to the particular people they have in mind. A will is the only way to insure this. Important as it is to her, however, it is even more important to you that your wife have a will and that its dispositive scheme be integrated with yours.

For example, suppose your will provides that half of your estate goes to your wife and that the other half be held in trust for your children, with life income from the latter half to go to your wife or perhaps be sprinkled between your wife and children as circumstances indicate. If you predecease your wife, your children receive only half of your estate under your will. What happens if your wife should die, say, eight months later without a will? The other half of your estate, which went to her, could be distributed only by the rules of intestacy.

Also, who is to be the guardian of the persons and property of your children? Your will and hers should agree on a guardian in the event that both of you should die or become incapacitated.

The Estate-Tax Marital Deduction

The estate-tax law allows as a deduction from the gross estate an amount equal to the value of any interest in property which passes from decedent to the surviving spouse, provided such interest is includable in the gross estate.

Qualification—the "terminable interest" rule. An interest will not qualify for the marital deduction if it will terminate or fail after a period of time or after the occurrence or nonoccurrence of an event or contingency where (1) an interest in such property will go or has gone to another person for less than full consideration and (2) that person may possess or enjoy any part of such property after such termination or failure. An example would be a life estate provided for your wife, with the remainder to your children at her death.

Two very important exceptions to the terminable-interest rule are (1) the life estate (legal or beneficial) with a power of appointment enabling the spouse to transfer all or a specific portion of it for herself or her estate (and thus a general power to transfer all of it to anyone) and (2) life insurance or an annuity with a comparable power of appointment given to the spouse.

An interest passing to a surviving spouse which will terminate only upon his or her death either within six months after the decedent's death or as a result of a common disaster is not treated as a terminable interest if, in fact, such termination does not occur.

Limitation to 50 percent of adjusted gross estate. The amount of the deduction is limited to 50 percent of the value of the "adjusted gross estate." This base is used to avoid a double deduction; that is, expenses, indebtedness of the decedent, taxes, and losses during administration are deducted to arrive at the adjusted gross estate. Similarly, the value of any community property (on which you already receive a "marital deduction" in the sense that your wife's half is not included in your estate) is also deducted to get the base on which the 50 percent is calculated. The effort to achieve the full 50 percent, when the size of your adjusted gross estate is constantly changing, has led to the development of several types of pecuniary and fractional-share formula clauses; these, in turn, have been complicated by the Internal Revenue Service, which has published a Revenue Procedure severely restricting the marital deduction allowed on interests which can be satisfied by a distribution in mind of appreciated property valued in accordance with estate-tax rules.

Reduction of the marital deduction. There are a few "hookers" that must be guarded against to avoid unintentional loss of the marital deduction. If care is not taken to identify the assets from which your bequest to your wife is to be satisfied and if the interest passing to her could have been satisfied by assets which do not qualify for the marital deduction, the value actually passing to her will be reduced by the value of such non-qualifying property even though she never actually received it. Other variations of the same theme are (1) reduction of the value of any interest passing to the surviving spouse by the amount of any federal estate or other death taxes imposed on such interest and (2), if property subject to an encumbrance passes to a surviving spouse, limitation of the marital deduction to the net value of the property—that is, fair market value less the mortgage or other lien.

Overqualification and redundant qualification. Overqualification is the transfer to the surviving spouse of more property than is necessary to qualify for the maximum marital deduction. Its vice is that it increases the potential estate tax on the spouse's estate without any benefit to the decedent's estate. It arises, usually through inadvertence, from the common practice of owning property jointly (including the owning of the home as tenants by the entirety) and from the tendency of husbands to name their wives as principal beneficiaries of their life insurance policies. The Form 706 simulation which was recommended previously will alert you to the magnitude of this problem, and your adviser can help you to minimize it.

Redundant qualification arises from failure to analyze your dispositions to make sure that property entitled to one form of tax-favored treatment is not used to secure another advantage which could have been obtained through the use of different property. For example, payment received by any beneficiary, other than an executor, from an employee's trust forming part of a qualified pension or profit-sharing plan is excluded from your gross estate to the extent that the payments are attributable to employer contributions. If you make a direct payment from such a plan to your wife, you could end up using both the marital deduction and the exclusion to get a single tax benefit. You should satisfy the 50-percent-of-adjusted-gross-estate requirement by passing her interests which would otherwise be taxable and which will qualify for the marital deduction. The "excluded" property should go into the nonmarital portion for your children.

Simultaneous death clauses. The marital deduction is dependent upon a surviving spouse. Under the Uniform Simultaneous Death Act, each spouse is presumed to have survived the other in respect to his own property. Hence, in order to obtain the marital deduction in such circumstances, you state explicitly in your will that your wife shall be deemed to have survived you. If you have succeeded in achieving substantially equal estates, you should both include this provision in your wills. If your estate is still substantially larger than your wife's, your will should include a presumption that she survived you, but hers should *not* presume that you survived her.

Bequests conditioned on survival. As previously mentioned, a bequest to a surviving spouse on the condition that she survives you by six months does not violate the terminable-interest rule. Thus you can elect to employ this device or not. It can be very useful to avoid the abortion of your entire estate plan after the death of both spouses within a brief span. To state it succinctly: If your wife's estate and yours are equal, use a survivorship-condition clause; if your estate is much greater than your wife's, do not use such a clause in your will but do include one in hers.

Testamentary Trusts

We have already mentioned the advantages of trusts—professional management, protection of one beneficiary as against another, avoidance or minimization of the successive estate problem, flexibility to sprinkle or to spray among beneficiaries as their changing circumstances warrant. Trusts are virtually mandatory when you have minor beneficiaries. We have also mentioned the possibilities of income-tax savings since the trust is another taxable entity and judicious spreading of income can bring the rates down substantially. All in all, this is so useful a device that it is naturally utilized in a will establishing a dispositive pattern to take effect at death. However, every one of these advantages may be secured by an intervivos trust without incurring such disadvantages of a testamentary trust as questions of validity, the unwillingness of insurance companies and employee benefit plans to permit designations to a testamentary trustee, and the opportunity for estate creditors to get at assets.

Powers of Appointment

Trust and powers of appointment go together like a horse and carriage. In tax law, a power of appointment confers the authority—with respect to property which the holder does not own—to transfer the legal or beneficial ownership, to invade or consume the capital (corpus) of a trust, or to affect the beneficial enjoyment of a trust by altering, amending, revoking, or terminating it.

Powers of appointment usually are classified into general powers and special powers. Under a general power, the donee can transfer the property to anyone, including himself, his estate, his creditors, or the creditors of his estate. If his power permits him to act in favor of any one of these four groups of beneficiaries, the estate tax will treat him as if he were the owner and include the value of the property in his estate. However, if his power to consume, invade, or appropriate income for his benefit is limited by an ascertainable standard relating to his health, education, support, or maintenance (that is, "support in his accustomed manner of living"), it will not be treated as a general power.

A power under which the donee can transfer only to a limited class of persons, which does not include the "fatal four" here named, is a special power. It does not pull the property involved into the donee's estate. This power may be expressed positively, as when you give your wife the authority "to appoint the property to such one or more of our children as she may select." It can also be expressed negatively, giving her the power to appoint to any person she may select except herself, her estate, her creditors, or the creditors of her estate.

THE MARITAL-DEDUCTION TRUST

A widely used testamentary plan calls for devising the residuary estate remaining after specific devises and the payment of funeral, administration expenses, taxes and losses to a trustee and creating a "marital deduction" trust (Trust A). This is measured by formula to amount to the maximum marital deduction allowable; it consists solely of property that qualifies for the deduction and includes none that is excluded from the gross estate. A nonmarital-deduction trust (Trust B) is created to receive the other "half" of the residuary estate.

The surviving spouse is to receive all the net income from Trust A. It is to be paid not less frequently than annually, and she is to be given a general power to appoint to whomever the corpus will go upon her death. Usually, but not invariably, the testator will provide that if, at her death, his wife has not exercised the power (by a will subsequently executed and making specific reference to the power), the estate will go over to his children, either to be distributed then or at some future time or times when the children individually attain a prescribed age. The wife may or may not be given a power to invade the corpus, and the trustee may or may not be given authority to do so on her behalf.

The income from Trust B will likewise go to the wife for life or be sprayed between wife and children. The corpus itself will be distributed to the children at the wife's death or at a subsequent time when they reach a specified age. This can be varied so as to give the wife a *special* power to appoint among the children, so as to give flexibility. The wife may be given power to invade the corpus of Trust B but *only* pursuant to a reasonably ascertainable standard along the lines discussed in the preceding section.

A Comparative Example

It may be well to tie together a number of the estate-planning tools which we have been discussing and illustrate their value. Let us assume that we have two executives, *A* and *B*, with the same assets except that *B* uses his tax adviser and *A* doesn't.

Each has an $80,000 home encumbered with a $50,000 mortgage. Each has stocks and bonds amounting to $110,000; cash and bank accounts in the amount of $20,000; and tangible personal property of $20,000 (including household furniture and furnishings of $10,000). Each has personal life insurance with a face value of $100,000 and a $50,000 group life policy financed by payroll withholding. Each participates in his company's qualified profit-sharing plan, which is funded two-thirds by the company and one-third by the employee, the balance standing to his credit being $120,000. The company also has a nonqualified death benefit plan, carried with a life insurance company and payable to preferentially ordered beneficiary classes (spouse, then children, and so on) with no right by the employee to designate. The amount of the policy is $100,000 in the case of both *A* and *B*. For the purpose of the example, we assume that each will have funeral expenses, debts, and administration expenses of $15,000.

A does no estate planning; and his ever-loving wife, striving always to be like *A*, prepares her own estate tax return. They both play a part in the tax debacle: he by creating a testamentary trust with life income to her and the remainder to the children (but giving her no power over the corpus); she by including the company benefits in the gross estate.

B listens to his estate advisers. More than three years ago, he gave his wife the house with its furniture and furnishings, along with $15,000 in a savings account. He also transferred $60,000 worth of life insurance to her, and she pays the premiums from the interest on the savings account. At the same time, he gave his children $40,000 of life insurance; and, before transferring it, he made it payable to the nonmarital portion of an intervivos trust he created to receive such proceeds and his company benefits (except for the survivor benefit, in which case he had no power to designate the beneficiary). Under the Uniform Gift to Minors Act, he transferred $30,000 of his stock to his wife as custodian for the children. Knowing that his children would be of college age shortly, he also provided in his will for $25,000 to Old Siwash, his college alma mater.

At this point, *A* and *B* died of simultaneous heart attacks while riding the 5:39 P.M. commuter train home. What are the results?

		A	B
1.	Gross Estate	$600,000	$185,000
2.	Debts and Expenses	(65,000)	(15,000)
3.	Adjusted Gross Estate (Line 1 minus Line 2)	535,000	170,000
4.	Marital Deduction (Maximum Half of Line 3)	0	85,000
5.	Charitable Deduction	0	25,000
6.	Total Allowable Deductions (Lines 2, 4, and 5)	65,000	125,000
7.	Exemption	60,000	60,000
8.	Total Deductions and Exemption (Line 6 plus Line 7)	125,000	185,000
9.	Taxable Estate (Line 1 minus Line 8)	475,000	0
10.	Gross Estate Tax (Line 9 times Rate)	137,700	—
11.	Maximum Credit for State Tax	(11,400)	—
12.	Net Estate Tax Payable	$126,300	0

DISPOSITION OF THE BUSINESS INTEREST

The penalties for failure to plan reach their highest point in connection with a family business. If this is incorporated, the stock in it, which may have been valued handsomely for estate-tax purposes, may not be salable at an acceptable price and cannot be redeemed; the business may have to be liquidated for lack of management; key assets may have to be sold; and the beneficiaries may find themselves minority owners without a voice in management and unable to obtain income from the business.

You are the person best able to plan ahead. You should therefore make a searching analysis of your business to decide the following key question: Should the business be continued in the family or sold? Subsidiary issues are

+ Is it worthwhile continuing; that is, is it a cyclical business, susceptible to severe shrinkage?
+ Is the success of the business so dependent on your knowledge and ability that it will be in jeopardy after you're gone, or could a good professional run it?
+ Will it produce an adequate and reasonably secure income for your beneficiaries?
+ Is there some member of your family who has the aptitude, training, and the desire to operate the business?
+ Do you have one or more faithful key employees who could and would provide the necessary continuity and support?

✦ Are you free from commitments to others who have built up the business with you?

If you're still "all lights green" on continuing the business within the family, you will have to provide against shrinkage from the estate-tax bite and maintenance of adequate working capital in the business. In short, you will face an acute liquidity problem.

With respect to the payment of funeral expenses, administration expenses, and death taxes, there is a special relief section in the Internal Revenue Code (Section 303) which is available if the value of the business's stock comprises more than 35 percent of the value of the gross estate or more than 50 percent of the net estate. To the extent that redemption of stock by the corporation does not exceed the sum of the foregoing expenditures, the proceeds are subject only to capital-gains rates and not to ordinary income-tax rates as dividend distributions. Unfortunately, solution of one problem raises another. The Tax Court has held that Section 303 does not override the accumulated earnings tax provisions; so "storing up" monies in the corporation to provide the funds to redeem stock from the estate of a majority shareholder will run afoul of the severe penalties of the accumulated-earnings tax to the extent that you exceed the permissible $100,000 credit. Insurance on your life, covered by and payable to the corporation, could provide an answer to this problem, and borrowing by the corporation also might be employed to secure the amount above the $100,000 credit. Be sure your attorney checks out the laws where your business is incorporated, shareholder agreements (if any), and loan agreements by the company for restraints against such arrangements.

There is another relief provision in the Code (Section 6166) applicable to the situation where 35 percent gross or 50 percent net of the estate value consists of interest in a closely held business. In this case, the executor may elect to pay that part of the estate tax which is attributable to such assets in as many as ten annual installments, with 4 percent simple interest on the unpaid balance.

Suppose that you decide that the business ought not to continue in the family, that it should be sold. You then face a question of timing. Do you wish to continue owning it until your death or to sell out earlier? You also must determine whom you wish to sell to, bearing in mind the effect on your employees. One device is a buy-sell agreement which continues you in the business during your lifetime and assures a sale on satisfactory terms at your death. It incidentally produces an income-tax saving because a present sale would create an immediate capital gains tax, which would be avoided if the estate were the seller, owing to the stepup in basis at your death.

On the other hand, maybe you are interested in selling the business when you know that it is at its peak value. If the company is listed on an exchange or has a widely accepted stock, you may want to consider this tax-free reorganization: You receive voting shares in the acquiring company in exchange for the assets of your business (a *C* reorganization) or for your shares in your company (a *B* reorganization). In either case, you will not be taxed on the exchange but will carry over your basis (cost) in the business to the shares of the buyer which you receive in the exchange. You then will have a much more flexible asset, and you will receive income in the form of dividends on such shares.

PLANNED PHILANTHROPY

Charitable giving has a definite place in planning larger estates because it has a number of tax advantages which, if skillfully used, will substantially increase the efficiency of your benevolence. The basic tax considerations are simply stated: Gifts made during your lifetime, especially of appreciated property, save both income taxes and estate taxes (because the property no longer is in the estate); testamentary devises to charity not only reduce estate taxes by virtue of the deduction allowed but do so without reducing the marital deduction.

There is an apparent dilemma here: If we wait until death, we forego income-tax savings; but, if we make lifetime transfers to get the income-tax savings, we lose some marital deduction. However, you can thread your way through the problem by making lifetime gifts to charity with a reserved lifetime income to you, to your wife, or to whomever survives the other. You get an income-tax deduction for the actuarial value of the charitable remainder, and, at the same time, since the property is part of the adjusted gross estate, it will enlarge the marital deduction at no increase in estate tax by virtue of qualifying for a charitable deduction.

If you are reluctant to part with property prior to your death, you can still receive all the benefit except the income-tax savings by bequeathing a portion of your estate in trust, the life income to go to your wife or other beneficiary and the remainder to charity. Of course, the value of the estate-tax deduction for the remainder is discounted by a factor dependent upon the then-attained age of your beneficiary. (For example, if she were 65 at your death, the deduction would be 66.58 percent of the property value.)

A liquidity problem is created when you have a high concentration of your assets in a single business. You have all your assets tied up in the stock, but you can't liquidate without giving up control. Perhaps a foundation may be the answer. Certainly, the savings in income taxes realized by a program of annual gifts to the foundation will be substantial and will increase the cash available to you. This device may have limited life, however, as Congressman Patman and others have severely criticized it.

Another situation in which liquidity may be needed is where you are "locked in" to some listed stock which has appreciated sharply; in this case, you can sell some to your favorite charity at your tax basis (cost). Not only will this put cash in your hand, but it may avoid the percentage limitation (20 percent of adjusted gross income, plus 10 percent in case of transfers to certain organizations such as church, educational, hospital, and governmental units), because the deduction in such cases is only the "profit element"—that is, the difference between your tax basis and the fair market value.

There are countless combinations and permutations in the design of charitable giving. The needs of your beneficiaries, the stature of your estate, the composition of your assets, your income-tax position, and the flexibility of your charitable organizations are all factors. Once again, refer to your attorney for consultation and planning.

KEEPING UP TO DATE

It was said of the French in World War II that they had planned brilliantly but, unfortunately, for another World War I. You, too, can become a victim of a "Maginot Line" estate plan in a blitzkreig estate situation. Not only can the tax laws change—and they will change most dramatically if the American Law Institute's proposals are accepted—but your circumstances can alter. You may move to, or from, a community-property state; your beneficiaries may die, their capabilities may grow or diminish, or your objectives for them may undergo a revision. All this suggests a program of review at biennial intervals and each time that a significant change in your circumstances occurs.

✦ ✦ ✦

A brief treatment of a complicated subject must have a limited objective. So it is with this chapter. If, as a result of your mental traverse over the tortuous paths of estate planning, you have developed an appreciation of the importance of having a good estate plan and have conceived a number of ideas about your estate that you wish to discuss with your estate-planning team, my modest purpose will have been achieved. The use of the phrase "estate-planning team" was deliberate; this is a complicated and important business. The minimum complement of such a team should be your attorney, your insurance agent, and your prospective trustee.

INDEX

Index

ABOUT
THE AUTHORS

About the Authors

LESTER E. DENONN, of Simpson, Thacher & Bartlett in New York City, holds a B.A. and J.D. from New York University and an M.A. from Cornell University. Over the years he has specialized in legal problems of banking and finance. He is a frequent lecturer on the Uniform Commercial Code before bar and banking associations and has chaired numerous forums on the subject. His books and articles in the field are widely consulted.

HERBERT GOLDENBERG is a member of the firm of Blum, Haimoff, Gersen & Szabad, which specializes in corporate and securities matters. He has served with the U.S. Government, including participation in the Nuremberg war crimes trials. He is a graduate of Columbia School of Law (Class of 1939), where he was an editor of the *Columbia Law Review*.

OLIVER P. HOWES, JR., is a partner in the New York law firm of Nims, Halliday, Whitman, Howes & Collison. He specializes in matters of trademark infringement and unfair competition. Mr. Howes is a graduate of the Columbia School of Law and is a frequent lecturer at the Practicing Law Institute and before various bar groups. He is admitted to practice before the Second, Sixth, and Seventh Circuit Courts of Appeal as well as before the New York Bar.

PETER BARTON HUTT is a partner in the law firm of Covington & Burling in Washington, D.C. He specializes in food and drug law. Mr. Hutt holds a B.A. degree from Yale University and an LL.B. from Harvard Law School, and he was awarded an LL.M. degree from New York University Law School under a fellowship from the Food and Drug Law Institute. He has been a consultant to the President's Commission on Law Enforcement and Administration of Justice.

FELIX H. KENT is a senior partner in the New York law firm of Lawler, Sterling & Kent, which for many years has been prominent in the advertising field as counsel to advertisers and advertising agencies. A graduate of Harvard Law School, he was a member of the CBS and the ABC legal departments before entering private practice. He has been a speaker and a participant in seminars, on various aspects of advertising and broadcasting law, before the Federal Bar Association, Bureau of National Affairs, American Association of Advertising Agencies, Fordham Law School, Practicing Law Institute, and other organizations.

WILLIAM R. LINKE is Director—Personnel for The Curtis Publishing Company in Philadelphia and a lecturer in labor legislation at Rider College. Prior to his present affiliation he was director of labor relations at American-Standard in New York City and had previous experience in personnel and labor relations at both Radio Corporation of America and Union Carbide. He is a frequent lecturer before American Association of Industrial Management groups.

MICHAEL MALINA is an attorney associated with Kaye, Scholer, Fierman, Hays & Handler in New York City. He graduated from Harvard Law School, magna cum laude, in 1960 and was an editor of the *Harvard Law Review*. He specializes in antitrust and trade regulation.

RICHARD M. MARKUS is a partner in the Cleveland law firm of Sindell, Sindell, Bourne, Markus, Stern & Spero; adjunct professor of law at the Cleveland-Marshall Law School; and chairman of the Products Liability Committee of the American Trial Lawyers Association. Before he began his practice in Cleveland, he served in the Appellate Section, Civil Division, of the U.S. Department of Justice. He is a graduate of Northwestern University (B.S. magna cum laude) and of Harvard University Law School (LL.B. cum laude). He is admitted to the bars of the District of Columbia, Ohio, the Supreme Court of the United States, and several of the federal courts of appeal.

WALTER S. ROTHSCHILD is a partner in the New York law firm of Cleary, Gottlieb, Steen & Hamilton. He graduated with honors from both Harvard College and Harvard Law School, and he studied at the University of Paris Law School on a Fulbright Scholarship. Mr. Rothschild is a member of the New York Bar and is currently vice chairman on employee pensions and benefits for the American Pension Conference. He is a frequent speaker at seminars sponsored by the American Management Association, the American Compensation Association, and the annual New York University Institute on Federal Taxation.

EUGENE F. ROWAN is personnel relations manager at the J. C. Penney Company in New York City. Prior to joining that organization in 1960, he was associated with the New York law firm of Davies, Hardy & Schenck, where he specialized in labor law. Mr. Rowan served as panelist at the White House Conference on Equal Employment Opportunity in 1965 and, in addition to serving as a member of the Advisory Council of Plans for Progress, was on loan as its Administrative Director in 1967. He is chairman of the American Retail Federation employee relations committee, a member of the American Arbitration Association, and director of the Robert Brunner Foundation.

PAUL D. SEGHERS is an attorney with his own law firm in New York City. He received his LL.B. degree from New York University and his B.C.S. degree from Southeastern University. Prior to organizing his own law firm, he was associated with Gary & Gary in New York City after earlier experience as a special examiner for the Internal Revenue Bureau. Mr. Seghers is the founder and past president of the Federal Tax Forum, Inc., and also founder and president of the Institute on U.S. Taxation of Foreign Income.

GEORGE M. SZABAD is vice president, counsel, secretary, and a director of Burndy Corporation, a leading manufacturer of electrical connectors. He also is a member of the firm of Blum, Haimoff, Gersen & Szabad. Mr. Szabad has served with the U.S. Government, including the State Department and the Department of Labor, where he was in charge of appellate litigation. He is a graduate of Columbia School of Law (Class of 1939), where he was an editor of the *Columbia Law Review*.

DAVID TOREN is a partner in the New York law firm of McGlew & Toren and specializes in international patent and trademark matters, including litigation. He is a graduate of the New York Law School and, in addition, holds a degree in chemical engineering from a Swedish college. He is a teacher of patent law and has lectured in Europe frequently on industrial property law. He is admitted to the bars of the Supreme Court of the United States, the U.S. Court of Claims, and several other federal bars in addition to the New York Bar.

GEORGE S. WOLBERT, JR., is a member of the New York Bar and general manager of the tax department of a large petroleum corporation in New York City. He holds a B.S. degree in petroleum engineering from Pennsylvania State University, an LL.B. degree from the University of Oklahoma, LL.M. and S.J.D. degrees from the University of Michigan, and an LL.M. in taxation from New York University. In addition to his extensive corporate experience, he has been a member of the law faculty at Washington and Lee University.

DATE DUE